WORLD HISTORY BY ERA

The Age of Monarchs

VOLUME 5

Other titles in the
World History by Era series:

The Age of Revolution
Ancient Civilizations
Classical Greece and Rome
Europe Rules the World
The Middle Ages
The Nuclear Age
The Renaissance
The Technological Revolution
The World Wars

WORLD HISTORY BY ERA

The Age of Monarchs

VOLUME 5

Clarice Swisher, *Book Editor*

Daniel Leone, *President*
Bonnie Szumski, *Publisher*
Scott Barbour, *Managing Editor*

Greenhaven Press, Inc., San Diego, California

Every effort has been made to trace the owners of copy-righted material. The articles in this volume may have been edited for content, length, and/or reading level. The titles have been changed to enhance the editorial purpose.

No part of this book may be reproduced or used in any form or by any means, electrical, mechanical, or otherwise, including, but not limited to, photocopy, recording, or any information storage and retrieval system, without prior permission from the publisher.

For Marion and George

Library of Congress Cataloging-in-Publication Data

The age of monarchs / Clarice Swisher, book editor.
    p. cm. — (World history by era; vol. 5)
    Includes bibliographical references and index.
    ISBN 0-7377-0763-1 (lib. bdg. : alk. paper) —
    ISBN 0-7377-0762-3 (pbk. : alk. paper)
    1. Civilization, Modern—17th century. 2. Civilization, Modern—18th century. 3. Europe—Colonies. 4. Culture—History. 5. Imperialism—History. 6. Europe—Territorial expansion. I. Swisher, Clarice, 1933–   II. Series.

D258 .D36 2002
940.2'52—dc21   2001042926
                                                                  CIP

Cover inset photo credits (from left):
Corel Professional Photos; Photodisc; Corel Professional Photos; Corel Professional Photos; Planet Art; Digital Stock; Photodisc
Main cover photo credit: Art Resource
Dover, 223
Library of Congress, 67, 118, 130, 167, 203
North Wind Picture Archives, 74, 187, 208

Copyright © 2002 by Greenhaven Press, Inc.
P.O. Box 289009 San Diego, CA 92198-9009

Printed in the USA

CONTENTS

Foreword   14
Introduction   16

Chapter 1: European Nations Struggle for Political Power

1. The Thirty Years' War in Europe
By Gerrit P. Judd   29
The Thirty Years' War, fought between 1618 and 1648,
had four stages. During the Bohemian and Danish
stages, religious conflicts between Catholics and
Protestants dominated the fighting. During the
Swedish and French stages, new alliances formed in
order to attain greater political power.

2. Civil War in England
By Robert Edwin Herzstein   36
King Charles I so antagonized Parliament and the
people with his arrogant demand for absolute power
and conformity to the Anglican Church that Puritan
opposition under Oliver Cromwell led to war against
the king in 1642. After a Puritan victory in 1646,
Cromwell ruled England and the military for nearly a
decade until the restoration of the monarchy in 1660.

3. The Glorious Revolution
By Will Durant and Ariel Durant   42
James II, in his actions to promote Catholicism and
diminish the power of the Anglican Church, offended
members of Parliament and the clergy and aroused
fear among the public. Political leaders secretly invited William of Orange, who was married to James's
daughter Mary, to invade from Holland and overthrow James. James fled, and the new government
laid a foundation for democracy.

4. The Ottoman Turks Are Defeated in Vienna
By Frederick L. Nussbaum   49
At a time when European powers fought among

themselves, the Ottoman Turks expanded their empire into Europe, much to the dismay of the pope and many national leaders. Finally, two Hapsburg armies organized to go against the Turks, and their combined forces defeated the Turks at Vienna in 1683.

5. Peter the Great and Russia's Emerging Role
By B.H. Sumner   56

Peter the Great was determined to bring Russia closer to European culture and to broaden its economic and political base. He sent expeditions into four fronts—Siberia, the Caspian Sea area, Persia, and the Baltic area—and founded the city of St. Petersburg. As a result of Peter's achievements, Russia became a major player in European history.

6. Louis XIV at the Peak of Absolutism
By T. Walter Wallbank and Alastair M. Taylor   64

Louis XIV fulfilled the role of absolute monarch with elegance, extravagance, and arrogance. He built the palace of Versailles at public expense and waged war against his neighbors to expand his state until his armies eventually lost.

Chapter 2: Economic Advancements and Natural Disasters in England

1. England's Transport Revolution
By Phyllis Deane   72

Starting in the mid–seventeenth century, English investors financed a canal network that connected existing rivers throughout the country to transport heavy goods regularly and cheaply. Once factory owners had necessary materials available, the factory system developed. And it, in turn, formed the basis of the Industrial Revolution.

2. The Development of Joint-Stock Companies
By George Clark   81

The structure of companies traded today on Wall Street developed during the seventeenth century, when nations formed large commercial trading companies for global commerce. Joint-stock companies allowed individuals to buy shares in large trading companies and receive dividends according to their investment.

3. New Institutions Revolutionize Finances

By Paul Kennedy 87

During the seventeenth century, success in war depended more on the availability of credit than on funds raised by local taxation. To expedite a system for borrowing, lending, repayment, and credit reliability, England created the Bank of England in 1694, streamlined the stock exchange, and regularized the repayment system.

4. Structural Groundwork for the Industrial Revolution

By François Crouzet 93

The factory system developed gradually during the century leading up to the Industrial Revolution as entrepreneurs learned to gather capital and centralize work. Innovations occurred first in the iron, brewing, metal, and textile industries until the large workshops could, indeed, be called factories.

5. The Plague of 1665

By Daniel Defoe 100

The plague brought terrible suffering and death to London, particularly affecting the city's poorer residents.

6. The Great Fire of London

By Samuel Pepys 109

Fire spread across central London in the fall of 1666. Residents tried to save their possessions by moving them to safe locations or by loading them on barges floating on the river. After five days the fire died out, leaving a devastating path of ruined churches, schools, and homes.

Chapter 3: The Age of Reason and the Arts

1. Modern Reason Supplants Medieval Philosophy

By Francis Bacon and René Descartes 116

Medieval philosophers reasoned deductively from

culturally accepted premises, which were seldom questioned. New methods for reaching conclusions were developed that replaced old ways of thinking.

2. The Scientific Revolution
By Fritjof Capra   122
Galileo overturned medieval philosophy when he insisted that nature be studied with experimentation and mathematics. Isaac Newton followed Galileo's method by recognizing the significance of gravity and using mathematics to formulate laws of motion. Together, these men revolutionized the study of science.

3. Bach and Handel: Two Baroque Masters
By Kenneth Clark   128
Johann Sebastian Bach and George Frideric Handel were both influenced by religion, and both musicians composed in the baroque style.

4. Five Baroque Painters
By Mary Ann Frese Will et al.   134
Baroque artists painted their subjects naturally and realistically, but they used new techniques to give emotion to the everyday subjects they chose. All five painters created effects with light, color, brush strokes, and composition, but each used the techniques in an individual way.

5. Literature in the Age of Reason
By George K. Anderson and Robert Warnock   142
During the late seventeenth and early eighteenth centuries, French and British writers emphasized reason over imagination and adhered to the form and style first developed by Greek and Roman writers. In French drama and British prose, writers promoted behavior according to reason and control over individual emotion.

Chapter 4: Power Shifts in Asia and Australia

1. Japanese Rulers Oust Foreigners and Isolate the Country

By G.B. Sansom   150

Early in the seventeenth century the Tokugawa family controlled Japan, but because it feared that Christians might incite uprisings in the north and the west, it persecuted them. After the Shimabara uprising occurred in 1637 in spite of intimidation, the ruling family drove all foreigners out of the country and forbade Japanese citizens from traveling abroad.

2. The Rise of the Ch'ing Dynasty in China

By Frederic Wakeman Jr.   157

Little by little the Manchu leaders Nurhaci, Abahai, and Dorgon increased the size and skills of their armies, making them able to extend their territory by conquering one tribe after another. Finally, with the help of defecting Chinese soldiers, they entered Beijing and declared an end to the Ming dynasty.

3. The Decline of the Mogul Empire in India

By Woodbridge Bingham, Hilary Conroy, and Frank W. Iklé   164

By the beginning of the seventeenth century, the Mogul ruler had made India a prosperous, united country. His descendants, however, were religious fanatics who spent lavishly on buildings and military exploits until the citizens were taxed into poverty. Their poor administration led to revolt and ruin.

4. The English East India Company Prevails in India

By J.H. Parry   172

Typical of European trading companies, the English East India Company established a trading depot in India and made a profit in Indian goods. When competing companies tried to overtake the East India Company, English sea power intervened. Eventually, the company acquired political dominance when the Indian dynasty declined.

5. The Evolving French Interest in Southeast Asia

By Richard Allen   179

During the mid–seventeenth century, France established missions in Southeast Asia to spread the Catholic faith in Indochina and Thailand. Although Thailand turned to the British for help, the French remained in Indochina, where missionary efforts evolved into military and administrative help; eventually the French colonized Indochina.

6. Cook Discovers Eastern Australia

By Roderick Cameron   185

While on a scientific mission, James Cook sailed around the islands in the South Seas and explored the east coast of what is now Australia, which had never before been seen by Europeans. Cook and his crew described plants, animals, and the activities of the Aboriginal people and claimed the territory for England.

Chapter 5: European Nations Dominate the Americas

1. The English Establish the American Colonies

By Allan Nevins and Henry Steele Commager,   192
with Jeffrey Morris

The English colonized the eastern seaboard of the United States throughout the 1600s as trading companies and grants of property made the venture financially feasible. Men and women from the English middle class left their homeland and immigrated to America when political events endangered their freedom and security at home.

2. The Colonial Governor Addresses the Problem of Witchcraft

By William Phips   200

As the British-appointed governor of New England, William Phips was uncertain how to cope with the witchcraft trials that had begun while he was on a mission. In these letters to British officials, he describes witchcraft activities, explains what procedures he has thus far taken, and pleads for further direction.

3. The Witchcraft Trial of Susanna Martin
By Cotton Mather   206

During court-held witchcraft trials, exemplified by
the trial of Susanna Martin, some victims were displayed falling to the ground when the accused witch
cast her eye on them. Other victims testified about
troubles caused by the witch, such as bewitching animals and attacking people.

4. Americans Rise Against Oppression
By Howard Zinn   213

After the Seven Years' War, the British looked to the
American colonies to provide needed revenue. The
lower classes, many of whom were unemployed and
near poverty, asserted their concerns at town meetings. Fueled by the rhetoric of leaders, they turned
their protestations to violence and attacks on the rich
Americans.

5. Two Perspectives on the Boston Massacre
By James Bowdoin et al.   220

Quartering British soldiers in Boston antagonized the
colonists and led to protests and violence. According
to the colonial report, the soldiers inflicted verbal
abuse and violence on innocent colonists.

6. The French Found New France in Canada
By Alfred Leroy Burt   228

The colony of New France in Canada developed with
the dedicated work of its leaders: Samuel de Champlain brought the new colonists, Jean Talon served as
an effective administrator, Bishop Laval founded a
church, and Count Frontenac protected the colony
from Indian raids.

7. The Fall of Quebec Ends the French Empire in Canada
By Guy Frégault   235

Before the American Revolution, when Britain and
France dominated North America, war broke out be-
tween the two countries, concurrently with the Seven
Years' War, fought in Europe from 1756 to 1763. The
English victory over the French at Quebec marked
the end of the French Empire.

8. Social Complexity in Colonial Mexico

By J.I. Israel 243

Seventeenth-century Mexico had developed a complex social and economic structure, but race, class, and ethnic conflicts lurked just below the surface. During the 1640s Jews, who had functioned by disguising their identity, became the target of the Inquisition, and, as a result, suffered torture and deportation.

Chapter 6: Decline and Unrest in the Middle East and Africa

1. The Slave Trade

By Paul Bohannan and Philip Curtin 251

Throughout the eighteenth century, plantations and ranches in the Americas needed an increasing supply of slaves. Because Africans had better resistance to diseases and were more efficient workers than slaves from the Americas, the slave trade mushroomed along the western coast of Africa and inland for some miles.

2. Early Petitions for Freedom

By Anthony Pieterson, Phillip Corven, and Peter Vantrump 258

Before the Revolutionary War, slaves in America could petition for their freedom. Three petitions citing reasons for seeking freedom are cited in the original form. One slave was granted freedom, one was denied, and the third outcome is unknown.

3. The Dutch Settle South Africa

By Harm J. de Blij 262

Cape Town was first settled by a Dutch group under the leadership of Jan van Riebeeck to establish a food-supply station for ships rounding the cape. Rich farmland and green slopes lured these farmers and cattlemen to form a permanent, independent colony.

4. The Decline of the Ottoman Empire

By Andrew Mango 268

By the late 1600s, the Turkish military had experienced two defeats on the European front. Roving bands and unemployed soldiers destroyed towns and cities in Turkey and left them in disorder. In this weakened state, the Ottoman Empire was vulnerable, and European countries moved in with trade and culture and brought changes the old order could not withstand.

Chronology   271

For Further Research   276

Index   280

About the Editor   288

The late 1980s were a time of dramatic events worldwide. Tragedies such as the explosions of the space shuttle *Challenger* and the Chernobyl nuclear power plant shocked the world out of its complacent belief that humankind had mastered nature and firmly controlled its technological creations. In U.S. politics, scandal rocked the White House when several high-ranking officials in the Ronald Reagan administration were convicted of selling arms to Iran and aiding the Nicaraguan contra rebels. In global politics, U.S. president Ronald Reagan and Soviet president Mikhail Gorbachev signed a landmark treaty banning intermediate-range nuclear forces, marking the beginning of an era of arms control. In several parts of the world—including Beijing, China, the West Bank and Gaza Strip, and several nations of Eastern Europe—people rose up to resist oppressive governments, with varying degrees of success. In American culture, crack cocaine and inner-city poverty contributed to the development of a new and controversial music genre: gangsta rap.

Many of these events were unrelated to one another except for the fact that they occurred at about the same time. Others were linked to global developments. Greenhaven Press's World History by Era series provides students with a unique tool for examining global history in a way that allows them to appreciate the seemingly random occurrences as well as the general trends of human progress. This series divides world history—from the time of ancient Greece and Rome to the end of the second millennium—into ten discrete periods. Each volume then presents a collection of both primary and secondary documents that describe the major events of the period in chronological order. This structure provides students with a snapshot of events occurring simultaneously in all parts of the world. The reader can then see the connections between events in far-flung corners of the world. For example, the Palestinian uprising (*intifada*) of December 1987 was near in time—if not in character and location—to similar protests in Beijing, China; Berlin, Germany; Prague, Czechoslovakia; and Bucharest, Romania. While these events were different in many ways, they all involved ordinary citizens striving for self-autonomy and democracy against governments that were attempting to impose strict controls on their civil liberties. By making the connections between these events, students can see that they comprised a global movement for democracy and human rights that profoundly impacted social and political systems worldwide.

Each volume in this series offers features to enhance students' understanding of the era of world history under discussion. An introductory essay provides an overview of the period, supplying essential context for the readings that follow. An annotated table of contents highlights the main point of each selection. A more in-depth introduction precedes each document, placing it in its particular historical context and offering biographical information about the author. A thorough chronology and index allow students to quickly reference specific events and dates. Finally, a bibliography opens up additional avenues of research. These features help to make the World History by Era series an extremely valuable tool for students researching the rise and fall of civilizations, social and political revolutions, cultural movements, scientific and technological advancements, and other events that mark the unfolding of human history throughout the world.

During the age of kings, the period from 1611 to 1774, absolute rulers gained power in Europe and developed national states. The states grew strong with kings who used their power and military might to gain territory and wealth. Historians T. Walter Wallbank and Alastair M. Taylor explain:

> In many countries of Europe the strong central government which was so outstanding a feature of the growth of the national state became so powerful as to be practically unrestricted by any class of people or institution of the realm. The king became, in theory and in fact, an autocrat responsible to God alone. This, then, was the great age of absolutism, the period of "the divine right of kings."[1]

The new power arrangement allowed many countries, especially those along the Atlantic coast, to develop trade and commerce and expand global influence out of proportion to their geographical size.

Before the age of kings, Europeans had already sent explorers, missionaries, traders, or colonizers to almost every area of the world. In the midst of political and economic change, European nations also experienced an artistic and intellectual revolution, which was often stimulated and supported by the kings and their courts. Eventually European political, economic, and intellectual ideas and events combined to become an identifiable culture, which Europeans exported around the globe.

THE POLITICAL TRANSFORMATION

During this period, the whole European continent was in the midst of political transformation. Europe had been fighting destructive religious wars for many years with Catholics and Protestants pitted against each other. During the Thirty Years' War, which lasted from 1618 until 1648, European countries stopped allying themselves with like religious groups and instead formed alliances to stop other countries from becoming too powerful. The ruling families of the time concentrated power into national states by ruthlessly carving out territory and then controlling it with their armies. Wallbank and Taylor describe it as "the golden age of European absolutism. . . . The concentration of power in the hands of ruling families that aspired to military glory or the extension of their dynasties' power does much to explain the epidemic of wars that convulsed Europe."[2]

These wars, fought for the extension of territory and power, changed the political landscape of northern and eastern Europe. As a result, the power of Sweden and Turkey declined; Poland lost its identity when pieces of its territory were seized by Russia, Austria, and Prussia; and Hungary became a province of Austria. At the end of the eighteenth century, Russia under the Romanov family, Austria under the Hapsburgs, and Prussia under the Hohenzollerns were the great powers that dominated eastern Europe.

Wars to extend power and territory also changed the landscape of western Europe as power shifted from southern to northern countries. The once-powerful Italians were defeated by the French. Spain and Portugal, at the height of their power, had sent out explorers and had established colonies in South America, but both countries were too small and resource-poor to compete with their neighbors to the north. Holland, France, and England used their armies and navies against Spain, causing its final decline. Holland, which had been part of the Spanish Netherlands, gained its independence under William the Silent of the House of Orange; he saw a strong national state as a contract binding the king and his subjects against invaders.

France, under the Bourbon family, became the most powerful European nation during the seventeenth century. Literary historians George K. Anderson and Robert Warnock identify French advantages:

> Her population was not only the largest in Europe, about eighteen million, but was almost equal to that of England, Spain, Austria, and the Dutch Republic combined. Her land was fertile and supported an industrious and energetic people. They had pioneered in new crafts and industries, especially because of the skill and organizing ability of the Protestant Huguenots. France had a homogeneous population and formed a truly national empire, unlike the international empires of Spain and Austria.[3]

France gained her power under strong leadership and an aggressive military. The statesman Cardinal Richelieu, minister to the French monarchy during the first years of the seventeenth century, centralized power and paved the way for Louis XIV. Richelieu established internal order by squelching protests, reducing the power of the nobles, and centralizing power in the monarchy. He rebuilt the army, launched a navy, and protected French frontiers. By the time Louis XIV came to the throne and took over state affairs, Richelieu had organized the government in a way that made the king synonymous with the state. Louis XIV vigorously continued Richelieu's work and made Paris the center of European culture, the envy of all other European countries.

GLOBAL EXPANSION

European monarchs used their acquired power to gain wealth by expanding global activity, which had begun in the 1400s. When Europeans ventured into new areas of the world, their goals and activities followed the same pattern: exploration, trade, settlements and colonies, and domination.

The goal of European exploration was to find riches that could enhance the king and his state. In the early stages of exploration, missionaries, especially from Spain and Portugal, often accompanied the explorers. Historian G.N. Clark explains the extent and effect of missionary work: "The missionaries, especially the Jesuits, had penetrated into every corner of the known world, and had been amongst the pathfinders into the unknown. They had done much to make the expansion of Europe into an extension of western civilization as well as western rule."[4] New explorations were initiated in each new century. For example, Portugal had explored Brazil and the Far East, and Spain had explored Mexico and South America before 1600; Captain James Cook explored Australia and the South Sea islands for England in the 1700s; but exploration of Africa did not begin until after the age of monarchs.

After exploring, nations traded and established foreign posts, and the work was done by trading companies. As trade increased and establishment of trading posts became too expensive for governments to fund alone, joint-stock, or trading, companies were formed. A trading company was created when wealthy investors pooled their resources to fund trading operations and posts; in exchange, investors received a share of the profits. European nations used these trading posts to manage imports and exports: The foreign country supplied raw materials for use at home and bought the products manufactured in the home country. Holland became a powerful commercial and financial center during the early seventeenth century. The Dutch East India Company, founded in 1602, was one of the first trading companies. Soon the Dutch company took territories from the Portuguese and established Dutch posts in Southeast Asia. France had four trading companies active in the Mediterranean and the Caribbean areas. England far exceeded other European countries in world trade. The British kings who followed William III left the tasks of government to the Whig political party, which favored commercial and financial interests. Through a combination of foresight and planning, English political leaders led the country to world supremacy.

European trading posts facilitated worldwide trade in a wide variety of products. For example, calicoes, chintzes, and ginghams from the Orient decorated the rooms of wealthy Europeans. The Americas introduced new products such as cocoa, potatoes, tobacco, corn, and coffee. Fish from New England shores increased the European food supply, furs came from the Hudson Bay, and sugar from the West Indies supplanted honey. In the 1500s the Spanish and Portuguese had begun a slave trade, buying natives on the western coast of Africa to sell as slaves on American plantations. During the 1600s, after the decline of Spain and Portugal, the English, Dutch, and French took up the slave trade and expanded it.

NEW PRACTICES AND INSTITUTIONS

As the volume of trade increased and trading posts extended into more and larger geographic areas, the governments had to refine practices in order to sustain profits for the trading-company investors. The Dutch, for example, built better ships and operated them more efficiently, keeping their freight rates down. The English government took the most active role. England had already built a vast merchant marine. In 1651 the Navigation Act stipulated that all products, both imports and exports from Africa, Asia, and the Americas, be carried by British ships manned by British sailors, an act that generated great wealth for England. The government actively aided trade by improving harbors and building a structure of canals to transport goods to and from the port cities.

The increase in trade also required changes in financial operations, and again England led the way by developing new and effective institutions. The government made the joint-stock trading companies financially safe by operating them under state-supervised regulations. In 1694 an act of Parliament established the Bank of England to market government securities, administer the currency, and make loans. New banking procedures, such as checking accounts and bookkeeping procedures, facilitated the

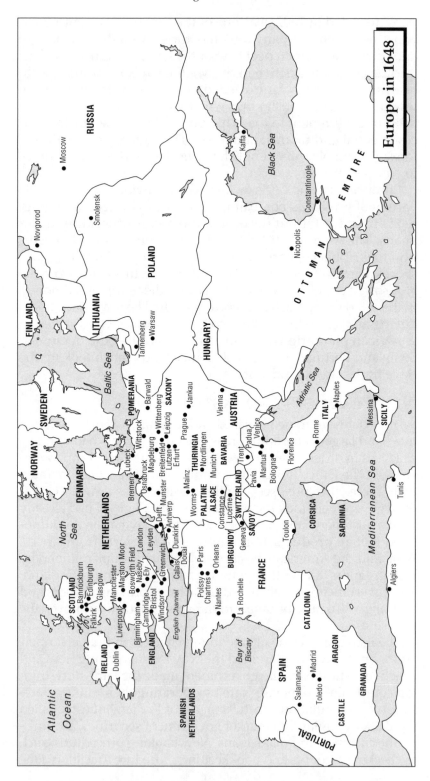

Europe in 1648

growing commerce. England developed marine insurance to protect ship owners. To facilitate the needs of investors who wanted in or out of the market, the government established stock exchanges that traded either products or stocks and bonds. These improvements in financial management continued to increase England's wealth and to sustain her leadership in the world of trade and commerce.

SETTLEMENTS AND COLONIES

The major trading nations, primarily England, found that trading posts around the globe were often insufficient to manage the growing operations and set about to form settlements and permanent colonies. Settlements were outposts where the home country sent governors and workers to stay for a period of years to build roads and buildings, manage plantations, and facilitate the trade, and then they returned home. Colonies were similar except that those who went to these outposts settled there permanently. With both settlements and colonies, the goal was the same: to gain wealth for the home country. For example, the American colonies, India, and Canada existed for exploitation, as sources of raw materials and as markets for British products. Colonies were not allowed to manufacture anything in order to prevent potential products from competing with manufacture at home.

Colonization, like exploration and trade, occurred not at a particular time but rather as part of the sequence of expansion. For example, since the Spanish and Portuguese had already established colonies in the Americas before the age of kings, the period from 1611 to 1774 was an interim for Mexico and South America when colonies operated under control of the mother country, but colonists had not yet revolted or fought for independence. Not until the early 1600s did the English establish colonies in North America because they had found other locations to be more lucrative in the early stages. Later, at the southern tip of Africa, the Dutch established a settlement at Cape Town, intended only to be a supply station for ships rounding the cape. When the Dutch found fertile land and good grazing hills, they made a permanent settlement, which they lost to the French in the late 1700s.

TIGHTER CONTROL AND POCKETS OF RESISTANCE

England and other powerful trading nations tightened controls and increased taxes in their colonies because those practices brought greater profit. In the Middle East, where the Ottoman Empire was in decline, individual countries lacked strong and consistent rulers. Those nations were particularly vulnerable to trading companies that came in to establish trading posts and colonies with the power that had been granted to them by their home government. In India, which also lacked a strong ruler, the Dutch, English, and French trading companies competed until England was granted India as compensation for having won the Seven Years' War. England eventually took over the government. By the end of the age of kings, American colonists, however, were already agitating against new taxes and restrictions.

A few places around the globe had rulers strong enough to resist European trade and commerce. China had had a series of dynasties dating back to 1500 B.C. and a rich cultural and artistic history. The Chinese did not explore or develop sea power because they viewed their culture as superior, their ruler as the ruler of mankind. Europeans, they thought, were barbarians and had little to interest the Chinese.

NEW INDUSTRIAL DEVELOPMENTS

The vast network of trade brought into Europe raw materials that were then turned into manufactured goods to be sold in trading posts and colonies. With the increase in these activities, new industrial developments were needed to keep up with the demand. Overseas colonies particularly stimulated the textile industry. For example, Italy had markets for silk, lace, and velvet. Holland produced woolen cloth and linens. France exported tapestries, and England marketed woolen cloth and cottons.

England not only led Europe in world trade and commercial practices but also led in the development of the textile and other kinds of industry. Advances in English technology, power supply, metallurgy, and mining contributed to increased industrial production. The invention of the flying shuttle for making cloth and the spinning jenny for making yarn increased output in textile factories. The steam engine, invented by Thomas Newcomen and improved by James Watt, ran cotton mills, locomotives, and steamships. Inserting a ventilation shaft and fans into coal mines made the mining industry safer and thus more efficient. The development of wrought, or malleable, iron made it possible to manufacture strong machines that did not break or crack. These advancements evolved as more raw material arrived from the colonies and as the colonial populations created an increasing market for manufactured goods.

To facilitate this increased production, England needed better transportation. Roads with better drainage and firmer roadbeds made land transportation faster. Canals connected England's numerous rivers for hauling heavy products like coal and iron. Although engineers were beginning to adapt the steam engine to railroads and ships, the greatest increase in train and steamship transport occurred in the century after the age of kings. By the end of the age of monarchs, however, the groundwork had been laid for the Industrial Revolution that followed.

THE INTELLECTUAL REVOLUTION

The intellectual revolution—the Enlightenment in the Age of Reason—developed concurrently with the revolutionary changes in politics and global trade and commerce. While kings kept armies to protect their borders from invaders, artists and intellectuals traveled freely across national boundaries, exchanging new ideas and artistic styles.

The term *Enlightenment* describes the multi-faceted transformations in European culture, and by 1770 the term *Age of Reason* had come to identify the period of these changes. Wallbank and Taylor elaborate on the importance of the Enlightenment:

> So important are these changes in European thought in early modern times, from the latter part of the seventeenth century through the eighteenth century, that they constitute what is known as the Enlightenment. During this epoch the mind, not faith, was regarded as the best source of guidance. Reason was elevated above everything else, and there was little use for what was regarded as emotion, myth, and supernaturalism. The main support of the new rationalism was science. Thinkers of the Enlightenment were so positive that reason could solve all human problems that their whole approach to man and society was colored by a vigorous optimism. . . . Faith in reason, exaltation of science, and belief in humanitarianism led writers and thinkers of the eighteenth century to carry on a strenuous campaign of stock-taking in all aspects of society.[5]

These changes in thought manifested themselves on three fronts: science, mathematics, and philosophy.

THE ENLIGHTENMENT IN SCIENCE, MATHEMATICS, AND PHILOSOPHY

The scientific revolution was based on the ideas that observation and experimentation formed the foundation for science and that mathematics was necessary to describe scientific results. For example, with observations made with the telescope, astronomers abandoned the belief in the geocentric, or earth-centered, universe and established that the Sun is at the center of the universe with the earth revolving around it. In chemistry Robert Boyle ushered in an age of progress with his discoveries regarding compounds and gases. Medicine advanced beyond the practice of barbers performing bloodletting to become a science based on physiological discoveries, such as William Harvey's discovery of the circulation of blood. In physics, Isaac Newton discovered laws in optics, motion, and gravity. Scientific observations yielded results in conjunction with mathematics. Advances in analytic geometry and calculus gave scientists the tools to describe their results.

Medicine and science were not the only disciplines affected during this time period. Philosophy during the age of monarchs was no longer a tool of religion but a new way of thinking set on developing schemes of thought that reconciled philosophy and science. One new scheme was inductive reasoning, which drew conclusions from a study of particular facts or events, a scheme that coincided with scientific experimentation. Another new method of thinking was deduction, a system for determining a truth from which further thought logically follows. Philosophers, for example John Locke and Immanuel Kant, applied the methods to such problems as the nature of reality, the meaning of matter, and the problems of knowledge.

NEOCLASSIC AND BAROQUE STYLES IN THE ARTS

The revolution in science and philosophy also affected the arts—literature, architecture, painting, and music. Anderson and Warnock elaborate:

> All the arts felt the rule of reason and assumed their proper places within the universal system. In this most intellectual of eras they took on a cold, even mathematical character in harmony with the Cartesian [Descartes's] principle. The formal pattern of a Bach fugue and the neat clockwork of a Haydn symphony reflect the rational ordering of music, as of all the arts, in the age of common sense.[6]

Artists carried out their rational goals in neoclassic and baroque styles, which were common to all of the arts. The neoclassic style signifies a preference for the classical ideals of reason, form, and restraint, which had been practiced by ancient artists and writers. Artists manifested those ideals in art by creating works with order, symmetry, and simplicity of style. Baroque style, on the other hand, is ornate and emphasizes dramatic effects carried out in bold, curving forms and elaborate ornamentation. In any work the structure may follow a neoclassic style and the execution of details may follow a baroque style. These common elements, however, did not prevent writers and artists from expressing their individuality.

Subordinating imagination and emphasizing reason, writers of poetry and prose followed formal rules during this period. They wrote in a formal style, using long, balanced sentences composed of elaborate abstract language, following the style of ancient Roman writers such as Virgil and Horace. An excerpt from British poet Alexander Pope's *An Essay on Man* illustrates the formal style and complex ideas based on reason:

> Know then thyself, presume not God to scan,
> The proper study of mankind is man.
> Placed on this isthmus of a middle state,
> A being darkly wise and rudely great:
> With too much knowledge for the skeptic side,
> With too much weakness for the stoic's pride,
> He hangs between; in doubt to act, or rest;
> In doubt to deem himself a god, or beast;
> In doubt his mind or body to prefer;
> Born but to die, and reasoning but to err;
> Alike in ignorance, his reason such,
> Whether he thinks too little, or too much.[7]

In all forms of literature—poetry, plays, and essays—many writers urged, directly or by satire, that readers strive to live a reasoned life.

Architects during the age of kings also expressed themselves in classical and baroque style. Important buildings were vast in size and rich in ornamentation. In France, for example, the palace of Louis XIV at Versailles was surrounded by formal gardens, flowing fountains, and rows of manicured hedges. Inside, the formal structure was ornamented with silks and velvet, mirrors, marble, and carvings. In England, Christopher Wren designed St. Paul's Cathedral in baroque style, creating a huge cathedral with ornate windows and elaborate design. In *Architecture Through the Ages*, Talbot Hamlin describes it:

> The history of the design of St. Paul's Cathedral is itself significant. After the Great Fire of 1666, in which such a large proportion of the city of London was destroyed, the old Gothic cathedral was a dangerous ruin, and its reconstruction became an absolute necessity. Sir Christopher Wren, the architect-in-chief of the court, prepared a design which was thoroughly Baroque in its conception. He envisioned a great domical area of enormous scale, so as to allow large unbroken congregations to attend the service. He surrounded this with a ring of eight

chapels, four larger and four smaller. . . . The diversity of shapes, the interesting diagonal and transverse arches, the alternation of dome and groined vault, all of this formed an artistic unit full of the true Baroque symphonic quality, and the domination of the central dome over this rich side aisle had the true Baroque drama.[8]

Baroque painting began in Italy but quickly spread throughout Europe. Baroque painters used light and shade to highlight their subjects. They painted portraits of kings and members of the court or portraits of peasants dramatized in light and color, still lifes and landscapes in rich color and detail, and religious scenes. For example, Flemish painter Peter Paul Rubens, who was one of the first baroque painters outside of Italy, painted a large landscape, *Landscape with the Chateau of Steen,* dramatically using light and shade to portray distance from the hunter in the foreground to the tiny trees on the far horizon. Sir Anthony Van Dyck painted British king Charles I standing with his horse. H.W. Janson, in *History of Art,* says, "The fluid Baroque movement of the setting contrasts oddly with the self-conscious elegance of the king's pose. . . . He [Van Dyck] created a new aristocratic portrait tradition that continued in England"[9] in the elaborate baroque portraits painted by Thomas Gainsborough. An example of a religious scene painted in high baroque style is Rembrandt's *The Blinding of Samson,* in which the central action is portrayed in a flood of light dramatically in contrast to the darkness of the tent in which the action takes place. Baroque painters had these themes and stylistic elements in common, but each, nevertheless, incorporated their own individual touches.

The finest music of the age of kings was composed in Germany and Italy. Though each major composer had his own style, all of them composed music with formal classical structure ornamented with baroque variations. Johann Sebastian Bach, influenced by the church, created great organ fugues and religious masses. George Frideric Handel composed court music, operas, and oratorios, the *Messiah* being the best known. During the eighteenth century Franz Joseph Haydn, who took advantage of the progress in the violin-making skill of the Stradivarius family, composed over a hundred symphonies and perfected a balanced orchestra made up of strings, woodwinds, brasses, and percussion. Claudio Monteverdi wrote the first important operas in Italy. His first ones were private court performances, but later operas were popular spectacular performances produced in public opera houses in Venice. Like baroque painters, composers constructed their works with classical forms and embellished them with dramatic baroque detail.

The intellectual ideas and the artistic styles developed during the age of kings had a less dramatic effect globally than the expansion in trade and commerce. Wherever Europeans settled colonies, however, they brought Western culture with them. It was further exported through the exchange between artists and intellectuals in the home country and their counterparts in the colonies. With the increase in British and French colonies around the globe, the English and French languages and European culture spread far and wide. Indeed, European events stole the limelight during the age of kings because European events touched, and often dominated, events in every other part of the globe.

NOTES

1. T. Walter Wallbank and Alastair M. Taylor, *Civilization Past and Present*. Vol. 2. Rev. ed. Chicago: Scott, Foresman, 1949, p. 83.

2. Wallbank and Taylor, *Civilization Past and Present*, p. 112.

3. George K. Anderson and Robert Warnock, *The World in Literature*. Vol. 2. Chicago: Scott, Foresman, 1951, p. 5.

4. G.N. Clark, *The Seventeenth Century*. Oxford, England: Clarendon, 1931, p. 200.

5. Wallbank and Taylor, *Civilization Past and Present*, p. 39.

6. Anderson and Warnock, *The World in Literature*, p. 21.

7. Quoted in Bernard D. Grebanier et al., eds., *English Literature and Its Backgrounds*. Vol. 1. *From the Old English Period Through the Age of Reason*. Rev. ed. New York: Dryden, 1949, p. 822.

8. Talbot Hamlin, *Architecture Through the Ages*. New York: G.P. Putman's Sons, 1940, p. 456.

9. H.W. Janson, *History of Art: A Survey of the Major Visual Arts from the Dawn of History to the Present Day*. 2nd ed. Englewood Cliffs, NJ: Prentice-Hall, 1977, pp. 506–507.

European Nations Struggle for Political Power

CHAPTER 1

THE THIRTY YEARS' WAR IN EUROPE

GERRIT P. JUDD

Gerrit P. Judd explains the alliances formed and battles fought during four stages of the Thirty Years' War, waged in Europe between 1618 and 1648. He explains that the first two stages revolved around religious conflicts between Catholics and Protestants. The war ended in 1648 with the Treaty of Westphalia. Gerrit P. Judd, an American historian who lived in and wrote about Hawaii, is the author of *From Kingdom to Statehood, The Story of America's Island Paradise.*

T he Thirty Years War (1618–48) brought to a climax a number of forces which had been building up in the sixteenth century. The German people, who bore the brunt of the fighting and suffered the most from it, called it the Great War. Actually it was a series of wars rather than a single conflict. Either name for it is somewhat artificial, for between 1450 and 1660 there were only four years (1548, 1549, 1550, and 1610) in which organized fighting did not occur in Europe. Nonetheless, the Thirty Years War, in its phases and results, had a certain unity. It originated as part of the continuing struggle of Catholic and Protestant forces for the religious control of the West. But in its later stages the character of the war shifted from religious to political. At the same time the war itself shifted Europe's balance of power westward from Germany to France.

Historians traditionally divide the Thirty Years War into four periods: the Bohemian (1618–25), the Danish (1625–9), the Swedish (1630–5), and the French (1635–48). In the first two periods the main objective was religious. But in the later periods

Excerpted from *A History of Civilization,* by Gerrit P. Judd. Copyright © 1966 by Gerrit P. Judd. Reprinted with permission from Pearson Education, Inc., Upper Saddle River, N.J.

this objective blurred, and the war became mainly a political struggle of Sweden and France against the Hapsburgs.

THE BOHEMIAN PERIOD: 1618–1625

The Thirty Years War began with a revolution in Bohemia. In 1617 the Bohemian Diet had elected as king Ferdinand II (1578–1637), a Hapsburg who became Holy Roman (German) emperor two years later. This plump and officious ruler was a religious enthusiast, one of the last militant champions of the almost extinct Catholic Reformation. Bohemian Protestants, such as Count Thurn, became alarmed when the new government not only permitted the closing of some Protestant churches but also appointed Roman Catholics to seven of the ten seats in the Bohemian royal council. In 1618, during the early stages of the revolt, the rebels threw two of these Catholic councillors from a window 70 feet high—an incident known as the Defenestration of Prague. Both councillors survived. A Catholic account insisted that angels had broken their fall. The Protestant version denied the miracle and stated instead that they had landed on a dungheap. The rebels seized Prague, established a provisional government, and deposed Ferdinand II. They elected as their king Frederick V (1596–1632), the Palatine elector of the Holy Roman empire. The new king, a well-meaning but ineffective Calvinist, was the son-in-law of James I of England. The German Protestant Union, of which Frederick V was head, gave him some military aid.

For a time Count Thurn had military success in defense of the new Protestant regime. But the emperor Ferdinand II made an agreement with Maximilian I (1573–1651) of Bavaria, a capable and dedicated ruler, who was head of the newly formed Catholic League. Maximilian's mercenary troops, including soldiers from Ireland, Poland, and Russia, invaded Bohemia under the Baron of Tilly (1559–1632), an experienced and able general. Jesuits who accompanied the invading army encouraged the troops, and the expedition assumed some of the characteristics of a crusade. Each of the twelve largest cannons, for example, was named after one of the apostles. Meanwhile the Lutheran elector of Saxony stayed neutral. He was jealous of Frederick V's new power as king of Bohemia. In addition, the German Lutherans generally disliked the Calvinists, in Bohemia as elsewhere, just as much as they disliked the Catholics. Their refusal to help Frederick V is similar in motivation to their earlier refusal to help the Dutch Calvinists during [the Spanish duke] Alva's reign of terror in the sixteenth century. Tilly's army won a decisive victory over Frederick V in the battle of the White Mountain near Prague in 1620, and subjected Prague to a hideous sack which lasted for a week. Frederick V, who had received no effective help from his father-in-law, James I of England, was forced to flee to Holland. In contemptuous reference to his short reign the Dutch called him the "Winter-King" of Bohemia. Tilly's troops, with Spanish help, ravaged Frederick's Palatine territories and broke up the Protestant Union. Ferdinand II regained the Bohemian throne, and Maximilian of Bavaria obtained the Palatine electorate. The imperial forces in Bohemia began a systematic campaign to destroy Protestantism. By 1623 the Protestant religion had all but vanished from this conquered and devastated nation. At the same time Ferdinand II undertook a vigorous anti-Protestant campaign in Austria. These events, apparently of secondary importance and mostly confined to Germany, released forces which in time involved almost all the states of Europe in an exhausting war which lasted over a generation.

THE DANISH PERIOD: 1625–1629

Emperor Ferdinand II's involvement in a German war tempted a number of foreign powers to intervene against the Hapsburgs. Christian IV (1588–1648), the king of Protestant Denmark, tried to form a coalition against the empire. But France was unable to take effective action because of the Huguenot [French Protestants] disturbances. James I of England, embroiled as he was in difficulties with Parliament, hesitated to ask it to vote taxes for a foreign war. The Dutch were afraid of an invasion from the Spanish Netherlands. Only Denmark was willing to uphold the Protestant cause in Germany by armed force. Christian IV, a zealous ruler somewhat lacking in judgment, raised an army of more than 20,000 men in 1625. With the help of some German princes he marched against the imperial forces. The emperor then received unexpected help from Albert of Wallenstein (1583–1634), a proud soldier whose wealth enabled him to put a private army in the field. Wallenstein, in a gesture reminiscent of the Roman republic, put his army at Ferdinand II's disposal. The combined armies of Tilly and Wallenstein defeated the forces of Christian IV and occupied his province of Holstein. Wallenstein's apparently invincible army met with a setback when it failed to take by siege the city of Stralsund. But Christian IV's position was precarious. At the treaty of Lübeck (1629) he recovered Holstein but promised not to interfere further in German affairs. Emperor Ferdinand II took advantage of his victories by issuing the Edict of Restitution (1629), which restored to the Catholic Church all properties confiscated in the empire since 1552, and which outlawed all Protestant denominations except the Lutherans. Tilly and others, jealous of Wallenstein's power, persuaded the emperor to dismiss him. The second phase of the Thirty Years War, like the first, ended in victory for the Catholic imperial forces.

The turning point in the Thirty Years War occurred, not in Germany, but in the Italian peninsula. In 1627 the duke of Mantua died without heirs. At the suggestion of the Spanish government, Emperor Ferdinand II occupied Mantua to exclude the French claimant, Charles of Nevers. Pope Urban VIII (1623–44), whose main objective was to protect the Papal States, supported France in the dispute. By 1631, after a short war, French forces drove the Hapsburgs from Mantua and established Charles of Nevers as ruler of the duchy. This trivial incident had wide implications. It revived the centuries-old papal fear of the empire. As had happened so many times before, the pope sought an ally, in this case France, against the emperor. Consistently, and despite angry imperial protests, the papacy refused to regard the warfare in Germany as a crusade against the Protestants. Instead of supporting Emperor Ferdinand II, and preserving the religious lines of conflict, the pope sided with France, and so split Catholic Europe into two rival interests. Urban VIII's action, based on political rather than religious considerations, made it possible for a Catholic state, such as France, to seek Protestant allies against the Catholic Hapsburgs.

THE SWEDISH PERIOD: 1630–1635

The Swedish period of the Thirty Years War opened in the summer of 1630, when King Gustavus Adolphus (1611–32) of Sweden landed in Pomerania with an army of 15,000 men. He was without question the most remarkable personality involved in the war. Handsome, physically strong, somewhat slow of movement but fast and imaginative in making decisions, he was a military genius who could inspire fervent loyalty among his followers. Before his intervention in Germany his reign had been conspicuously successful in both domestic and foreign affairs. In the year of his accession he granted a charter of liberties to the Swedish legislature. He also introduced reforms in Sweden's law courts and administration. In warfare against Russia (1617) and Poland (1621–9), Sweden made important territorial gains. The army which Gustavus Adolphus commanded had the highest standards of conduct of the time, with the possible exception of [Oliver] Cromwell's Ironsides in the English Civil Wars. The troops, mainly Swedish and Finnish peasant boys, were well disciplined and well paid. They had the best muskets of the period. To keep order on the confused and smoke-filled battlefields, Gustavus Adolphus revolutionized tactics by clothing his troops in uniforms of blue and yellow. He was the first European commander to make extensive use of uniforms in the field. Others soon followed his example. In entering the war he had mixed motives. He wished to defend the Protestant religion against the aggression of the emperor. He dreamed also of uniting Germany in a mainly Protestant confederation. But many German princes interpreted his arrival as a sign of Swedish imperialism. Simply because he was a foreigner, Gustavus Adolphus never received full cooperation from the German Protestants. For the same reasons of political jealousy Christian IV of Denmark failed to support him.

Six months after the landing of Gustavus Adolphus in Pomerania, France and Sweden signed the Treaty of Barwald. By this treaty Richelieu [the French minister and director of war strategy] gave Sweden a large subsidy for the conduct of the war. The split within Catholic Europe, precipitated by Pope Urban VIII in the Mantuan crisis, now had its full effect on the Thirty Years War. The character of the war changed from a German and mainly religious struggle to one throughout Europe which was mainly political, as Protestant Sweden and Catholic France joined forces to oppose the Catholic Hapsburgs.

Gustavus Adolphus drove the imperial forces from Pomerania. He then obtained military aid from his brother-in-law, the handsome and bewildered elector George William (1619–40) of Brandenburg. Meanwhile the imperial forces under Tilly invaded Saxony. In May, 1631, they captured Magdeburg, the most important trading city in north Germany, and burned the entire city except for the cathedral. Two-thirds of the population died in this disaster, the most terrible episode of the Thirty Years War. The elector of Saxony consequently abandoned his position of neutrality and allied himself with Gustavus Adolphus. At the battle of Breitenfeld near Leipzig the combined Swedish and Saxon armies defeated Tilly. Gustavus Adolphus occupied all of Bohemia, including the city of Prague. He moved into southern Germany and formed a new Protestant Union. Nothing, it seemed, could prevent his capture of the Hapsburg capital of Vienna. Richelieu was astonished at the unexpected and overwhelming success of France's new ally. At the same time he was disturbed that Sweden might dominate Germany without regard for French interests. The rapid advance of Gustavus Adolphus frightened Emperor Ferdinand II. He asked Wallenstein to form a new army. Wallenstein counterattacked and recaptured Bohemia. After defeating Tilly, who died of battle wounds, Gustavus Adolphus invaded Bavaria and took Munich. At the battle of Lützen (November 16, 1632) he defeated

Wallenstein but lost his life in the fighting.

After the death of Gustavus Adolphus the Swedish army deteriorated in discipline and morale. About the same time Wallenstein's career reached a climax of folly and egomania. He opened secret negotiations with Sweden, Saxony, and France. His hope seems to have been to dominate the empire, and he probably also aspired to the Bohemian throne. Emperor Ferdinand II removed him from his command early in 1634 and rejoiced when he was assassinated a week later. In the fall of that year the imperial forces inflicted a decisive defeat on the Swedish army at Nördlingen. At this time the emperor was in firm possession of southern Germany east of the Rhine. The Swedish rout at Nördlingen wiped out almost all of Gustavus Adolphus' military accomplishments. The treaty of Prague (1635), which restored Catholic and Protestant lands to their status as of 1627, strengthened the Hapsburgs and weakened the authority of the German princes.

THE FRENCH PERIOD: 1635–1648

The last and most devastating part of the Thirty Years War is known as the French, or the Swedish-French, period. In general French and Swedish armies fought, with the help of various allies, against the Hapsburgs of Austria and Spain. In these 13 years religious motives gave way to political motives. Germany became a battleground of rival imperialisms, much like the Italian peninsula in the early sixteenth century. Neither side could muster enough strength for a decisive victory, and the war degenerated into one of attrition. But the French and Swedish forces, separately or in combination, won a number of battles over their opponents: at Wittstock (1636), Leipzig (1642), Jankau in Bohemia (1643), and in Bavaria (1646 and 1648). As an indication of the purely political motives which prevailed, Christian IV of Denmark, fearful of Sweden's continuing power in the Baltic, fought and lost a short war (1643–5) against Sweden, and actually received military aid from his former enemy, the Hapsburgs. In this instance Protestant Denmark and the Catholic Hapsburgs fought against Protestant Sweden, the ally of Catholic France.

The Peace of Westphalia ended the Thirty Years War. The Swedes and the German Protestant princes negotiated with the empire at Osnabrück. The French and the German Catholic princes held their meetings at Münster. The negotiations, begun in 1645, were frequently interrupted by squabbles over ceremony and precedence. Since the war continued during the making of the treaty, the changing course of the war influenced the discussions. The chief territorial gainers were Sweden, Brandenburg, and France. Sweden and Brandenburg acquired western and eastern Pomerania, respectively. France received formal sovereignty over part of Alsace and the bishoprics of Metz, Toul, and Verdun. The Dutch and Swiss republics received formal recognition of their independence. The treaty also granted to the various German states the right to make alliances and treaties, a concession which weakened the already precarious control of the Hapsburg emperors over their imperial domains. In ecclesiastical affairs, the Augsburg settlement of 1555 was extended to include Calvinism, as well as the Catholic and Lutheran faiths, as a denomination which a German prince might declare to be the official religion of his principality. This extension in practice meant a much broader measure of religious toleration than Europe had experienced in the past. . . .

The war had a number of far-reaching political effects. Within Germany the various princes gained important rights, among them the power to make alliances and treaties. The increased independence of the many German states delayed the political unification of Germany for over 200 years and reduced the prestige of the Holy Roman Empire to a ridiculously low level. Within the empire only Austria and (later) Brandenburg-Prussia achieved the status of major powers. The war also shifted the balance of international affairs. It was now impossible for the Hapsburgs to dominate European politics. By 1648, if not before, France had scored a major triumph over Austria and had become Europe's foremost state.

After the Thirty Years War ended, Pope Innocent X published a heated denunciation of the Peace of Westphalia, in particular because it continued the official recognition of the Lutherans and extended that recognition to the Calvinists. His protest was for the most part ignored. This incident reveals the declining prestige of the papacy in European politics. It also reveals the decline of religion and the rise of secularism as a guiding force in Western civilization.

Civil War in England

ROBERT EDWIN HERZSTEIN

Robert Edwin Herzstein analyzes the reign of King Charles I and the religious conflicts that led to civil war. When Puritans in Parliament wanted their power to be as absolute as that demanded by the king, moderates sided with the king, Puritans sided with Oliver Cromwell, and war broke out in 1642. Cromwell led his forces to victory in 1646. Herzstein describes the troubled settlement that led to a second brief war before Cromwell organized a government that lasted until his death in 1658; by then the country was ready to restore the monarchy. Robert Edwin Herzstein taught history at the University of South Carolina. He is the author of *The Holy Roman Empire in the Middle Ages: Universal State or German Catastrophe?*, *Adolf Hitler and the German Trauma 1913–1945*, and *Roosevelt and Hitler: Prelude to War.*

C harles I (1625–1649) did nothing to heal the breach between the king and people. He heartily subscribed to his father's theories of divine right. Charles continued to govern through the ministry of worthless favorites. He was even more strongly opposed than his father had been to Puritanism. Charles was a dignified, cultured, and kindly man, loyal to his friends but woefully lacking in the kind of imagination that is essential to a statesman. Though brought up in England, he had no more understanding of the English people than had the Scottish James, and much less understanding of the Scots, whom he was also called upon to rule.

The events of the early years of Charles' reign ended all hope

Excerpted from *Western Civilization*, by Robert Edwin Herzstein. Copyright © 1975 by Houghton Mifflin Company. Reprinted with special permission from Houghton Mifflin Company. All rights reserved.

of cooperation between king and Parliament. The duke of Buckingham [George Villiers], a favorite of both James and Charles, was the power behind the throne until he was assassinated in 1628. His wars with Spain and in aid of the Huguenots against the French king should have won the support of Parliament, but his utter incompetence served only to enrage the Commons, while Charles' French marriage aroused the old fear of Catholicism. Parliament, therefore, refused supplies and threatened to impeach Buckingham. The king dismissed one Parliament after another with nothing accomplished and finally tried to raise money for the war by forced loans. In 1628, Charles was forced to call Parliament again, and as the price of its cooperation in raising taxes he accepted the Petition of Right. One of the cornerstones of British freedom, the petition is a clear statement of the illegality of the exercise of absolute power on four crucial points: martial law, the billeting of soldiers on the civilian population, arbitrary taxation, and arbitrary imprisonment. These provisions, if respected, would have made absolute government impossible. Charles accepted them, then broke them. When Parliament in protest again refused supplies, he determined to rule without it.

For eleven years, from 1629 to 1640, Charles tried the experiment of personal government without calling Parliament. To the king, it seemed the only alternative. If he could not rule with Parliament—and he could not without abandoning his principles—he would rule without it. This policy aroused resentment among the people whom he could least afford to offend and did not bring in enough money to maintain an army with which to suppress a rebellion. One factor, however, worked in the king's favor: as long as he could avoid calling Parliament, the general discontent had no forum for expression.

So it might have remained if Charles had not, in addition to imposing economic and political oppression, trespassed upon freedom of conscience. He gave a free hand to Archbishop [William] Laud, the most thorough exponent of a "high church" Anglicanism, so that Laud might enforce conformity to the strictest form of Anglican ritual. Laud's plan was to smother Puritanism by denying it every means of expression.

THE LOWLAND SCOTS RISE AGAINST CHARLES

The people who sat sullenly through the prescribed services of the Anglican Church and muttered threats against the government when they returned home to read their Bibles in privacy were characterized by some or all of the following: a Calvinist belief in predestination; a strict morality that showed itself in stern simplicity of life and disapproval of Sunday games; a growing hatred of ritualistic church services, bishops, and Laud's hand-picked clergy; and hatred of royal despotism. It was Scotland that gave the signal and provided the opportunity for rebellion. In 1637, Laud and the king determined to extend the enforcement of the Anglican service to Scotland, to replace the traditional Presbyterianism. This was sheer madness, as James I, who knew the stubborn Scots even if he never came to know the English, might have told them. More accustomed to the ways of rebellion than their law-abiding English neighbors, the Lowland Scots rose as one and swore to a covenant to defend their religion. Charles then marched north with a meager army to force them to obedience, only to find a nation in arms awaiting the attack with a godly fervor. Lacking money and confronted with a people heartily out of sympathy with his plans, Charles could not raise anything like an adequate army.

Absolutism without adequate financial resources had failed. In October 1640, Charles summoned a Parliament to raise money and to re-establish the royal finances on a firmer basis. This was the Long Parliament, which lasted through years of opposition, civil war, and the experiment of the Commonwealth. It provided the long-awaited opportunity to organize opposition to the king.

The members of the new Parliament were almost unanimous in their determination to curb the absolute powers of the monarchy. In the course of a few months, this determined Parliament destroyed absolutism in England forever.

A DIVIDED PARLIAMENT

So far Parliament had been nearly unanimous. The members of the Puritan majority, however, were not content to stop there. They went on to a "root and branch" attack on the episcopal system in the Anglican Church and claimed powers over the army and the executive authority that would have made Parliament as absolute as the king had ever been. Divisions now began to appear in the ranks of the Commons. Many men who had heartily supported acts to curb royal absolutism hesitated at proposals to transfer full authority from king to Parliament, contrary to constitutional precedent. The same men, though willing enough to check the power of Laud's "high church" bishops, whom they suspected of leaning toward Catholic practice, balked stubbornly at Puritan proposals to do away with the Book of Common Prayer, endeared to them by years of familiarity.

Parliament was dividing on religious and political grounds, with Puritans and Parliamentarians on one side, moderate Anglicans and rather reluctant Royalists on the other. At last in 1642 the crisis came, and Parliament and the nation had to make a definite choice. In January, Charles made a frustrated attempt to arrest five members of Parliament recognized as the leaders of the opposition. In self-defense, the Commons took unconstitutional measures to raise an army. The king fled to Oxford and with him went the Royalists in Parliament, a minority of the Commons and a majority of the Lords. Open war was now in effect between king and Parliament, or what was left of it.

The volunteers of the Parliamentary Army were yeoman farmers, gentlemen, and the industrial and commercial classes of the towns. The line between Royalist and Parliamentarian, however, corresponded to no clear class division. Yeomen and gentlemen fought on both sides, and, though London and the seaports were the strongholds of Parliament, there were Royalists in every city, and they were a majority in some. In general the Royalists were stronger in the north and west, and Parliament could count on a majority in the eastern and midland counties. But this geographical alignment was not absolute. It was not a war of sections any more than it was a war of classes.

In the final analysis it was a war of opposing political and religious principles or sentiments. The ancient feeling of loyalty to the crown was the force that rallied people around the royal banner. Some of those who found that they could not ignore the king's call to arms were Puritans, but most were Anglicans, Catholics, and men to whom religion was not a dominating passion. Among them were enough of the hard-drinking, hard-riding gentry to give the whole Royalist party the name Cavaliers. Not all Parliamentarians were Puritans, and not all Puritans were of the strict type of popular fancy. There were enough of the latter, however, to win their party the name Roundheads, for their refusal to wear the flowing curled hair affected by their less austere opponents.

The civil war lasted four years (1642–1646). In the long run, the deciding factor was the New Model Army, recruited from among the most extreme Protestants and organized by a genuine military genius, Oliver Cromwell. Well-armed, well-drilled, and kept under a strict military and moral discipline, the New Model Army formed the shock troops of the parliamentary side. Cromwell's "Ironside" cavalry proved their disciplined worth against the Royalist commander Prince Rupert's wild Cavaliers at Marston Moor in 1644. By the end of the war the New Model represented about a fourth of the Parliamentary forces, by far the most effective part.

With the surrender of the king in 1646, Parliament faced the difficult problem of arranging a permanent settlement. As the price of the Scottish alliance, Parliament in 1645 had agreed to make Presbyterianism the state religion of England. This compromise satisfied most Puritans, who believed some kind of state church to be necessary, though few were really Presbyterian in the Scottish sense. It did not, however, satisfy the members of the New Model Army, recruited from extreme Protestants whose individualistic love of religious freedom made them oppose any state-controlled church. They were the Independents, differing among themselves in theological views but united in the conviction that each congregation must be free to determine its own religion.

The Presbyterian Parliament, flushed with victory, made two serious mistakes. It persecuted Anglicans, thus embittering the defeated Royalists, and, forgetting who had won the war, it also passed persecuting acts against the Independents and proposed to disband the New Model without back pay. The result was a second brief civil war, uniting Royalists, Parliamentary Presbyterians, and Scots in a curious alliance against the Independents. The latter, led by Cromwell, were again victorious, and not to be cheated of the fruits of victory, the army chiefs took control. In December, 1648, they forcibly purged Parliament of its Presbyterian members, leaving only a small minority who could be trusted to do what the army wished. Two months later, this "Rump Parliament" abolished the House of Lords.

For the first and last time in its history, England was subject to a military dictatorship, one which brought about the execution of the defeated king. The Independent army was in the saddle, and in no temporizing mood. In 1649 Charles Stuart met his death with dignity. England staggered under the shock, and men who had fought against him united with those who had rallied round his banner to hail him as a martyr. The execution of the king erased the memory of his oppressive government and made the great majority of the English Royalists at last. After the king's death England was a republic, but a republic ruled by a small minority of armed men who could not count on popular support. During the next eleven years (1649–1660), England passed from one experimental form of government to another. Whatever the form, however, in actual fact England was ruled by Oliver Cromwell, or his son Richard, with the backing of the army. Such a government could not last long, but under the capable guidance of Cromwell it lasted long enough to give England time to recover from the civil war and to restore its prosperity and prestige abroad.

GOVERNMENT UNDER CROMWELL

The internal government of England under Cromwell was peaceful and orderly, but the warlike spirit of the Puritan army had plenty of opportunity to express itself in Ireland, Scotland, and the neighboring states on the Continent. During the period of the Commonwealth (as Cromwell's government was called), Cromwell had to crush strong opposition in both Ireland and Scotland. In the former, the Catholic majority rose in support of the Stuart heir, the future Charles II. The Puritan army invaded Ireland and suppressed the Catholics with barbarous cruelty that they had never exhibited when dealing with their Protestant enemies. To this day, the "curse of Cromwell" is deeply etched in the memory of the Irish people. In Scotland, where the opposition was Presbyterian rather than Catholic, Cromwell was much more merciful. After defeating the Scots, he left them with a settlement that was eminently fair, though unpopular because it was forced upon them by the English and because Cromwell insisted on toleration of other Protestant sects. Having restored peace to the British Isles, the militant Commonwealth turned to war with the Netherlands, the chief commercial rival of England. Before his death in 1658, Cromwell had made England once more a ranking power among the nations of Europe.

On the whole, Cromwell accomplished a great deal of permanent value, for many of his economic policies were carried on by the restored Stuart monarchy. Yet his government grew steadily more unpopular. Under the pressure of what would today be called blue laws [regulating Sunday activities], enforced by the army, many a former Puritan turned Cavalier and many a former Parliamentarian turned Royalist. When the death of Cromwell left the government to his son, the nation was very nearly unanimous in the opinion that only one course lay before it—to restore the Stuart monarchy in the person of Charles II, with adequate guarantees that the powers of Parliament, as determined by the acts of 1640–1641, would be respected. This decision was put into effect without further civil war, thanks to the intervention of General [George] Monk, in command of the army, who used his power to secure a freely elected Parliament which invited Charles II to return. In 1660, the new king was welcomed home with delirious demonstrations of joy. The Anglican Church was restored and for a time persecuted dissenters, but the principle of religious freedom was soon to come into its own, at least as far as dissenting Protestants were concerned.

THE GLORIOUS REVOLUTION

WILL DURANT AND ARIEL DURANT

Will Durant explains how William of Orange of the Netherlands invaded England in 1688 and overthrew King James II, who had ruled since 1685. In his determination to promote Catholicism, James had violated numerous traditions: He had appointed Catholics to ministerial posts and had openly attended Catholic mass. According to the Durants, leading members of Parliament secretly invited William to invade; James was defeated when he realized that his daughters had turned against him and his army had deserted him. James fled to France and never returned to England. The government set up under King William and his wife, Queen Mary, laid the foundation for democracy. Will Durant was a journalist and a professor of Latin, French, and philosophy. He and his wife, Ariel Durant, wrote a popular multivolume work, *The Story of Civilization*, which covers 110 centuries of world history.

James, brooding in defeat [after losing a trial against several Protestant bishops], consoled himself with the infant to which the Queen had given birth on June 10, a month before her expected time. He would bring up this precious boy as a loyal and devoted Catholic. Day by day father and son, over every opposition and discouragement, would move a step nearer to the sacred goal—the old [absolute] monarchy living in concord with the old [Catholic] Church, in an England pacified and reconciled, in a Europe repenting its apostasy [abandonment of religion], and united again in the one true, holy, universal faith.

Perhaps it was the premature birth that brought disaster to the

Excerpted from *The Story of Civilization*, vol. 3, part 4: *The Age of Louis XIV*, by Will and Ariel Durant. Copyright © 1963 by Will and Ariel Durant. Reprinted with permission from Simon & Schuster.

precipitate King. Protestant England agreed with James that this boy might continue the effort to restore Catholicism: it feared him for the same reason that the King loved him. It denied, at first, that this was the King's son; it accused the Jesuits of having brought in some purchased infant to the Queen's bed as part of a plot to keep the King's Protestant daughter Mary from inheriting the throne. It turned more and more to Mary as the hope of English Protestantism, and reconciled itself to another revolution to make her queen.

EXPLORING THE PROSPECT OF A NEW MONARCHY

But Mary was now the wife of William III of Orange, Stadholder [chief magistrate] of the United Provinces; what would proud William say to being merely the consort of a queen? Why not offer him co-ordinate rule with Mary? After all, he too had royal English blood; his mother had been another Mary, daughter of Charles I. In any case William had no intention of playing consort to his wife. It was probably at his suggestion that Bishop [Gilbert] Burnet, who had exiled himself to the Continent on the accession of James, persuaded Mary to pledge her full obedience to William "in all things," whatever authority might devolve upon her. . . .

William, fighting Louis XIV for the preservation of Dutch independence and Protestantism, had hoped for a time to win his father-in-law to an alliance against a French King who was destroying the balance and liberties of Europe. When this hope faded, he had negotiated with those Englishmen who led the opposition to James. He had connived at the organization, on Dutch soil, of [James Scott, duke of] Monmouth's [unsuccessful 1685] expedition against the King, and had allowed it to depart unhindered from a Dutch port. He had reason to fear that James planned to disqualify him as a successor to the throne; and when a son was born to the King, the rights of Mary were obviously superseded. Early in 1687 William sent Everhard van Dykvelt to England to establish friendly contacts with Protestant leaders. The envoy returned with favorable letters from the Marquis of Halifax, the Earls of Shrewsbury, Bedford, Clarendon (son of the former Chancellor), Danby, Bishop Compton, and others. The letters were too vague to constitute clear treason, but they implied warm support for William as a contender for the throne.

In June, 1687, Kaspar Fagel, Grand Pensionary, issued a letter authoritatively stating William's views on toleration: the Stadholder desired freedom of religious worship for all, but opposed the abrogation of the Test Act confirming public office to adherents of the Anglican faith. This cautious pronouncement won him the support of prominent Anglicans. When the birth of a son to James apparently ended William's chances of succeeding James, the Protestant leaders decided to invite him to come and conquer the throne. The invitation (June 30, 1688) was signed by the twelfth Earl of Shrewsbury, the first Duke of Devonshire, the Earls of Danby and Scarborough, Admiral Edward Russell (cousin of the William Russell executed in 1683), Henry Sidney (brother of Algernon), and Bishop Compton. Halifax did not sign, saying that he preferred constitutional opposition; but many others, including Sunderland and John Churchill (both then in the service of James), sent William assurance of their support. The signers recognized that their invitation was treason; they deliberately took their lives in their hands, and dedicated their fortunes to the enterprise. Shrewsbury, a former Catholic converted to Protestantism, mortgaged his estates for forty thousand pounds, and crossed to Holland to help direct the invasion.

William could not act at once, for he was not sure of his own people, and he feared that at any moment Louis XIV would renew his attack upon Holland. The German states also feared attack by France; nevertheless they raised no objection to William's invasion, for they knew that his ultimate aim was to check the Bourbon King [Louis XIV]. The Hapsburg governments of Austria and Spain forgot their Catholicism in their hatred of Louis XIV, and approved the deposition of a Catholic ruler friendly to France. Even the Pope gave the expedition his *nihil obstat* [official approval], so that it was by permission of Catholic powers that Protestant William undertook to depose Catholic James. Louis and James themselves precipitated the invasion. Louis proclaimed that the bonds of "friendship and alliance" existing between England and France would compel him to declare war upon any invader of England. James, fearing that this statement would further unify his Protestant subjects against him, denied the existence of such an alliance, and rejected the offer of French help. Louis let his anger get the better of his strategy. He ordered his armies to attack not Holland but Germany (September 25, 1688); and the States-General of the United Provinces, freed for a time from fear of the French, agreed to let William proceed on an expedition which might win England to alliance against France.

WILLIAM INVADES AND JAMES FLEES

On October 19 the armada set forth—fifty warships, five hundred transports, five hundred cavalry, eleven thousand infantry, including many Huguenot [French Protestant] refugees from the French dragonnades. Driven back by winds, the fleet waited for

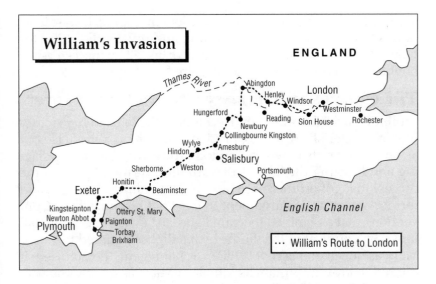

William's Invasion

ENGLAND

··· William's Route to London

a "Protestant breeze," and sailed again on November 1. An English squadron sent to intercept it was scattered by a storm. On November 5—the national holiday commemorating the Gunpowder Plot [an attempt by Catholics to blow up Westminster Palace when the king and Parliament were there]—the invaders landed at Torbay, an inlet of the Channel on the Dorsetshire coast. No resistance was encountered, but no welcome was received; the people had not forgotten Jeffreys and Kirke [officials who tortured and killed men involved in Monmouth's revolt]. James ordered his army, under command of Lord John Churchill, to assemble at Salisbury, and he himself joined it there. He found his troops so lukewarm in their allegiance that he could not trust them to give battle; he ordered a retreat. That night (November 23) Churchill and two other high officers of the King's army deserted to William with four hundred men. A few days later Prince George of Denmark, husband of James's daughter Anne, joined the spreading defection. Returning to London, the unhappy King found that Anne, with Churchill's wife, Sarah Jennings, had fled to Nottingham. The spirit of the once proud monarch broke under the discovery that both his daughters had turned against him. He commissioned Halifax to treat with William. On December 11 he himself left his capital. Halifax, back from the front, found the nation leaderless, but a group of peers made him president of a provisional government. On the thirteenth they received a message from James that he was in hostile hands at Faversham in Kent. They sent troops to rescue him, and on the sixteenth the humiliated King was back in Whitehall Palace. William, advancing toward London, sent some Dutch guardsmen with instructions to carry James to Rochester, and there let him escape. It was done; James fell into the trap laid for him, and quitted England for France (December 23). He would survive his fall by thirteen years, but he would never see England again.

THE CONVENTION FORMS A NEW GOVERNMENT

William reached London on December 19. He used his victory with characteristic firmness, prudence, and moderation. He put an end to the riots in which London Protestants had been pillaging and burning the houses of Catholics. At the request of the provisional government he summoned the lords, bishops, and former members of Parliament to meet at Coventry. The "Convention" that assembled there on February 1, 1689, declared that James had abdicated the throne by his flight. It offered to crown Mary as queen and accept William as her regent; they refused. It offered to crown William as king and Mary as queen; they accepted (February 13). But the Convention accompanied this offer with a "Declaration of Right," which was re-enacted by Parliament as the "Bill of Rights" on December 16, and (though not explicitly agreed to by William) became a vital part of the statutes of the realm:

> Whereas the late King James II . . . did endeavor to subvert and extirpate the Protestant religion, and the laws and liberties of this Kingdom:
>
> 1. By assuming and exercising a power of dispensing with, and suspending of, laws, and the execution of laws, without consent of Parliament; . . .
>
> 3. By . . . erecting a . . . "Court of Commission for Ecclesiastical Causes";
>
> 4. By levying money for and to the use of the Crown, by pretense of prerogative, for other time and in other manner than the same was granted by Parliament.
>
> 5. By raising and keeping a standing army . . . without consent of Parliament; . . .
>
> 7. By prosecutions in the Court of King's Bench for matters and causes cognizable only in Parliament . . .
>
> All which are utterly and directly contrary to the known laws and statutes and freedom of this realm; . . .
>
> Having therefore an entire confidence that . . . the Prince of Orange will . . . preserve them [the Parliament] from the violation of their rights which they

have here asserted, and from all other attempts upon their religion, rights, and liberties, the . . . lords spiritual and temporal and commons, assembled at Westminster, do resolve that William and Mary, Prince and Princess of Orange, be and be declared King and Queen of England, France, and Ireland . . . and that the oaths hereafter mentioned be taken by all persons of whom the oaths of allegiance and supremacy might be required by law. . . .

"I, A. B., do swear that I do from my heart abhor, detest and abjure, as impious and heretical, this damnable doctrine . . . that princes excommunicated or deprived by the pope, or any authority of the see of Rome, may be deposed or murdered by their subjects, or any other whatsoever. And I do declare that no foreign prince, person, prelate, state, or potentate has, or ought to have any jurisdiction, power, superiority, . . . or authority . . . within this realm. So help me God."

. . . And whereas it hath been found by experience that it is inconsistent with the safety and welfare of this Protestant kingdom to be governed by a popish prince, or by any king or queen marrying a papist, the said lords spiritual and temporal, and commons, do further pray that it may be enacted that all and every person and persons that is, are, or shall be reconciled to, or shall hold communion with, the see or Church of Rome, or shall profess the popish religion, or shall marry a papist, shall be excluded and be forever incapable to inherit, possess, or enjoy the crown and government of this realm. . . .

THE GLORIOUS REVOLUTION LAYS THE FOUNDATION FOR DEMOCRACY

This historic proclamation expressed the essential results of what Protestant England called the "Glorious Revolution": the explicit assertion of the legislative supremacy of Parliament, so long contested by four Stuart kings; the protection of the citizen against arbitrary governmental power; and the exclusion of Roman Catholics from holding or sharing the throne of England. Only next to these results in importance was the consolidation of governmental power in the landowning aristocracy; for the revolution had been initiated by great nobles and carried through with the landowning gentry as represented in the House of Commons;

in effect, the "absolute" monarchy by "divine right" had been changed into a territorial oligarchy characterized by moderation, assiduity, and skill in government, co-operating with the princes of industry, commerce, and finance, and generally careless of the artisans and peasantry. The upper middle classes benefited substantially from the revolution. The cities of England recovered their freedom to be ruled by mercantile oligarchies. The merchants of London, who had shied away from helping James, lent £200,000 to finance William between his arrival in the capital and his first reception of parliamentary funds. That loan cemented an unwritten agreement: the merchants would let the landowners rule England, but the ruling aristocracy would direct foreign policy to commercial interests, and would leave merchants and manufacturers increasingly free from official regulation.

There were some inglorious elements in the Glorious Revolution. It seemed regrettable that England had had to call in a Dutch army to redress English wrongs, that a daughter should help oust her father from his throne, that the commander of his army should go over to the invader, and that the national Church should join in overthrowing a King whose divine and absolute authority it had sanctified against any act of rebellion or disobedience. It was regrettable that the supremacy of Parliament had to be vindicated by opposing freedom of worship. But the evil that these men and women did was interred with their bones; the good that they accomplished lived after them and grew. Even in establishing an oligarchy they laid the foundations of a democracy that would come with the broadening of the electorate. They made the Englishman's home his castle, relatively secure against the "insolence of office" and "the oppressor's wrong." They contributed some part to that admirable reconciliation of order and liberty which is the English government today. And they did all this without shedding a drop of blood—except the repeated nosebleeds of the harassed, helpless, deserted, witless King.

THE OTTOMAN TURKS ARE DEFEATED IN VIENNA

FREDERICK L. NUSSBAUM

Frederick L. Nussbaum analyzes the defeat of the Turkish army at Vienna in 1683, marking the end of Turkish expansion in Europe. He describes the disunity and disorganization that prevailed among European powers before forces joined under two Hapsburg commanders, whose armies together defeated the Turkish stronghold at Vienna. Though this area of the Balkans has been politically and economically European since 1683, remnants of Muslim culture still remain. Historian Frederick L. Nussbaum is the author of *The Economic Institutions of Modern Europe* and *Commercial Policy in the French Revolution: A Study of the Career of G.I.A. Ducher.*

T he great, truly world-historical action of these years developed not in the arena of Louis XIV but along the roads which with all their limitations the Austrian monarchy and its allies trod. Here were achievements begun, relations established, which outlasted the centuries.

In these decades of the seventeenth century, while Europe was spreading over all the seas and continents, it was confronted by its final and most serious threat from Islam. In spite of its apparently hopeless disruption and anarchy, it met and surmounted the crisis. The defeat of the Turks before Vienna in 1683 meant that for centuries to come Europe was supreme in its world, without effective external challenge.

Excerpted from *Triumph of Science and Reason,* by Frederick Nussbaum. Copyright © 1953 by Harper & Brothers. Reprinted with permission from HarperCollins Publishers, Inc.

Europe could carry on its conquest of the world in security. The nationalistic prepossessions, markedly baroque, with which the Europeans have made their picture of the past, have focused attention on the record of internal conflicts for power and perquisites. Yet at the time Europeans were fully conscious of the greatness of their salvation. The wars against the Turks, and notably the liberation of Vienna and the recovery of Buda, were celebrated in chronicles and relations, gazettes and geographical descriptions, panegyrics [eulogies of praise] and poems, addressed to the pope, the emperor, the generals and the twenty-seven cardinals elevated in honor of the event. The municipal library of Budapest compiled a bibliography, *Litteratura contemporanea della reconquista el Buda e Pest, 1686–1718;* no less than sixteen hundred of such items are still extant.

TURKISH EXPANSION IN EUROPE

Since the Turks had crossed into Europe, they had expanded their conquests until they faced the Russia of the Romanovs, the Hungary of the Hapsburgs, and the Poland of the Jagellons. They controlled all of the lower Danube, the entire shores of the Black Sea and the Caspian, and disputed the Ukraine with Poland and Russia, Podolia with Poland and Transylvania and the valley of the Theiss with the Hapsburgs. Throughout the Balkans and southern Russia they exercised an imperial authority that did not merely exploit the subject populations as passive victims but organized them to contribute positively to the strength of the empire in wealth, in soldiery and in brains. The harem, the Janizaries [soldiers in the elite Turkish guard], the civil service and the councils utilized this cosmopolitan power, if not without regard to race and religion, at least with a high degree of flexibility and intelligence.

The haremlik, which in the sixteenth century could produce a Suleiman the Magnificent [the sultan of Turkey (1520–1566), under whose governance the Ottoman Empire reached the height of its power], in the seventeenth was producing petty and unmanly specimens such as Mohammed IV. This padishah [sultan of Turkey], under whose reign Christendom was to tremble for the last time before the Turks, left the command of his armies to his grand vizier [high officer in Muslim government] and spent his days hunting. While he was yet a child, his mother as regent had initiated a revival of Turkish vigor. Mohammed Kuprili, the first of a dynasty of strong grand viziers furnished by his family, was called to power in 1656 at the age of seventy. With an administration and an army disciplined to complete responsibility, he made the Turkish empire once more a threat to Europe.

The problem from the Turkish point of view was twofold, to thrust back the advanced position of Venice in the Mediterranean and to utilize the restless Magyars [the principal ethnic group of Hungary] as a base for advance up the Danube at the expense of the Hapsburgs and into the Ukraine and White Russia at the expense of the Poles and the Russians.

On the Danube the Magyars were as unsatisfactory allies for the Turks as they were for the Hapsburgs. When Mohammed Kuprili removed George II Rákóczy for involving himself and the Empire in a war with Poland, Rákóczy rose in rebellion. Kuprili II Ahmed, the son of Mohammed, sent an army into Transylvania and Hungary which was so successful that Ahmed himself entered the campaign with an army of nearly 250,000. Not only Hungary but Moravia and Silesia were devastated. Eighty thousand Christians were carried off into slavery. The Emperor Leopold seemed wholly unable to repulse such forces. Pope Alexander VII bestirred himself to form a Holy League among the Christian princes. Louis XIV was the first to adhere to the League. . . .

DISUNITY AMONG EUROPEANS

Meanwhile, the uncertainties of the Ukrainian situation involved Turkey in wars with Poland and Russia. The hetman [captain] Dourochenko of the western Ukraine, in rebellion against Poland, recognized Turkish suzerainty [in control of international affairs] and brought the Turks into war with the Poles, out of which they won possession of Podolia (1672, 1676). When Dourochenko was driven out by the Muscovite party (1677), war with Russia resulted finally in the surrender by the Turks of Kiev and eastern Ukraine (1681). The peace left Kara Mustapha, the pupil and son-in-law of Kuprili I and third in this dynasty of effective grand viziers, free to take advantage of the rebellion of Emmerich Tököli against the Hapsburgs (1682) to attack Austria. He invaded Hapsburg Hungary with 100,000 troops, won some easy victories and resolved to march directly on Vienna, sure of succeeding where Suleiman the Magnificent had failed a century and a half before.

The situation was wholly favorable to the Turkish hopes. Under Ahmed Kuprili, Crete had been recovered and Podolia conquered from the Poles. Under his successor, Kara Mustapha, peace had been made with Russia by surrendering Turkish claims to the Ukraine. In spite of the conciliatory diet of 1681, Hungary was in rebellion. Tököli had refused the settlement that made an Esterhazy [of Hungary] the palatine and had offered the Turks suzerainty over Hungary. Europe was divided. Not only was

France actively aiding the Hungarian rebels with money and recruits from Warsaw; the French king had defeated the statesman-like plan of Sobieski [the Polish commander of the Hapsburg army] to organize a European defense against the Turks by refusing a truce in his cold war against the Empire. His troops had besieged Luxemburg in full peace and had thus paralyzed the German states to which Leopold might look for assistance. Spain, Austria's natural ally, could hardly provide for the defense of the Netherlands. The United Provinces, torn by the divergences of policy between the estates-general and [Dutch] William of Orange, raised not a hand to save from destruction an ally whose loss would have been fatal to themselves. Frederick William of Brandenburg, betrayed as he believed at Nimwegen, had allied himself with France. His offer of twelve thousand troops was declined at Vienna.

EUROPEANS ORGANIZE TO STOP THE TURKS

On the other hand, the pope succeeded in rendering effective assistance in the organization of European public opinion in response to the danger. At Vienna and Warsaw the papal diplomats played an important part. For a few years, however, the central figure in the organization of the defense was John III Sobieski, king of Poland. As hetman he had made his reputation by defeating the Turks in Podolia. As king he undertook a statesman-like program: peace between Russia and Poland, truce between the Bourbon and the Hapsburg, alliance between Poland and Austria.

Sobieski's program was crippled from the start by the refusal of Louis XIV to commit himself to a truce. Although France had favored his election, Sobieski gradually drew away from France and undertook a rapprochement with Austria. When French diplomats attempted by bribes to bring about the dissolution of the diet, Sobieski exposed them and for the time ended French influence. The emperor, meanwhile, was not eager for the alliance. The Hungarian rebels had received assistance from Poland and had even offered Sobieski the suzerainty of Hungary. It was not until the threatened invasion had become actual that terms were arrived at by which Sobieski was to receive a subsidy of 1,200,000 florins and furnish 40,000 men to make up a force of 100,000. When Louis XIV, under what was made to seem a response to public opinion, volunteered to raise the siege of Luxemburg, the German states responded to the emperor's appeals with respectable contingents.

In December, 1682, Kara Mustapha in effect declared war by demanding impossible conditions for the renewal of the truce which an Imperial mission had been seeking. An attack on the Empire had been the focus of the grand vizier's policy since the beginning of his career. In 1676 his announcement of this intention had been noted with satisfaction in the French council of state. War with Poland and then with Russia had prevented its execution. Now, at peace with both, he formally recognized Emmerich Tököli as vassal king of Hungary and organized an army at Adrianople. As it advanced through the Balkans reinforcements from the vassal states joined until it amounted to about 250,000 men, a very large proportion of which was service forces.

TWO ARMIES UNITE TO DEFEAT THE TURKS

[A commander of a Hapsburg army] Charles of Lorraine, in command of the [Hapsburg] Imperial forces, had only about thirty thousand men and was obliged to adopt a Fabian policy [of avoiding direct confrontation] until reinforcements could reach him from the German states and Poland. By defeating the attempt of Tököli to take Pressburg, he was enabled to effect a junction with the Poles at Hollabrun and with the Germans at Tuln. The whole Christian force, numbering about seventy thousand, crossed the Danube and, without interference by the Turks, marched along the south bank to the Kahlenberg, a height that looked down on Vienna and the plain to the east.

The siege had begun on July 16, 1683. The heroic story of the defense has become the keystone of Vienna's legend. Under Count Rüdiger von Stahremberg some thirteen thousand regular troops, reinforced by all the able-bodied citizenry, maintained an obstinate resistance in spite of the ravages of famine, disease and bombardment. More than once Kara Mustapha might have taken the city by storm. He chose to wait until the rigors of the siege would compel surrender. The limit of human endurance was almost reached when, on September 11, the relieving army appeared on the slopes of the Kahlenberg.

Under the command of Sobieski, the European forces took advantage of the unpreparedness of the besiegers and promptly attacked on September 12. The result was a surprisingly easy victory. The Moldavian and Wallachian auxiliaries on the Turkish right were overrun by the Imperial forces. The whole line then threw itself on the Turkish camp and routed its guards. The Janizaries were caught in the siege trenches between the defenders and the vanguard of the relieving army and cut to pieces. In eight hours' combat the relief of Vienna had been accomplished.

The galvanic spasm of delight that shook Europe and found expression in hundreds of retellings of the story and eulogies of the leaders was not matched by a corresponding resolution of the political issues. The participants in the battle themselves fell at once into jealous conflicts over their relative merits. The Imperials complained because they had borne the brunt of the battle and the Poles got the glory and most of the booty. The Polish king in turn was aggrieved because Leopold failed to show adequate gratitude and recognition. Louis XIV ordered the siege of Luxemburg re-established. The Spanish, hopeful of Dutch and Imperial support, declared war on France. The Imperial government faced again the same issue it had faced when the Turkish threat was developing, whether its principal interest was in the east or in the west. After a long debate, Leopold followed the urging of the pope and his victorious generals, rather than that of Spain, and entered upon a Holy League with Poland, Venice and the Knights of Malta to fight "the thirteenth crusade" (March 5, 1684) and developed the campaign against the Turks. France held off to pursue its own campaign against the Barbary pirates, but Russia adhered in 1686.

The exploitation of the Turkish defeat developed rapidly to such a degree of success that eastern Europe was transformed. Kara Mustapha laid the responsibility for the defeat on Ibrahim, pasha of Buda, and had him executed, but a few days later, by order of the sultan, was himself executed at Belgrade. The Turks were unable to find a point of resistance. In 1684 Pest was taken, Buda besieged and a Turkish army destroyed in Croatia. In 1685 the Imperial forces recovered Gran and Neuhaüsel. Tököli was chased into exile. On the famous battlefield of Mohács another destructive defeat was inflicted on the Turks. Buda was finally taken in 1687. [Prince of Transylvania George] Apaffy did homage to the emperor and a Hungarian diet at Pressburg declared the crown of Hungary hereditary in the house of Austria. The Venetians under Morosini, the hero of Candia, made their way into the Morea and besieged Athens, destroying the Parthenon, which the Turks had turned into a powder magazine (1687). The Turks at last sought to negotiate peace, but the demands of the Imperials were such that the Turks determined to continue the war. They were saved by Louis XIV. In September, 1688, the War of the League of Augsburg began. In spite of the mediatory efforts of England and Holland, the war in the Balkans dragged on until 1699, when Turkey had to give up Hungary and Transylvania to the Empire, Podolia and the western Ukraine to the Poles, Dalmatia and the Peloponnesus (less Corinth) to the Venetians as well as the islands of Aegina and Saint Maur, and to the Russians, Azov.

In spite of division, conflict and confusion, Europe had ended the threat of conquest by Islam. It had preserved not only its system of power but its secularism and segmentation. The Balkans continued to be governed from Constantinople but the powerful forces of economic and technological advance and of intellectual adventure at first slowly and then, with the French Revolution, more rapidly penetrated the areas where once Islam had brought a civilization of a different order. Europe's conquest in cultural terms was never complete. Not only Islam but Byzantium still differentiates the southeast section of the European peninsula from the north and west. Nevertheless, the essential condition of European advance was established. Europe was still capable of suicide, but it was secure against catastrophe from the outside.

PETER THE GREAT AND RUSSIA'S EMERGING ROLE

B.H. SUMNER

B.H. Sumner portrays Peter the Great as an energetic leader and strategist who set extravagant goals that others predicted would fail. Peter was active on four fronts—Siberian, Caspian, Persian, and Baltic—and he founded the city of St. Petersburg in 1703. Despite poor health, he charged ahead with his plans until he died at age fifty-two, following a rescue operation in icy water. According to Sumner, Peter transformed Russia from a country seldom regarded by other Europeans to a major participant in European history. Sumner taught Russian history at Oxford University in England. He is the author of A Short History of Russia and Survey of Russian History.

U nder Peter, Russia was active on every frontier. In 1700 and 1703 he received embassies from the khan of Khiva appealing for protection from Bokhara [one of the oldest cultural and trade centers of Asia]. He was too engrossed in war with Sweden to take any practical action, but eleven years later when another appeal came from the khan his hands were less tied. He was at that same time drinking in tales from a Turkoman adventurer of river gold in the Central Asian sands, of the old course of the Oxus flowing into the Caspian instead of the Aral Sea, and of the routes to India. Thereupon (1714) Peter decided to mount a large expedition to explore, trade, and seek gold; to bring Khiva, and Bokhara if it proved possible, into subjection, and to

Excerpted from *Peter the Great and the Emergence of Russia* (New York: Collier Books, 1962) by B.H. Sumner. Copyright © 1962.

send forward a detachment up the Oxus and on to India. The expedition, 3,500 strong, explored the eastern Caspian, and then struck across the desert for Khiva (1716–17). There it found a new, unfriendly khan. After beating his troops, it ignominiously fell into the simplest of traps and was butchered almost to the last man.

THE SIBERIAN FRONT

This signal disaster coincided with Russian thrusts from the side of Siberia, whence Peter sent out four expeditions into the Central Asian steppes (1714–22). The quest for gold, which was uppermost, proved fruitless, but the confines of Siberia were successfully advanced; [the city of] Omsk was founded (1717); with the Kazakhs [pastoral Muslims in Kazakhstan and northern China] closer relations were knit, which twenty years later were to have important consequences. Russian knowledge of these steppe regions was greatly extended, and the first history and geography of the Kalmuk lands [a region of southwest Russia occupied by Buddhist Mongols] was written. Siberia under Peter became not only a land of convict labour (and of Swedish prisoners of war), but also a land with growing agriculture and with the first beginnings of mining. It was ceasing to be dominated by the fur interest, but it did not become what he hoped it would, a land of gold, until the nineteenth century.

THE CASPIAN FRONT

The Khivan expedition coincided also with further activity on the Caspian and in Persia. In 1715 Peter appointed one of his most energetic "fledglings," Volynsky, to undertake a mission to the shah. His instructions, revised by Peter's own hand, included a commercial treaty and full information on the condition, resources, and communications of Persia, especially those with India, as well as on the silk trade and the possibility of killing the overland route through Turkey by diverting the whole trade to Russia. Special attention was to be given to the Armenians. Volynsky concluded a commercial treaty (1717), which gave Russian merchants valuable openings, but the most important consequences of his mission were that it revealed to Peter the extreme weakness into which Persia had sunk and created additional links with the Georgians and Armenians in Transcaucasia. Further reconnaissances were made to chart the Caspian and spy out routes. Volynsky was made governor of Astrakhan [a city on the Volga River], whence he continued to prepare the ground and sent Peter reports urging that with but a small army the Persian silk provinces along the Caspian could be seized.

In December 1721 Peter received the news of outrages committed on Russian merchants in Transcaucasia by the wild Lesghian mountaineers of Daghestan [a region bordering the Caspian Sea], nominal subjects of the shah. "Now is the very occasion for which you were ordered to prepare"; so Peter wrote to Volynsky. Immediately news followed that the shah had been deposed by an Afghan revolt. The Safavi dynasty was at the last stage of collapse and Persia in the throes of anarchy. Peter launched out on his Caspian venture.

He found Transcaucasia divided between Persia and the advancing Ottoman empire. To the north of the Caucasus along the Terek river, flowing into the Caspian, ran the shadowy southern limits of his own empire, the rough, frontier land of the Terek Cossacks [people of southern Russia and adjacent parts of Asia, noted as cavalry men]. For the last century and a half Muscovite connections had been slowly increasing with the peoples of the Caucasus, and with the two ancient Christian peoples, the Georgians and the Armenians, living beyond the mighty range.

Armenian merchants played a great rôle in the silk trade, so much coveted by Peter, and were regular go-betweens with Muscovy through Astrakhan. The various Georgian principalities were divided amongst themselves in internecine rivalry. Many of their nobility were much Persianized and often found it convenient to embrace Islam. Yet they also found it convenient to look northwards to the Orthodox tsar, far away though he was in Moscow. . . .

THE PERSIAN FRONT

Unlike the earlier Romanovs [Russian ruling dynasty], Peter was less interested in Georgia than in the coastal Caspian provinces of Persia. These were the main object of the war that he began in 1722. Nominally it was to aid the helpless shah to restore order in his own dominions. Actually it was to forestall the Turks and establish Russian control of the western and southern shores of the Caspian and thereby capture the silk trade.

Peter led his army in person, accompanied by Catherine. He sailed down the Volga to Astrakhan, where he had mustered a force of 30,000 troops and 5,000 sailors, in addition to large numbers of Cossacks and other irregular cavalry. Thence he sailed across to the Terek region with his infantry, while the cavalry went round by land, facing "indescribable labour in their march on account of lack of water and bad grass." Meeting with little organized resistance, he occupied without difficulty his first main objective, Derbent, an important strategical and trading centre on the coast. Thence he planned to seize Baku [a city on the western shore of the Caspian] and send up a force to Tiflis [the capital of Georgia; modern-day Tbilisi] to clinch the adherence of the strongest of the Georgian princes and of certain groups of Armenian mountaineers.

Both were in sizable strength and professed to be ready for action, once Russian support arrived on the scene. But the Georgian had to admit being challenged by a rival prince, and he could make no impression on the Lesghian confederacy in Daghestan. Peter did not repeat the gamble of thrusting forward in expectation of a Christian rising. It was late summer, and sickness took a terrible toll of his troops and horses. His supply fleet suffered severely in a storm. The Daghestan mountaineers were in dangerous force on his flank. He decided to withdraw to the Terek and Astrakhan. Once again Peter had showed himself far too over-confident and had trusted too much to uncompleted or extemporized plans. But he had no intention of abandoning his Caspian venture, and in those regions, with the star of the Persians at its lowest, a daring policy might reap a rich harvest.

In that same autumn (1722) a small detachment was sent to seize the Persian port of Resht, and in the next year Baku was occupied by larger forces. Simultaneously, a treaty was signed with the now derelict shah by which Peter undertook to defend him against his foes in return for the cession of the Persian seaboard provinces, already occupied at key-points by his troops.

At the same time the Turks entered upon the scene to vie with the Russians in annexations. They soon came to the edge of war with Peter. He was determined to block their path to the Caspian and to keep his hold there, but he continued to be cautious in his dealings with the Armenians and Georgians inland, whom the Turks were equally determined to keep from Russian clutches. After much entangled diplomatic wrestling a troubled agreement was reached (1724): Peter kept his coastal strip, and the Turks kept Georgia, which they had overrun, and suzerainty over their Sunni [a branch of Islam] brethren in the fastnesses [strongholds] of Daghestan. . . .

THE BALTIC FRONT

Internal divisions in Sweden gave Peter every opportunity to establish his influence at Stockholm. Both George I and Frederick IV of Denmark feared the worst from the far-reaching designs they attributed to him in Holstein [a region of northern Germany] and Mecklenburg [a region of northeast Germany on the Baltic Sea], and Frederick [king of Prussia] was also faced with demands for Russian exemption from the Sound dues. Their alarms were further increased when early in 1724 Russian influence in Stockholm rose so high that a defensive alliance was made between the two ex-enemies, which included an ominous provision for joint action to obtain satisfaction for the duke of Holstein. A British diplomat belittled such an alliance as being "like Daniel's dream, a toe of clay to an image of brass, which can never consolidate." In the long run he was right, but for the time being the newcomer in the Baltic had preponderant power. . . .

In 1720 Peter concluded a treaty with Frederick William, the first of a long series of similar treaties with Prussia and Austria culminating in the first partition of Poland (1772). Thereby the free, elective constitution of the Polish monarchy and the "liberties" of Poland, including the famous *liberum veto* [freedom to vote], were to be preserved intact. This was the riposte of Peter to the lining up of Augustus II with the emperor and George I. The treaty meant, in effect, a Russo-Prussian combination to keep Poland weak, distracted, and unreformed. It did not, however, mean a Russian intention to partition Poland.

Schemes of partition had been broached already in the seventeenth century, though not by Muscovy, and were repeatedly put forward by Frederick William and by Augustus himself. They involved the lopping off of portions of Poland, then the second largest country in Europe, but by no means the disappearance of Poland as a state. Peter neither proposed nor planned any considerable diminution of Poland, save as regards the vassal fief of Courland [a region of southern Latvia], which he succeeded in keeping as a Russian pawn. He preferred to hold fast to what had become his policy of checkmating Augustus's designs and of maintaining Russian influence in Poland by bribery, intimidation, and force, playing off against each other Augustus and the confederation of his Polish opponents. It was aptly said at the time: "He has built his system upon the dissensions of this country and with the design of making them arise should they not appear of themselves.". . .

THE FOUNDING OF ST. PETERSBURG

At times Peter was gay and confident that his labours were bearing good fruit and that his heritage was secure. Few shared such optimism. St. Petersburg was almost as unpopular as ever. The labour gangs still toiled there, as on the Ladoga canal: "This is, as it were, the bottomless pit in which innumerable Russian subjects perish and are destroyed." The upper class cursed as ever the expense of having to build houses and live in a remote marsh, far from supplies and their regular haunts.

None the less, St. Petersburg was growing fast, and its position as a great port assured. Ten years earlier one foreign diplomat compared it to "a heap of villages linked together, like some plantation in the West Indies." Later he styled it "a wonder of the world, considering its magnificent palaces . . . and the short time that was employed in building it." In actual fact, it was very far from being as yet the majestic capital that [architect] Rastrelli and others created in the second half of the century. Peter had no taste for sumptuous buildings, and was economical, even parsimonious, in his personal expenditure and his own court, though he allowed his wife ample scope and required of his grandees lavish hospitality.

The capital was graced now, if boorishly in western eyes, by Peter's new "assemblies"; mixed evening parties, two or three times a week, with dancing, cards, chess, and forfeits. These he had instituted immediately after returning from Paris in 1717. The hosts were designated by Peter himself, and he required that the guests should be drawn from a wide variety of persons and not confined to the aristocracy. Unlike most of his entertainments, there was no heavy drinking at the "assemblies," and they were a genuine and successful essay in accustoming Russian society to the novelty of social intercourse between men and women on a more or less western model.

PETER'S FINAL YEARS

Peter spent the last year of his life in St. Petersburg and thereabouts. His health grew steadily worse, and at times he would withdraw in unaccustomed, morose aloofness. Despite his doctors, he was frequently on the move—to visit his new residence at Peterhof near by, with its fountains which he prized so highly (now utterly ruined by the Germans); to inspect salt works near Novgorod [a city south of St. Petersburg important as an old trade route of eastern Europe] and the Ladoga canal, new factories and neighbouring shipyards; to take the Olonets waters and there enjoy himself hammering out sheets of iron. He was constantly cruising, constantly carousing, rather less constantly at work. A few weeks before his death he was not only taking the final decisions for the creation of his long-meditated Academy of Sciences, but was also revising details of the bacchanalian rites that he had instituted thirty years before and never abandoned.

Always he had lived at full stretch; he had grown to great stature as a statesman, warrior, and ruler, but in his grosser man he remained as he was as a youth. One of his doctors, a Scotsman, high in eulogy of "the unbounded genius of this great and active prince," declared that his "failings . . . principally, if not solely, arose from his inclination to the fair sex." Another admirer, at second hand, appositely summed up: "In short, for a king he was as little elegant as expensive in his amours: as in things of the highest moment, so in this he acted according to his inclinations without any regard to forms."

In mid-November 1724, when he was sailing off to visit some iron-works, a boat was shipwrecked before his eyes. He leapt into the icy water and laboured indefatigably at rescue work. He was inflamed with a fever, and though he was soon intermittently hustling about again, he was a stricken man. The strangury and stone [a bladder condition] returned. At the end of January 1725 he was in great pain and unable to leave his bed. In the early morning of February 8, unconscious for the last thirty-six hours, he died.

The death of Peter was acclaimed abroad with jubilation everywhere, save in Berlin where Frederick William alone of sovereigns ordered court mourning "for his dearest friend." No longer would the "northern Turk" disrupt the balance of Europe; now his surcharged country would relapse into internal broils and impotence. No one indeed could fill the place of so wholly an exceptional ruler as Peter, and decline there was bound to be; but there was no such breakdown as many expected. Catherine was immediately proclaimed empress without opposition, thanks to swift last-minute decisions . . . and to the devotion of the guards to their dead emperor and his consort.

Peter's Legacy

At once the official paeans began. Peter was lauded as "a Joseph who hath enlarged thy stores, and enrich'd thee with all good things, such as thou never before enjoyd'st! A Joseph, who hath brought thee out of darkness into light, out of ignorance into knowledge, out of contempt into glory . . . !" So Russia was told in funeral sermons, and for long afterwards in orations, odes, and anniversary outpourings. It is true that much genuine pride was felt in the new position in the world that Russia now occupied, thanks to Peter, but most of his subjects were far more conscious of the price they had to pay for "glory." Nothing is more revealing than a vivid, popular woodcut issued at this time and widely circulated for long afterwards which bore the title "The mice bury the cat."

What was the legacy of Peter? How much of it survived? What is his place in history?

First and most obviously, he transformed Russia's foreign relations. For a century before Peter, Muscovy had been tentatively and spasmodically linking herself closer with the West. Now henceforward Russia played her part as one of the main participants in European history. One dry, prosaic fact speaks for much: on Peter's accession he found his country with only one regular mission abroad, in Warsaw; on his death he left his representatives accredited to almost all the courts of Europe. For long Russia's part was confined to diplomacy, politics, and war. Within ten years of Peter's death she [Catherine] decided the issue of the Polish succession; within forty years the issue of the Seven Years' War in Europe; within ninety years the issue of Napoleon. Later her contribution was enlarged to cover the arts and sciences; and in [the twentieth] century it [was] transformed by the Soviet revolution into one of the greatest world influences of our day.

LOUIS XIV AT THE PEAK OF ABSOLUTISM

T. WALTER WALLBANK AND ALASTAIR M. TAYLOR

Authors T. Walter Wallbank and Alastair M. Taylor portray the Sun King, Louis XIV, who reigned from 1643 until 1715, as an absolute monarch whose power regulated all aspects of French life. Wallbank and Taylor describe Louis XIV's excesses: the palace of Versailles and the lavish lifestyle prevalent in the palace. The authors also describe the king's military exploits and the Treaty of Utrecht that ended Louis XIV's wars. Wallbank taught history at the University of Southern California in Los Angeles, and Taylor taught history at the University of Edinburgh, Scotland, and at Queen's University, Kingston, Ontario. They are coauthors of *The World in Turmoil, Promise and Perils,* and *Western Perspectives: A Concise History of Civilization.*

T he seventeenth and eighteenth centuries saw monarchical absolutism reach its height. Practically everywhere [in Europe] the power of the nobles had been destroyed, the government centralized, the Church brought under royal control, and all power lodged in the hands of absolute kings. Only in England, the Swiss cantons, and the Netherlands were there governments which rested even to a limited degree on the consent of the governed. . . .

Under the system of absolutism the king's power reached every aspect of his subjects' existence. The king regulated every phase of economic life, from the establishment of new industries to working conditions and standards of quality. As head of the Church he decided what religion his subjects were to follow and

Excerpted from *Civilization: Past and Present,* vol. 2, revised edition, by T. Walter Wallbank and Alastair M. Taylor. Copyright © 1949 by Scott Foresman and Company. Reprinted with permission from Scott Foresman-Addison Wesley.

persecuted those who dissented. He was the supreme and only lawgiver, the fountain of justice, the arbiter of manners and fashion, the patron of arts and letters, the personification of national glory. A vast and obedient bureaucracy and a powerful royal army enforced his will.

Though such a system of all-pervasive absolutism seems abhorrent to a modern generation nurtured in freedom and democracy, in the seventeenth century it was generally unquestioned and often very popular. A powerful king stood for order, efficiency, prosperity, and security—values willingly exchanged for the uncertainties of upheaval and bloodshed such as had been experienced during the Religious Wars. Furthermore the tradition of obedience to authority was still strong, as it had been in the Middle Ages. The ideas of individualism and liberty born of the Renaissance were not to bear political fruit until a later day. . . .

RICHELIEU CREATES THE STRUCTURE OF ABSOLUTISM

For "eighteen years the biography of [cardinal] Richelieu is the history of France." As chief adviser to Louis XIII, "the grim cardinal" set about restoring and furthering the work of his royal master's father [Henry IV, whose death left Louis XIII, a boy of nine, on the throne]. His basic objective was to exalt the power of the monarchy, to make Louis' power unchallengeable.

The structure of absolutism quickly took shape under Richelieu's direction. Castles of the nobility were torn down, their power as governors in the local districts was eliminated, local officials, called *intendants*, were superimposed on the governors, and finally the Estates-General—a body that might have challenged the power of the king—was shelved. . . .

Richelieu died in 1642, just a year before the passing of Louis XIII. Again the throne of France was occupied by an infant, Louis XIV, who was less than five years old. But Richelieu had anticipated this emergency. Before he died he had carefully schooled a promising young Italian to carry on his work. This was Cardinal Mazarin, who governed France with a firm and efficient hand during the minority of the king. Following the death of Mazarin in 1661, Louis XIV, then twenty-three years old, took over the personal management of state affairs. He found an obedient and docile people to govern. Henry IV, Richelieu, and Mazarin had done their work well. During the incredibly long reign (1643–1715) of Louis XIV the French people "worked, fought, lived, conquered for him alone."

In personal appearance Louis XIV was well qualified to play the role of absolute king. He was regal and dignified, whether in his dressing gown or in his most magnificent robes of state, and has been described as "the greatest actor of majesty that ever filled a throne." While not possessing a creative mind, the young king was of much more than average intelligence. He certainly was far superior to his mediocre father and to his degenerate great-grandson, Louis XV. Louis XIV worked assiduously at what he described as "the business of being king." His duties in the council chamber and the many documents which accumulated on his desk demanding attention took from six to eight hours of his time every day. This did not include Louis' attendance at court ceremonies and palace fetes.

A burning ambition to make his reign glorious possessed Louis. Believing implicitly in the divine right of kings, he chose the sun as the symbol of his power. There was no one to curb his inordinate pride. His fawning courtiers dubbed him *le roi-soleil* (sun king) and he became known throughout Europe as the Grand Monarch.

THE MAJESTY AND POMP OF VERSAILLES

The palace of the Louvre in Paris had been good enough for his predecessors, but Louis wanted a more magnificent symbol for his greatness. Nine miles from Paris, midst barren marsh land, the king began in 1669 to build the palace of Versailles. At one time more than thirty thousand men were employed on this project, and the total cost of construction probably exceeded one hundred million dollars. André Lenôtre, the master gardener of his time, transformed the marsh land into the most beautiful park in Europe. Versailles when completed had a façade over a quarter of a mile in length.

Its interior consisted of great rooms richly decorated with gilding, carvings, tapestries, and statues. The most famous of these rooms were the Salon of Apollo, with a solid silver throne, and the Grand Hall of Mirrors. The latter has seen much history. Besides its association with the military glories of Louis, in this room [Otto von] Bismarck proclaimed the new German Empire after the defeat of France in 1871. In 1919 the great mirrors reflected an equally momentous occasion when the representatives of Germany signed the Treaty of Versailles [ending World War I].

Versailles Palace is a depressing place today. The huge building seems lifeless, a symbol of royal elegance and tinsel court life that has no place in our modern world. But two hundred years ago Versailles was the most fashionable spot in Europe. Here during the day the French nobles promenaded with their king among the woods, terraces, and fountains of the park. Or they hunted and hawked in the nearby woods and meadows. At night thousands of candles transformed Versailles into a blaze of light.

Lords and ladies, in powdered wigs, silks, and laces, attended balls, masquerades, and concerts. Or if the weather was unusually fine, aquatic carnivals were held on the Grand Canal in the park.

The pomp and circumstance of Versailles had many unfortunate results, one being the excessive cost and the consequent economic burden on the masses. Perhaps most regrettable, however, was the fact that Versailles acted as a barrier between king and people. Louis XIV was isolated from his people. He lived in a world of glitter and luxury removed from the realities of the world of his subjects.

Louis XIV

Perhaps the most interesting aspect of life at Versailles was its "cult of majesty." Palace etiquette was carried to ridiculous extremes. The king was treated practically as a god. Life at Versailles was a continuous pageant and Louis as the symbol of the state was the center of it. The court nobles now lived a purposeless existence, dependent upon the favor of the king and in no position to challenge his word. Surrounded by fawning toadies and satellites, Louis' every action was made a regal ceremony based on the strictest precedent. For example, a nobleman of designated rank was required to dry the king after his bath, and only a very illustrious noble could hand the king his royal shirt or breeches during the public ceremony of dressing.

LOUIS XIV SERVES AS A EUROPEAN ROLE MODEL

During the seventeenth century France was the premier nation of Europe. The absolute monarchy of the Bourbons [the French royal family] was the inspiration for most of the ruling houses on the continent. The splendor and formality of Versailles was meticulously copied. In the words of [historian] Professor L. B. Packard, "From Versailles emanated the dress, manners, speech and fashions of civilized Europe." In nearly every phase of government—in diplomatic practice, the functioning of the central government, the organization of the army—the absolute state of Louis XIV was the model.

It was Louis' desire to strengthen even further the system of absolutism handed on to him by Richelieu and Mazarin. To that end he increased the powers of the *intendants* instituted by Richelieu, reorganized the army, drawing it more closely under state control, and instituted a wide variety of economic reforms designed to increase revenue and strengthen the competitive position of France. To carry out his economic policies Louis was fortunate in possessing as his finance minister the able Jean Baptiste Colbert. Under Colbert's guidance new industries were encouraged, agriculture flourished, colonies were founded, the navy was strengthened, and a surplus was accumulated in the treasury. Imports from other countries were excluded by high tariff barriers, while within France the removal of many provincial customs duties enabled trade to move more freely than ever before. Business practices and standards of quality and workmanship were minutely regulated. This systematic embodiment of mercantilist doctrines came to be known as Colbertism and served as the model for would-be despots all over Europe. . . .

The prosperity of France cultivated so assiduously in the days of Colbert did not long endure. Nearly all the achievements of that great minister went for naught in the face of the king's reckless expenditure of money at Versailles and his costly wars. Instead of social progress Louis chose military glory.

LOUIS XIV WAGES WARS

Louis' thirst for conquest kept Europe in almost constant turmoil for nearly fifty years. Fortified by the knowledge that he possessed the strongest army in existence and the most capable generals of the age, he embarked on a career of conquest whose basic objective was to attain for France her "natural boundaries." This meant extending French territory on the north at the expense of the Spanish Netherlands, and on the east to the Rhine. . . .

During the numerous wars which agitated Europe from 1667 to 1713 there evolved what was to become the guiding principle of international diplomacy in modern times—the concept of the balance of power. . . . To prevent France from dominating Europe, coalition after coalition was formed to resist the aggression of Louis XIV. From this time on relations among European nations tended to fall into a definite pattern whereby the various powers refused to permit any single state or combination of nations to exercise too much power. In maintaining this delicate diplomatic equipoise, England, . . . because of her relative geographical isolation from the continent, assumed the role of diplomatic balance wheel, throwing her support from one side to the other in order to maintain the balance of power on the continent.

Another important development was that wars were becoming worldwide in scope. In the War of the Spanish Succession the struggle was carried on by fleets in the Mediterranean and Atlantic and by armies along the Rhine and in Spain, Italy, and even far-off colonial America. Warfare from now on became less and less localized and hence more dangerous and destructive to civilization. During the period just reviewed, however, and throughout the eighteenth century until the French Revolution, warfare was largely confined to the soldiery and did not involve civilian populations as it had done in the Thirty Years' War and was to do again in more recent times.

THE TREATY OF UTRECHT AND THE END OF LOUIS XIV'S WARS

Of the several treaties which ended the wars of Louis XIV, the Treaty of Utrecht was most important in shaping the map of modern Europe. This peace settlement, made in 1713, is comparable in its importance to the Peace of Westphalia, concluded in 1648. The Treaty of Utrecht arranged with France a relatively moderate settlement. No nation was excessively weakened, no single power was made too strong, and a fairly satisfactory balance of power was maintained without any major conflicts for nearly thirty years. The terms of the Treaty of Utrecht were as follows:

(1) Louis' grandson was permitted to remain king of Spain so long as the thrones of France and Spain were not united.

(2) England obtained important colonies from France and Spain: Nova Scotia, Newfoundland, and the Hudson's Bay territory, and valuable naval bases in the Balearic Isles and Gibraltar in the Mediterranean.

(3) The Duke of Savoy, an Italian ruler, was given the title of king, and Sicily was added to his possessions.

(4) To Austria the allies gave Naples, Milan, Sardinia, and the Spanish Netherlands—the last to discourage the further expansion of France.

(5) The Dutch were allowed to regain certain important fortresses on their southern frontier as a protection from any future aggression from France.

(6) The Hohenzollern elector of Brandenburg was recognized as "king in Prussia" in recognition of his support of the alliance against France.

(7) France was allowed to retain most of the conquests along her boundaries made in preceding years. This gave her more defensible frontiers.

The significance of several provisions in this peace should be noted. The partition of the Spanish domains in Europe and the accession of the Bourbons to the throne of Spain after almost two centuries of Hapsburg rule marked the end of an era. The long-standing French-Spanish rivalry was now replaced by a strong French-Spanish family alliance as Bourbons occupied the two thrones. The English acquisition of important colonies and naval bases marks a significant stage in the rise of England to world power. The Treaty also gave recognition to two aggressive ruling families, the House of Savoy and the House of Hohenzollern. In the nineteenth century . . . the House of Savoy succeeded in unifying Italy politically, and the Hohenzollerns did the same for Germany.

Economic Advancements and Natural Disasters in England

—— | CHAPTER 2 | ——

ENGLAND'S TRANSPORT REVOLUTION

PHYLLIS DEANE

Phyllis Deane analyzes the financing, building, and significance of the English transport system on which the Industrial Revolution was built. England had had roads and coastal routes for centuries, but the canal network built from the mid–seventeenth century on made possible the movement of heavy goods, such as coal and iron, which were necessary for manufacture. According to Deane, government financing is usually necessary for projects as costly and time-consuming as transportation infrastructure, but in England private investors financed most of the canals. Because the canal system reduced costs in several ways, factory building became feasible. Phyllis Deane taught economic history at the University of Cambridge in England. She is the author of *Growth During the Industrial Revolution* and *The Evolution of Economic Ideas*.

A great deal has been written . . . about the "social overhead capital" which must be provided before an underdeveloped economy can expand its output of goods and services at a rate which will produce an appreciable growth in incomes per head. If we begin to define this "social overhead capital" in concrete terms, most of it seems to consist of capital embodied in basic transport facilities—harbours, roads, bridges, canals and, nowadays, railways. Without this sort of capital an economy's richest natural resources may remain inaccessible and underdeveloped.

Excerpted from *First Industrial Revolution*, 2nd edition, by Phyllis M. Deane. Copyright © 1965, 1979 by Cambridge University Press. Reprinted with permission from Cambridge University Press.

Now it is characteristic of such investments (1) that they require much greater outlays of capital than the individual entrepreneur can normally be expected to get access to, (2) that they take a long time to construct and an even longer time to yield a substantial profit, and (3) that the gross return on the investment comes indirectly to the community as a whole rather than directly to the initiating entrepreneurs. The consequence is that social overhead capital generally has to be provided collectively, by governments or international financial institutions rather than individuals, and that the mobilization of the large chunks of capital required is most easily achieved through taxation or through foreign borrowing. The interesting thing about the British experience, however, is that it was almost entirely native private enterprise that found both the initiative and the capital to lay down the system of communications which was essential to the British industrial revolution. . . .

ROADS AND SEA ROUTES

Some improvement in the roads dates from the 1750's, *before* the industrial revolution had gathered momentum sufficiently to add greatly to the internal traffic of goods. It was largely a consequence of the growth of towns with their mounting demands for basic food and fuel supplies which had to be drawn from a wider and wider agricultural hinterland. The main driving force for road improvement throughout the country was London. Most of the new roads and the best-kept roads led to London, although the influence of other towns—Liverpool, Birmingham and Manchester for example—began to show itself in the quality of their feeder-roads as the century wore on. The growing towns called for rapid and regular transport of foodstuffs and fuel over distances of 30 to 50 miles or so, and for comfortable, safe and speedy transport of passengers and mail between the main towns; and it was this kind of localized or light traffic that benefited most directly and impressively. The extent of the improvement may perhaps be gauged from the evidence of a clergyman before the 1808 Highways Committee, to the effect that three horses could then do what five had been required for 30 years before, and from [historian W.T.] Jackman's avowedly conservative estimate that "on the great highways of trade the time consumed on a journey between the termini of the longer routes was in 1830 only from one third to one fifth of what it had been in 1750."

If Britain had had to depend on her roads to carry her heavy goods traffic the effective impact of the industrial revolution might well have been delayed until the railway age. She started off, however, with transport advantages which none of her contemporary rivals [in Europe] could equal. The cheapest way of transporting bulky, weighty, goods was by water and Britain scored heavily in this respect by being narrow and insular—no part of the British Isles is more than 70 miles from the sea—and by having a considerable length of river which, if not naturally navigable, could readily be made so. The sea-coast route was the main highway of the British Isles in the eighteenth century and that required relatively little in the way of maintenance except to harbour installations. [Economist] Adam Smith, exaggerating a little perhaps, declared that "Six or eight men by the help of water carriage can carry and bring back in the same time the same quantity of goods between London and Edinburgh as 50 broadwheeled wagons attended by a hundred men and drawn by 400 horses." London indeed was built up on the strength of its sea routes, and the growth of this vast city—it had more than half a million inhabitants at the end of the seventeenth century and more than a million at the end of the eighteenth—was an important factor in England's transition from a regionally based subsistence economy to an integrated exchange economy. A fleet of vessels averaging a little over 200 tons in weight plied along the eastern coast between the Scottish ports and Newcastle, Hull, Yarmouth and London bringing coal, stone, slate, clay and grain, commodities whose transport through the miry roads of

England's river and canal network made possible the movement of heavy goods, such as coal and iron.

eighteenth-century England would have cost a fortune. According to [historian J.H.] Clapham the major portion of the coasting trade existed that Londoners might be housed, warmed and fed.

The sea had its hazards and delays, of course. Shipping might be held up in the Tyne and the Thames for weeks in succession in stormy seasons. When war broke out ships and seamen were liable to be summarily pressed into the navy and foreign privateers menaced the English sea lanes. Heavy duties were put on coastal shipping and enormous losses are reported to have resulted from the pilfering of the London dockers. Nevertheless, for all its vicissitudes coastal shipping was the main means of handling bulky, heavy commodities in the eighteenth century and without it there could have been no large-scale heavy industry and no large towns.

THE DEVELOPMENT OF A CANAL SYSTEM

No revolutionary developments took place in coastal shipping during the late eighteenth and early nineteenth centuries and it is to the transformation of the inland system of water navigation that we must look for the most spectacular and typical innovations of this period. The industrial revolution called for a reliable, high-capacity, low-cost transport system and this is what the canals provided. Moreover they were of the essence of the industrial revolution in that they were man-made, that they represented an application of scientific knowledge to practical engineering problems, that they catered for a mass market (albeit a producers' market) and that they involved heavy capital outlays involving a long time-horizon.

The canal age took place mainly in two hectic bursts of construction; the first in the 1760's and early 1770's was inspired by the success of the Duke of Bridgewater's canal between Worsley coal mine and Manchester and then stifled by the trade recession resulting from the American War; the second started up in the 1780's, after the war was well over, and became a national mania in the 1790's. It had been preceded by a century and a half of steady river improvement also financed capitalistically by groups of local landowners and businessmen. [According to historian C. Skempton,]

> It has been established that by the end of the eighteenth century some 2,000 miles of navigable water existed in England, of which approximately one third was in the form of canals built between 1760 and 1800: one third was in the form of "open" rivers which were naturally navigable: and the remaining third had been

created as a result of the work of engineers, chiefly between about 1600 and 1760.

It may seem surprising that a few hundred miles of canal could
make a significant addition to the basic industrial communications of an economy of the size and complexity of England. But
the canals were not cut into an empty map. Often a short canal
represented the last strategic link in a network of navigable rivers
and its construction might bring to fruition investments on river
improvement made over a century before.

The main motive-power behind the early development of the
canals was the same as that which was gradually pushing up the
standards of the roads at this period. It was the growth of the
towns. Later the prospects and needs of large-scale industry
helped to rocket the canal age into its grand mania; but, to begin
with, the operative force was the towns with their insatiable demand for coal to supply fuel for domestic needs and for the whole
host of little industries that are required even in a pre-industrial
community—bakeries, smithies, tanneries, sugar-refineries, breweries. It must be remembered that apart from coal there was no
fuel available in eighteenth-century England other than wood
and this was already an exhausted resource in most centres of
population and industry. [Clapham says,] "The fuel famine of the
eighteenth century would have stopped the growth not solely of
industry but of population in many districts had not means been
found for overcoming it." The canals were the means. More than
half the Navigation Acts passed between 1758 and 1802 to set up
a canal or river-improvement company were for concerns whose
primary aim was to carry coal. This was one of the crucial bot-
tlenecks that had to be broken before the industrial revolution
could take shape in England. It was crucial, first because it removed the main barrier to the urbanization which is generally
associated with industrialization as both cause and effect; and
secondly because the first industrial revolution grew up on a basis of coal and iron and it was necessary to be able to move these
bulky raw materials and their finished products quickly and
cheaply across the face of the country.

THE FIRST CANALS

The first wholly man-made inland navigation in this country was
the Sankey Brook, inspired by the coal needs of Liverpool, then
Britain's premier port outside of London. But it was the Duke of
Bridgewater's Canal from Worsley to Manchester that is generally regarded as the first great achievement of the canal age. Built
by James Brindley, it was designed to carry coal from the Duke's

colliery at Worsley to the up and coming industrial town of Manchester. It was an immediate social and commercial success. Its tunnel at Worsley and its aqueduct at Barton were engineering achievements which stirred the imagination of a public that believed passionately in man-made improvement. The fact that it halved the price of coal in Manchester further impressed itself on hard-headed businessmen and wealthy landowners and encouraged them to risk their savings, mortgage their lands and borrow from their relatives to finance similar expensive schemes of capital accumulation. Eight years later Birmingham businessmen had a similar success with the opening of the first section of the Birmingham canal, and by the end of the century the Hereford-Gloucester canal had reduced the price of coal at Ledbury from 24s. [24 shillings] to 13s. 6d [6 pence].

Success on this grand scale was bound to encourage imitation. It is amazing nevertheless that so much private capital was raised in England to finance the construction of costly capital assets which generally took several years before they began earning at all and which could not, in the nature of things, be expected to yield a quick return. The Duke of Bridgewater's canal cost nearly a quarter of a million pounds to complete—which was a great deal of money at a time when the average Lancashire labourer earned less than £20 [20 pounds] per annum; it took five years to complete it as far as Runcorn and another nine years to link up with the Mersey so that vessels could go on to Liverpool. The Leeds and Liverpool Canal took 46 years to complete and there were many which took 10 years or more. . . .

FINANCING THE CANALS

Where did all this capital come from? For the most part it was raised locally in the region the canal was to serve. [Clapham says,] "It was only among men to whom solid advantages were promised that money could be got for a canal that might take many years to build." Sometimes a local landowner or industrialist took the initiative and used his lands or his stock as collateral for borrowing the money; colliery owners like the Duke of Bridgewater or industrialists using heavy raw materials like Josiah Wedgwood, the pottery manufacturer, had most to gain. Occasionally a local merchant was able to raise the bulk of the funds necessary to cut a short canal. In most cases the new navigations were the product of corporate enterprise initiated by local businessmen and landowners and supported by local shareholders and bankers and city corporations and even sometimes by universities. During the mania the geographical basis of the capital raised for the canal companies began to spread beyond the regional level and many individuals with quite small capital resources and no direct interest in the enlargement of transport opportunities were tempted by the offer of glittering prizes to have their flutter among the canal shares.

There is no doubt that some of these ventures paid off extremely well. [Historian Asa Briggs says,] "Fantastic dividends were sometimes paid—the Oxford Canal for instance paid 30% for more than 30 years—although the average dividend was under 8%." The shares of the old Birmingham Canal, originally £140 each, were selling at £900 in 1792, at the height of the canal mania, and by 1825 an eighth share of this canal, originally worth £17. 10s., was selling for £355. A writer who picked out the ten most successful canals in 1825 calculated that they were then paying an average of 27.6 per cent. Not all the canal companies fulfilled the hopes of their investors, however. Some of the projects foundered on unexpected engineering difficulties, some on post-war depression and some on the inefficiency of their managers. Jackman has estimated, for example, that "fully one half of the number of canals and probably considerably more than one half of the capital expenditure realized returns that were inadequate in order to maintain the canals as effective agents for the work they were intended to accomplish."

CANALS YIELD A VARIETY OF BENEFITS

In the last analysis, however, it is inappropriate to judge the contribution of the canals to British economic growth in terms of the returns they yielded to their shareholders. What mattered was that the coal got to the consumers at reasonable prices, that the iron-foundries and potteries could reduce costs, that the factory worker could warm his family in winter and still have some money left over to buy the products of British industry and that the bread-and-cheese-eating labourers of Southern England could have cooked meals occasionally. In these terms the Canal Age made a massive contribution to the first industrial revolution and was a worthy forerunner of the railway age. [According to Clapham,]

> Throughout the country, stone for building, paving and roadmaking; bricks, tiles and timber; limestone for the builder, farmer or blast furnace owner; beasts and cattle; corn, hay and straw; manure from the London mews and the mountainous London dustheaps; the heavy castings which were coming into use for bridge-building and other structural purposes—all these and whatever other bulky wares there may be, moved along

the new waterways over what, half a century earlier, had been impossible routes or impossible distances.

In effect, what the canals did was to make possible enormous ultimate savings in man-power and horse-power at the cost of heavy preliminary outlays of capital. A single horse plodding along a canal towpath typically dragged a load of 50 tons of merchandise; on the banks of a navigable river its average load was 30 tons: on iron rails it pulled 8 tons and on macadam roads 2 tons. The typical goods carrier of the early eighteenth century, the packhorse, carried an average load of only about one-eighth of a ton. The effect was to produce what a development theorist would describe as a "radical transformation of production functions"; for it revolutionized the respective contributions of the main factors of production—labour, capital and natural resources—to the business of transport; and it permitted significant savings in raw materials and in the kind of capital that gets tied up in stocks of goods when delivery dates are uncertain.

In addition it is worth noticing that the canals produced a new class of investor, the canal shareholder, a non-participant investor who was readily transformed into a railway shareholder when the infinitely greater demands for railway capital were made in the 1830's and 1840's. This was an important new development. Most economies in the early stages of industrialization have some economic surplus, the problem is to channel it into the kind of large-scale investments which do not guarantee immediate return and which may be of more value to the community as a whole than to the chief investors. Even where incomes are unequally distributed it is rare to find many individuals with the enterprise, the far-sightedness *and* the access to capital necessary to launch one of these ventures. The Duke of Bridgewater was a rarity in eighteenth-century England. Hence the development of the joint-stock company system, whereby a large group of impersonally associated individuals could pool their capitals in a corporate venture, was a major step in permitting private enterprise to undertake costly capital projects on a wide scale. The joint-stock company established by Act of Parliament was not, of course, a new institution in the second half of the eighteenth century but it was the canal age that familiarized the small saver with this type of investment.

CANAL BUILDING IS INEFFICIENT BUT SIGNIFICANT

One consequence of building up the social overhead capital involved in the canal network by the agency of private enterprise was that it was not very efficiently done. The miscellany of widths, depths and transport charges made the network less integrated than it could have been. The opportunities open to some carriers to charge monopolistic rates limited the social gain and restricted the potential traffic; the nil returns which characterized a large proportion of the capital invested and the fantastically high share prices of the mania resulted in some capital wastage: and many of these wastages could have been avoided had there been effective centralized planning of the canal network. Nevertheless the job was done, and before the railway age revolutionized the transport situation a second time, England had been endowed with a solid and worth-while capital asset in the shape of more than 2,000 miles of heavy-traffic lanes, many of which are still in economic use today. . . .

It seems particularly worth emphasizing that the transport revolution had effectively begun and was affecting the productivity of the economy as a whole before the changes in other industries were at all sizeable in their impact, and that it was an absolutely crucial factor in facilitating the cost-reducing innovations which characterized the other transforming sectors of the first industrial revolution.

THE DEVELOPMENT OF JOINT-STOCK COMPANIES

GEORGE CLARK

Today's stock market had its beginnings in seventeenth-century Europe, when nations needed large trading companies for commerce around the world. Sir George Clark explains the historical background, showing how the new joint-stock companies differed from any companies that had previously existed. Moreover, he explains the role governments played in the venture and delineates differences in the ways English, Dutch, and French companies developed. Clark, who taught at Oxford University in England, is the author of *Science and Social Welfare in the Age of Newton* and *Early Modern Europe*.

T he seventeenth and eighteenth centuries were the age of the great trading companies, and these companies were the expression of the needs of the new age in commerce. They were created by the states, because the states could not but concern themselves in commerce and this commerce could not live without the support of the states; but they were owned and managed by private enterprise because private men were still the only source of that energy which was needed for such great undertakings. The states could make men serve them directly as soldiers or officials, but they had not yet reached the stage in which they could make economic activities a part of the public service. . . .

When the three nations [England, Holland, and France] which were to be the economic leaders of the seventeenth century came

Excerpted from *The Seventeenth Century*, by George Clark. Copyright © 1945 by Oxford University Press. Reprinted with permission from Oxford University Press.

to develop a considerable distant trade, new forms of organization sprang up amongst them, with many variations and from many causes, but yet with broad similarities and with broad differences from the medieval forms. This development was to lead ultimately, long after our period, to a state of things in which a special form of joint-stock company, the limited liability company, should be the normal legal form of all kinds of business enterprises all over the world. That was still far in the future. What was achieved in the seventeenth century was that the joint-stock enterprise established itself as the form for the greater commerce, that is the company which traded for itself and distributed the profits to its shareholders in proportion to the amounts of capital which they had contributed to it.

THE GRADUAL DEVELOPMENT OF JOINT-STOCK COMPANIES

No great institution begins at a definite moment. It must be the result of long preparation and its leading features must be to some extent anticipated before any birthday that may be selected. It is more accurate therefore to date the origin of any such institution vaguely than to date it precisely. Again a type of organization may be devised to meet certain conditions, then given up and forgotten, but revived or invented again when similar conditions return. There had been joint-stock companies in both Italy and Germany in the late Middle Ages; but those of the seventeenth century are not continuous with them. With this explanation of what is meant by the phrase, it may be said that it was in England that the joint-stock principle first definitely emerged, with the foundation of the Russian Company in 1553 and the first African Company in the same year. From the legal point of view it was a fusion of the principle of the guild or association with the principle of partnership. Common measures were still taken as they had been by the medieval associations, some of them, such as the defence against armed attack, being simply the continuation of the old functions, but to these was now added the new task of common trading: the members of the association were now also partners in an enterprise. A deliberate effort was being made at that time to improve the economic position of the country and the financial position of the government by opening up new foreign trades with countries in which English trade had hitherto been little developed. Russia was typical of these countries: it was more distant than the European countries with which the old "regulated companies" had traded, and it was less civilized. The individual member of the company was so much the less likely to find his advantage in using his own capital as he thought best. Larger ships were required, but at the same time the amount ventured by the individual trader was, for this new and less certain trade, relatively if not absolutely smaller, so that instead of a number of separately owned and managed portions of the cargo, it was an economy to have the whole in one ownership.

THE ENGLISH AND DUTCH COMPANIES

The principle, once evolved, spread rapidly. Some of the old regulated companies survived—in [economist] Adam Smith's time there were still five, the "Hamburgh," Russian and Eastland, which he called merely useless, the Turkey and African which he thought abusive—but the main work of the greater commerce and much other work in colonization and industry came to be done by joint-stock companies. The names of the three greatest, the East India Company, the Bank of England, the South Sea Company, sum up in themselves a great part of English history, but these were only the greatest among many. In all, good, bad, and indifferent, short-lived or long-lived, sound or fraudulent, Professor [W.R.] Scott reckons 49 founded between 1553 and 1680 and 56 between 1680 and 1719. The increase in the amount of capital employed by the joint-stock system was equally striking. It financed English shipping and colonization, the extension and consolidation of distant foreign trades, the organization of credit, and the carrying on of new manufactures, for instance those which were made possible by the skill of the immigrant Huguenots [French Protestants]. Other reasons, besides the general favouring conditions already mentioned, may be ascribed for its success. It broke down the quasi-monopoly of mercantile capital as such, that is, it enabled others than merchants to put their money into trade, thus increasing the available stores of capital. It united different classes of men in the ventures, and so was able to associate the technical knowledge of the merchant with the political influence and the judgement of the man of larger affairs, who was equally needed in that adventurous and difficult stage of commercial development. . . .

The Dutch East India Company was not only formed by the union of pre-existing companies but was, even after their coalescence, federal in structure. It was more like a modern trust than a simple modern company. The shareholders all got the same dividend, whatever "chamber" they belonged to; but the separate local "chambers" had their own directors, ships, selling-places, and so forth. This was due not solely to economic causes, but also to special local conditions. There were many towns in Holland capable of having "chambers" in them. The political organization of the country was such that each of them could make its influence tell. The shareholders were predominantly traders, not *rentiers* [persons of independent means], and they wanted to have the "chambers" in their towns because of the business which they brought to the localities. The federal division into "chambers" is thus typically Dutch. It is found even more markedly in the Dutch Northern Company than in the East India Company: the Northern Company has been called a production-cartel held together by the common enjoyment of a monopoly. The only parallels outside Holland seem to be in the plan made by the Dutchman Usselincx for a Swedish South Sea Company, and in the Prussian companies, which were much influenced by Dutch emigrants, but in which the same result was furthered by another cause, the scarcity of capital in Prussia, which made it necessary to interest all the available towns.

THE ROLE OF GOVERNMENT IN JOINT-STOCK COMPANIES

The comparison between these seventeenth-century companies and modern trusts is misleading unless the fundamental difference is also borne in mind. Modern trusts and combines are based on voluntary agreement or on the triumph of some firms over others purely in the sphere of trading competition. In the seventeenth century something more was needed before it was possible to eliminate competition. Every one of these companies in every country owed its existence to an act of the state. Government aid, often in other forms as well, but always in one indispensable form, was necessary for them, and that indispensable form was the grant of a monopoly. It was the continuation of the medieval régime of privilege: the state granted to certain men, and to them only, the right to carry on a certain branch of business. The grants were sometimes nominally to all who would engage in a trade, but in practice the admission came to be limited to those who bought shares. The main line of criticism against the companies in both England and Holland came from those who wished to be allowed to compete against the favoured monopolists, interlopers who objected to being excluded from the same trade, or producers who wished to compete against the imported articles, as, for instance, calico-printers wished in various countries to compete against the authentic calicoes of Calicut [a city of southwest India]. Never, broadly speaking, was the criticism from the point of view of the consumer, who had to pay more for an article because the sellers were monopolists: thus the opposition to the companies differed in its turn from that against modern trusts. It was often disingenuous: the interloper often wished to derive advantage from the forts and other services of the companies without paying his share towards them.

THE FRENCH COMPANIES

The distinctive characteristic of the French companies is their close dependence on the state. In England and Holland the state had sometimes taken the initiative, but the main impulse of foundation and expansion came from the trading classes. The French companies were formed partly in rivalry with the Dutch and partly in imitation of them. . . .

The condition of France was much less favourable for their establishment than that of Holland, and consequently their history was less successful. Most of them underwent many changes of ownership—that of (North) Africa was reconstructed or revived half a dozen times in the century—or failed and were revived only to fail again. In Asia and Africa they had not achieved much solid foothold by the end of the seventeenth century, though they, like the English companies, outdid the Dutch in the settlement of North America. They were able to do this partly because they had a very powerful state behind them; but this connexion with political power was not always advantageous: the wars of Louis XIV did them much harm. [Louis XIV's finance minister Jean-Baptiste] Colbert's Northern Company was ruined by the Dutch war of 1672; his East India Company suffered much in the wars from 1691 to 1713, which were largely wars of commerce, and was prostrate when John Law took over its management in 1720; his Africa Company was practically destroyed by the fighting against the Algerines in 1682. Thus their legacy to the eighteenth century cannot be compared with that of the English companies or the Dutch. . . .

In structure the French companies differed from those of other countries. They were artificial creations of government. The kings took up large holdings of shares in them, and the men who surrounded the kings, no doubt not altogether of their own free will, followed suit. Colbert used strong administrative pressure to raise capital for his companies. In return the king's financial advisers had much to do with their management. The monopolies were more rigid than those of Holland, which in turn were more rigid than those of England. The companies were hampered by political interference: those of [Cardinal] Richelieu, for instance, were not allowed to have Protestants as members. . . .

In France the government did more than was done elsewhere to encourage the companies by exempting them from tolls and duties; but Holland was far less a protectionist country than France or England, and Dutch duties were light to start with, so this was an advantage over the English rather than the Dutch. Some of the French companies were too ambitious and took over privileges of an unpractical magnitude, a temptation into which projectors were always liable to fall in other countries as well. It is, however, only in France that there are instances of companies handing over part of their functions to the Crown. The Levant [countries bordering on the eastern Mediterranean Sea] Company founded in 1670 had the most favourable field for French enterprise, but it failed through bad trading methods and its privileges were handed over to an individual merchant in 1690. It was to private enterprise that the success of the French Levant trade in the eighteenth century was due. It does not seem unfair to say that the comparative ill-success of the French companies of the seventeenth century sprang from their failure to use private enterprise in the way in which it was used by the English and Dutch, and ultimately from the lack of a sufficiently vigorous trading community. France, after all, made demands on her citizens for the purposes of war which left little to spare for this less glorious work. . . .

The history of joint-stock companies affords a clear illustration of the general fact to which we have already adverted, that the French, English, and Dutch were economically moving in advance of the rest of Europe.

NEW INSTITUTIONS REVOLUTIONIZE FINANCES

PAUL KENNEDY

Paul Kennedy explains that new financial institutions were developed in the seventeenth century to fund wars. He argues that a country needed both taxation and credit in order to supply its military. Besides developing an efficient taxation system, England created the Bank of England, an effective stock exchange, and a system of repayment to ensure that lenders continued to supply the government with money on a regular basis. Paul Kennedy has been a visiting fellow at the Institute for Advanced Study at Princeton and a professor of history at Yale. He is the author of several books, including *The Rise and Fall of British Naval Mastery* and *The Realities Behind Diplomacy*.

The importance of finance and of a productive economic base which created revenues for the state was already clear to Renaissance princes. . . . The rise of the *ancien régime* [a social and political system of the past] monarchies of the eighteenth century, with their large military establishments and fleets of warships, simply increased the government's need to nurture the economy and to create financial institutions which could raise and manage the monies concerned. Moreover, like the First World War, conflicts such as the seven major Anglo-French wars fought between 1689 and 1815 were struggles of endurance. Victory therefore went to the Power—or better, since both Britain and France usually had allies, to the Great Power coalition—with

Excerpted from *The Rise and Fall of the Great Powers*, by Paul Kennedy. Copyright © 1987 by Paul Kennedy. Reprinted with permission from Random House, Inc.

the greater capacity to maintain credit and to keep on raising supplies. The mere fact that these were *coalition* wars increased their duration, since a belligerent whose resources were fading would look to a more powerful ally for loans and reinforcements in order to keep itself in the fight. Given such expensive and exhausting conflicts, what each side desperately required was—to use the old aphorism—"money, money, and yet more money." It was this need which formed the background to what has been termed the "financial revolution" of the late seventeenth and early eighteenth centuries, when certain western European states evolved a relatively sophisticated system of banking and credit in order to pay for their wars.

NONMILITARY AND MILITARY REASONS FOR FINANCIAL CHANGES

There was, it is true, a second and nonmilitary reason for the financial changes of this time. That was the chronic shortage of specie [coined money], particularly in the years before the gold discoveries in Portuguese Brazil in 1693. The more European commerce with the Orient developed in the seventeenth and eighteenth centuries, the greater the outflow of silver to cover the trade imbalances, causing merchants and dealers everywhere to complain of the scarcity of coin. In addition, the steady increases in European commerce, especially in essential products such as cloth and naval stores, together with the tendency for the seasonal fairs of medieval Europe to be replaced by permanent centers of exchange, led to a growing regularity and predictability of financial settlements and thus to the greater use of bills of exchange and notes of credit. In Amsterdam especially, but also in London, Lyons, Frankfurt, and other cities, there arose a whole cluster of moneylenders, commodity dealers, goldsmiths (who often dealt in loans), bill merchants, and jobbers in the shares of the growing number of joint-stock companies. Adopting banking practices which were already in evidence in Renaissance Italy, these individuals and financial houses steadily created a structure of national and international credit to underpin the early modern world economy.

Nevertheless, by far the largest and most sustained boost to the "financial revolution" in Europe was given by war. If the difference between the financial burdens of the age of Philip II [*r.* 1556–1598] and that of Napoleon [1804–1814] was one of degree, it still was remarkable enough. The cost of a sixteenth-century war could be measured in millions of pounds; by the late–seventeenth century, it had risen to *tens* of millions of pounds; and at the close of the Napoleonic War the outgoings of the major combatants occasionally reached a hundred million pounds *a year*. Whether these prolonged and frequent clashes between the Great Powers, when translated into economic terms, were more of a benefit to than a brake upon the commercial and industrial rise of the West can never be satisfactorily resolved. The answer depends, to a great extent, upon whether one is trying to assess the *absolute* growth of a country as opposed to its *relative* prosperity and strength before and after a lengthy conflict. What is clear is that even the most thriving and "modern" of the eighteenth-century states could not immediately pay for the wars of this period out of their ordinary revenue. Moreover, vast rises in taxes, even if the machinery existed to collect them, could well provoke domestic unrest, which all regimes feared— especially when facing foreign challengers at the same time.

Consequently, the only way a government could finance a war adequately was by borrowing: by selling bonds and offices, or better, negotiable long-term stock paying interest to all who advanced monies to the state. Assured of an inflow of funds, officials could then authorize payments to army contractors, provision merchants, shipbuilders, and the armed services themselves. In many respects, this two-way system of raising and *simultaneously* spending vast sums of money acted like a bellows, fanning the development of western capitalism and of the nation-state itself.

DUTCH SUPERIORITY IN FINANCIAL MACHINERY AND CREDIT RATING

Yet however natural all this may appear to later eyes, it is important to stress that the success of such a system depended on two critical factors: reasonably efficient machinery for raising loans, and the maintenance of a government's "credit" in the financial markets. In both respects, the United Provinces led the way—not surprisingly, since the merchants there were part of the government and desired to see the affairs of state managed according to the same principles of financial rectitude as applied in, say, a joint-stock company. It was therefore appropriate that the States General of the Netherlands, which efficiently and regularly raised the taxes to cover governmental expenditures, was able to set interest rates very low, thus keeping down debt repayments. This system, superbly reinforced by the many financial activities of the city of Amsterdam, soon gave the United Provinces an international reputation for clearing bills, exchanging currency, and providing credit, which naturally created a structure—and an atmosphere—within which long-term funded state debt could be regarded as perfectly normal. So successfully did Amsterdam become a center of Dutch "surplus capital" that it soon was able to invest in the stock of foreign companies and, most important of all, to subscribe to a whole variety of loans floated by foreign governments, especially in wartime. . . .

THE BRITISH MANAGE TAXES SUCCESSFULLY

The English system possessed key advantages in the financial realm which enhanced the country's power in wartime and buttressed its political stability and economic growth in peacetime. While it is true that its *general* taxation system was more regressive than that of France—that is, it relied far more upon indirect than direct taxes—particular features seem to have made it much less resented by the public. For example, there was in Britain nothing like the vast array of French tax farmers, collectors, and other middlemen; many of the British duties were "invisible" (the excise duty on a few basic products), or appeared to hurt the foreigner (customs); there were no *internal* tolls, which so irritated French merchants and were a disincentive to domestic commerce; the British land tax—the chief direct tax for so much of the eighteenth century—allowed for no privileged exceptions and was also "invisible" to the greater part of society; and these various taxes were discussed and then authorized by an elective assembly, which for all its defects appeared more representative than the *ancien régime* in France. When one adds to this the important point that per capita income was already somewhat higher in Britain than in France even by 1700, it is not altogether surprising that the population of the island state was willing and able to pay proportionately larger taxes. Finally, it is possible to argue—although more difficult to prove statistically—that the comparatively light burden of direct taxation in Britain not only increased the propensity to save among the better-off in society (and thus allowed the accumulation of investment capital during years of peace), but also produced a vast reserve of taxable wealth in *wartime,* when higher land taxes and, in 1799, direct income tax were introduced to meet the national emergency. Thus, by the period of the Napoleonic War, despite a population less than half that of France, Britain was for the first time ever raising more revenue from taxes each year in *absolute* terms than its larger neighbor.

FINANCIAL INSTITUTIONS

Yet however remarkable that achievement, it is eclipsed in importance by the even more significant difference between the British and French systems of public credit. For the fact was that during most of the eighteenth-century conflicts, almost three-quarters of the *extra* finance raised to support the additional

wartime expenditures came from loans. Here, more than any-
where else, the British advantages were decisive. The first was
the evolution of an institutional framework which permitted the
raising of long-term loans in an efficient fashion and simultaneously arranged for the regular repayment of the interest on (and
principal of) the debts accrued. The creation of the Bank of England in 1694 (at first as a wartime expedient) and the slightly
later regularization of the national debt on the one hand and the
flourishing of the stock exchange and growth of the "country
banks" on the other boosted the supply of money available to
both governments and businessmen. This growth of paper
money in various forms *without* severe inflation or the loss of
credit brought many advantages in an age starved of coin. Yet the
"financial revolution" itself would scarcely have succeeded had
not the obligations of the state been guaranteed by successive
Parliaments with their powers to raise additional taxes; had not
the ministries—from [Robert] Walpole to the younger [William]
Pitt—worked hard to convince their bankers in particular and
the public in general that they, too, were actuated by the principles of financial rectitude and "economical" government; and
had not the steady and in some trades remarkable expansion of
commerce and industry provided concomitant increases in revenue from customs and excise. Even the onset of war did not
check such increases, provided the Royal Navy protected the nation's overseas trade while throttling that of its foes. It was upon
these solid foundations that Britain's "credit" rested, despite
early uncertainties, considerable political opposition, and a financial near-disaster like the collapse of the famous South Seas
Bubble of 1720. "Despite all defects in the handling of English
public finance," its historian [G.M. Dickson] has noted, "for the
rest of the century it remained more honest, as well as more efficient, than that of any other in Europe."

THE RESULTS OF BRITAIN'S FINANCIAL FOUNDATION

The result of all this was not only that interest rates steadily
dropped, but also that British government stock was increasingly
attractive to foreign, and particularly Dutch, investors. Regular
dealings in these securities on the Amsterdam market thus became an important part of the nexus of Anglo-Dutch commercial
and financial relationships, with important effects upon the
economies of both countries. In *power-political* terms, its value lay
in the way in which the resources of the United Provinces repeatedly came to the aid of the British war effort, even when the
Dutch alliance in the struggle against France had been replaced

by an uneasy neutrality. Only at the time of the American Revolutionary War—significantly, the one conflict in which British military, naval, diplomatic, and trading weaknesses were most evident, and therefore its credit-worthiness was the lowest—did the flow of Dutch funds tend to dry up, despite the higher interest rates which London was prepared to offer. By 1780, however, when the Dutch entered the war on France's side, the British government found that the strength of its own economy and the availability of domestic capital were such that its loans could be almost completely taken up by domestic investors.

The sheer dimensions—and ultimate success—of Britain's capacity to raise war loans can be summarized as in Table 1.

Table 1. British Wartime Expenditure and Revenue, 1688–1815
(pounds)

Inclusive Years	Total Expenditure	Total Income	Balance Raised by Loans	Loans as % of Expenditure
1688–97	49,320,145	32,766,754	16,553,391	33.6
1702–13	93,644,560	64,239,477	29,405,083	31.4
1739–48	95,628,159	65,903,964	29,724,195	31.1
1756–63	160,573,366	100,555,123	60,018,243	37.4
1776–83	236,462,689	141,902,620	94,560,069	39.9
1793–1815	1,657,854,518	1,217,556,439	440,298,079	26.6
Totals	2,293,483,437	1,622,924,377	670,559,060	33.3

And the strategical consequence of these figures was that the country was thereby enabled [as historian Dickson says] "to spend on war out of all proportion to its tax revenue, and thus to throw into the struggle with France and its allies the decisive margin of ships and men without which the resources previously committed might have been committed in vain." Although many British commentators throughout the eighteenth century trembled at the sheer size of the national debt and its possible consequences, the fact remained that (in Bishop Berkeley's words) credit was "the principal advantage that England hath over France." Finally, the great growth in state expenditures and the enormous, sustained demand which Admiralty contracts in particular created for iron, wood, cloth, and other wares produced a "feedback loop" which assisted British industrial production and stimulated the series of technological breakthroughs that gave the country yet another advantage over the French.

STRUCTURAL GROUNDWORK FOR THE INDUSTRIAL REVOLUTION

FRANÇOIS CROUZET

François Crouzet traces the development of the factory system by citing individual men who centralized production to increase the size of companies. He identifies the factors that contributed to these changes: the growth of the iron industry, the technical inventions leading to mass production in the brewing industry, and the metal and textile workshops that gathered various tasks into a central location. The largest workshops became the first factories. French scholar Crouzet taught history at the University of Paris, Sorbonne; the University of Bordeaux; and Columbia University in New York. He is the author of *L'Economic Britannique et le Blocus Continental, 1806–1813.*

The industrialist was undoubtedly a new man, who emerged with the factory system during the Industrial Revolution. But, one might wonder, was he completely new? Or did he have some forerunners before the mid eighteenth century? Were there any individuals who might be called "pre-industrialists," or rather "paleo-industrialists" ("proto-industrialist" is tempting, but would be misleading, because the leaders of "proto-industrialization" were merchant-manufacturers, who put out

Excerpted from *The First Industrialists: The Problem of Origins,* by François Crouzet. Copyright © 1985 by Cambridge University Press. Reprinted with permission from Cambridge University Press.

work to domestic workers and were therefore quite different from industrialists)?

Although the basic unit of production in most of traditional industry was the domestic workshop, there were a number of branches in which "centralized," non-domestic production prevailed, basically for technical reasons: one cannot have a blast-furnace or a glass-oven in a cottage's backyard. Such were the furnace industries, where intense heat was needed (the increasing use of coal in English industry from the sixteenth century onwards worked towards greater centralization), and the mill industries, which required the use of water (or wind) power. The primary iron industry is both a furnace and a mill industry; it is typical of this small, but not unimportant, sector.

However, the word "centralized" must not delude. In the overwhelming majority of cases such establishments were very small affairs: the state of demand did not warrant large-scale production, for which in any case the necessary technology was not available and few economies of scale were possible. In the charcoal iron industry, the problems of wood and water power supplies severely limited the size of ironworks. Although these centralized works involved some investment in fixed capital, this remained modest, both in absolute terms and as a percentage of the firm's total capital. Although they "concentrated" workers on a single site, the numbers involved remained generally quite low (and liable to seasonal fluctuations). By the early eighteenth century, an average ironworks (markedly larger than 100 or 200 years earlier) employed seven people at its blast-furnace, which made 300 tons of pig-iron per annum, and three or more in its forge, together with several score casual labourers, such as miners, woodcutters, charcoal-burners and carriers; this was a "large" undertaking. More typical as a centralized unit of production was a paper mill, which was usually no bigger than an ordinary corn mill, which had only one vat and half a dozen to 15 employees. And by the mid eighteenth century, a Staffordshire potbank [pottery] employed a maximum of ten hands. This point has been made again and again by economic historians of the early modern period and there is no need to dwell upon it. . . .

However, among this army of pigmy firms arose a few giants, some really large, concentrated units of production, and also some industrial "empires." Eventually, during the half-century or so which preceded the Industrial Revolution, there was a clear trend in English industry towards more capital intensity, towards concentration of capital and labour. . . .

One thinks at once of the outstanding and exceptional career of Sir Ambrose Crowley (1658–1713): his three vertically integrated factories near Sunderland constituted the largest unit of concentrated industrial production in Britain, with about a thousand workers; he was the largest maker of iron goods in the world in his time. Still, Crowley's undertakings were atypical, owing to their gigantic size and to the special circumstances—large contracts with the Royal Navy in wartime—which had greatly helped their growth. On the other hand, Sir Ambrose remained a merchant in some ways: he resided in London, then in Greenwich, far from his northern factories which he rarely visited—hence the elaborate written constitution, the "Law Book," which he gave them; he also continued to employ many domestic workers in the Midlands. Accordingly [historian] Michael Flinn concluded that Crowley and his factories do not fit well into the mainstream of British economic history.

More typical of the iron industry in the seventeenth and early eighteenth centuries were the interlocking partnerships which integrated and brought under the control of a few men a large number of small or medium-sized units of production: blast-furnaces, forges, slitting [cutting] mills. The largest was the Foley empire in the Midlands, but later there was also the Spencer family's syndicate in south Yorkshire. The men who managed these combines were neither absentee grandees nor peasants nor craftsmen but professional ironmasters. This is clear for several members of the Foley family, who were active managers of their business—Richard, the founder (1588–1637), his third son, Thomas (1617–77), and two of the latter's sons, Paul (1650–99) and Philip (1653–1716), who established in 1692 "The Ironworks in Partnership," which associated them with three senior employees, John and Richard Wheeler and Richard Avenant, who as both full partners and managers were also fully fledged industrialists. Owing to the dispersion of the works, the partners were absentees from most of them, but they received weekly reports from their subordinates, and these at the end of the year were collected in "quarter books," from which consolidated accounts were compiled. The accounting was detailed, adequate, and became more and more sophisticated. The chief owner of the works took all the main policy decisions, fixed prices and wages, looked after sales; he followed a genuine strategy, including experiments for technical improvements.

This kind of attitude was not restricted to the heads of large combines; it was shared by some gentlemen who personally managed the ironworks they owned, such as Major John Hanbury (1664–1734), who was an innovator and developed processes for rolling iron-plates and making tin-plates. A similar case is that of William Rawlinson and John Machell, the two chief partners of the Backbarrow Company (founded in 1711), who were landowners of some standing in Furness, but devoted almost all their energies to the administration of their ironworks. Professionalism was also, of course, prevalent among the dissenting ironmasters who played such an important role—in the early eighteenth century Quakers alone owned or operated over half of all ironworks active in England. The story of the Darby dynasty and of their friends and relatives who ran Coalbrookdale during "interregnum" periods does not need retelling, but it provides further proof that ironmasters were the first group of professional industrialists to emerge (though the low level of English output—18,000 tons of pig-iron per annum by 1717—meant that this was not a large group or a very wealthy one).

PAPER MILLS AND BREWERIES

Likewise, though most paper mills were small, some were "large"—with three or four vats—and the large paper-makers of the early and mid eighteenth century can be regarded as industrialists, while being also gentlemen and founders of dynasties (like the Portal family, which descended from a Huguenot [French Protestant] who had fled from Languedoc to England).

The brewing industry is a quite different branch, in which striking developments took place, at least in London, where an enormous and intensive market created special conditions. From the sixteenth century, the capital had some relatively large "common breweries," the number and size of which increased during the seventeenth century and especially towards its end. Then, after 1720, came the "porter revolution": the new brew was suited to mass-production involving economies of scale, so that a technical invention brought about structural change—a phenomenon which was to be repeated time and again. The combination of the two factors favoured the rise, well before the accepted beginnings of the Industrial Revolution, of large undertakings, employing substantial amounts of fixed capital and capturing a growing share of the market. By 1740, the Great Common Brewhouse had clearly emerged in London and by 1760 it was close to perfection. During the year 1748 Sir William Calvert made 55,700 barrels of porter; ten years later, the five leading houses brewed between 55,000 and 60,000 barrels each. By 1778, the six "capital houses" of the metropolis were the largest undertakings in the land apart from a couple of ironworks and the Navy dockyards, and they retained that position up to the rise of the large cotton mills. Nevertheless, the great brewer was—and remained—a peculiar sort of industrialist; his work was more seasonal than full-time, and, for various reasons, including close links with the land, was considered to be gentlemanly. Moreover, the contagion of industrial brewing was restricted, by transport costs, to London and a few large towns, so that a multitude of brewing victuallers [innkeepers] and many small common brewers survived.

MULTIPLE TASKS IN A SINGLE WORKSHOP

As for Birmingham, by the mid eighteenth century, it had a few "gentlemen manufacturers," who combined production and marketing, which had previously been separated; they gathered their workpeople into large workshops, where division of labour was pushed far, under close and direct supervision, and they displayed an innovating spirit, for instance in the adoption of pressing and stamping machinery. The three outstanding cases were John Taylor, John Baskerville and Matthew Boulton, but they had some smaller colleagues. Of course, such establishments might be regarded as the beginning of the Industrial Revolution in Birmingham, but they were to remain exceptional for a long time, in a branch—the secondary metal trades—where the small family workshop was the typical unit. Still, they were a sign of the greater capital intensity which British industry displayed from the late seventeenth century, as well as of the disposition of merchants to extend their control over production and to assume some industrial functions (many cloth merchants took over dyeing and finishing, in their own workshops)—though this did not go very far. In several cases, it involved the mechanization and concentration in some central workshop of one or two processes, while most of the work continued to be done on a domestic basis. For instance, needle-making was a putting-out industry, but in the mid eighteenth century scouring [a method for cleansing wool] was mechanized and done in water-driven mills. . . .

There were also workshops in which were gathered a number of machines which had previously been used in the homes of outworkers, the idea being to supervise workpeople more closely and to improve the quality of products. In such workshops, in which there was no use of power, one could find either weaving looms or knitting frames or the so-called Dutch looms for making small wares, ribbons and tapes—complicated and costly machines of which a dozen or a score could be gathered on the same premises. These undertakings were owned sometimes by merchant-manufacturers, sometimes by small masters belonging to a superior class of artisan—like the "master weavers," who ran the small wares workshops: they worked on orders from merchants, but were above ordinary domestic weavers. In a few cases, bleaching, dyeing and finishing were done in the same building as weaving, for instance in the "manufactory" for linen ribbons which was established in 1747 by John and Nathaniel Philips. With a few exceptions, these small men hardly qualify as industrialists, but it happened that some of these "embryo-factories" deserved their name literally, either because they later developed into true factories, or because they had been the training ground for future factory masters; they helped to increase the human capital of skilled businessmen, which was vital to the starting of the Industrial Revolution.

THE FIRST FACTORIES

Quite different were the silk mills and the bleaching and printing works, but there is no need to dwell upon these well-known developments. After an unsuccessful attempt by Thomas Cotchett, the brothers (or rather half-brothers) John and Thomas Lombe opened in 1721, on the same site at Derby, a large water-powered mill for throwing silk. [Historian] W.H. Chaloner has rightly called this "the first modern British textile factory," which was automated and had a narrowly specialized function; and indeed it was to be used as a model for the cotton factories which [Richard] Arkwright and his imitators set up fifty years later. The Lombes have been called "projectors," but they were genuine industrialists, though neither for very long—John, the technician, died in 1722, Sir Thomas in 1739, and the mill was sold after his death—nor very successfully. After the expiry of their patent in 1732, they had a number of imitators. . . .

It was also technical innovation which produced bleaching works, which could employ up to a hundred people, and calico, fustian- or linen-printing works—the two processes sometimes being combined by the same firm and on the same site. Printing workshops have been described as "a highly significant transitional stage in the evolution from dispersed domestic industry to the fully evolved factory system," and [historian] S.D. Chapman ranks them in his Type II of factory development, because they centralized several processes—though with little mechanization. But, if some "large" undertakings appeared at an early date, there were actually very few of them before the last quarter of the century: in 1719 London had 23 calico-printers, but only three of them had a "large" labour force—205, 121 and 49 employees respectively. In 1760, the number of calico-printers in Britain was 23 plus, and it is likely that some of them were not "large." As for the multi-process sailcloth factories, which prospered in wartime, there were only a handful of these.

If ironworks are excluded, therefore, the number of large undertakings and genuine industrialists was quite small in mid-eighteenth-century Britain. Of course, below these, there was a vast penumbra zone of small "embryo-factories" or "proto-factories" and of large workshops (the dividing line between them being blurred), a number of them purpose-built, and therefore, I would suggest, of "embryo-industrialists." This zone was historically important and formed a link between the domestic and the factory system. But fully fledged industrialists had still to rise in large numbers.

THE PLAGUE OF 1665

DANIEL DEFOE

Daniel Defoe describes occurrences during the London plague of 1665 as if he were on the streets observing them. He was, however, a child of five during the plague; he writes his account from stories he heard and from accounts of the earlier Elizabethan plague described by Thomas Dekker in *Wonderful Year*. Though the details of Defoe's account may be fictional, they give a true general picture of the city during the 1665 plague. Daniel Defoe was a writer and a political reformer and dissenter. Besides writing pamphlets such as "The Shortest Way with the Dissenters" and "Giving Alms to Charity," he prepared the way for the novel with his works *Robinson Crusoe* and *Moll Flanders*.

I nnumerable dismal stories we heard every day on this very account. Sometimes a man or woman dropped down dead in the very markets; for many people that had the plague upon them knew nothing of it till the inward gangrene[1] had affected their vitals, and they died in a few moments. This caused that many died frequently in that manner in the street suddenly, without any warning; others, perhaps, had time to go to the next bulk[2] or stall, or to any door or porch, and just sit down and die, as I have said before.

These objects were so frequent in the streets that when the plague came to be very raging on one side, there was scarce any passing by the streets but that several dead bodies would be lying here and there upon the ground. On the other hand, it is observable that, though at first the people would stop as they went along, and call to the neighbors to come out on such an occasion,

1. decay of body tissue 2. any mass of material to sit upon

Excerpted from *A Journal of the Plague Year,* by Daniel Defoe.

yet afterwards no notice was taken of them; but that, if at any time we found a corpse lying, go across the way and not come near it; or, if in a narrow lane or passage, go back again, and seek some other way to go on the business we were upon; and in those cases the corpse was always left till the officers had notice to come and take them away, or till night, when the bearers attending the dead-cart would take them up and carry them away. Nor did those undaunted creatures who performed these offices fail to search their pockets, and sometimes strip off their clothes, if they were well dressed, as sometimes they were, and carry off what they could get.

But to return to the markets. The butchers took that care, that, if any person died in the market, they had the officers always at hand to take them up upon handbarrows, and carry them to the next churchyard; and this was so frequent that such were not entered in the weekly bill, "found dead in the streets or fields," as is the case now, but they went into the general articles of the great distemper. . . .

As for my little family, having thus, as I have said, laid in a store of bread, butter, cheese, and beer, I took my friend and physician's advice, and locked myself up, and my family, and resolved to suffer the hardship of living a few months without flesh-meat rather than to purchase it at the hazard of our lives.

But though I confined my family, I could not prevail upon my unsatisfied curiosity to stay within entirely myself, and, though I generally came frighted and terrified home, yet I could not restrain, only that, indeed, I did not do it so frequently as at first.

WALKS TO HIS BROTHER'S HOUSE

I had some little obligations, indeed, upon me to go to my brother's house, which was in Coleman Street Parish, and which he had left to my care; and I went at first every day, but afterwards only once or twice a week.

In these walks I had many dismal scenes before my eyes, as, particularly, of persons falling dead in the streets, terrible shrieks and screechings of women, who in their agonies would throw open their chamber windows, and cry out in a dismal, surprising manner. It is impossible to describe the variety of postures in which the passions of the poor people would express themselves.

Passing through Token-House Yard in Lothbury, of a sudden a casement violently opened just over my head, and a woman gave three frightful screeches, and then cried, "Oh! death, death. death!" in a most inimitable tone, and which struck me with horror, and a chillness in my very blood. There was nobody to be seen in the whole street, neither did any other window open, for people had no curiosity now in any case, nor could anybody help one another; so I went on to pass into Bell Alley.

Just in Bell Alley, on the right hand of the passage, there was a more terrible cry than that, though it was not so directed out at the window. But the whole family was in a terrible fright, and I could hear women and children run screaming about the rooms like distracted, when a garret[3] window opened, and somebody from a window on the other side the alley called and asked, "What is the matter?" Upon which from the first window it was answered, "O Lord, my old master has hanged himself!" The other asked again, "Is he quite dead?" and the first answered, "Ay, ay, quite dead; quite dead and cold!" This person was a merchant and a deputy alderman, and very rich. I care not to mention his name, though I knew his name too; but that would be a hardship to the family, which is now flourishing again.

VICTIMS REACT TO SWELLINGS AND TOKENS

But this is but one. It is scarce credible what dreadful cases happened in particular families every day,—people, in the rage of the distemper, or in the torment of their swellings, which was indeed intolerable, running out of their own government, raving and distracted, and oftentimes laying violent hands upon themselves, throwing themselves out at their windows, shooting themselves, etc.; mothers murdering their own children in their lunacy; some dying of mere grief as a passion, some of mere fright and surprise without any infection at all; others frighted into idiotism and foolish distractions, some into despair and lunacy, others into melancholy madness.

The pain of the swelling was in particular very violent, and to some intolerable. The physicians and surgeons may be said to have tortured many poor creatures even to death. The swellings in some grew hard, and they applied violent drawing plasters, or poultices, to break them; and, if these did not do, they cut and scarified them in a terrible manner. In some, those swellings were made hard, partly by the force of the distemper, and partly by their being too violently drawn, and were so hard that no instrument could cut them; and then they burned them with caustics,[4] so that many died raving mad with the torment, and some in the very operation. In these distresses, some, for want of help to hold them down in their beds or to look to them, laid hands upon themselves as above; some broke out into the streets, perhaps naked, and would run directly down to the river, if they were not stopped by the watchmen or other officers, and plunge

3. attic   4. substances capable of burning or eating away

themselves into the water wherever they found it.

It often pierced my very soul to hear the groans and cries of those who were thus tormented. But of the two, this was counted the most promising particular in the whole infection: for if these swellings could be brought to a head, and to break and run, or, as the surgeons call it, to "digest," the patient generally recovered; whereas those who, like the gentlewoman's daughter, were struck with death at the beginning, and had the tokens[5] come out upon them, often went about indifferently easy till a little before they died, and some till the moment they dropped down, as in apoplexies[6] and epilepsies is often the case. Such would be taken suddenly very sick, and would run to a bench or bulk, or any convenient place that offered itself, or to their own houses, if possible, as I mentioned before, and there sit down, grow faint, and die. This kind of dying was much the same as it was with those who die of common mortifications, who die swooning, and, as it were, go away in a dream. Such as died thus had very little notice of their being infected at all till the gangrene was spread through their whole body; nor could physicians themselves know certainly how it was with them till they opened their breasts, or other parts of their body, and saw the tokens.

CARETAKERS REPORTEDLY GUILTY OF MURDER

We had at this time a great many frightful stories told us of nurses and watchmen who looked after the dying people, that is to say, hired nurses, who attended infected people, using them barbarously, starving them, smothering them, or by other wicked means hastening their end, that is to say, murdering of them: and watchmen being set to guard houses that were shut up, when there has been but one person left, and perhaps that one lying sick, that they have broke in and murdered that body, and immediately thrown them out into the dead-cart; and so they have gone scarce cold to the grave.

I cannot say but that some such murders were committed, and I think two were sent to prison for it, but died before they could be tried; and I have heard that three others, at several times, were executed for murders of that kind. But I must say I believe nothing of its being so common a crime as some have since been pleased to say; nor did it seem to be so rational, where the people were brought so low as not to be able to help themselves; for such seldom recovered, and there was no temptation to commit a murder, at least not equal to the fact, where they were sure persons would die in so short a time, and could not live.

5. sores of the plague   6. sudden impairment of neurological function, especially that resulting from a stroke

Looters Rob the Dead

That there were a great many robberies and wicked practices committed even in this dreadful time, I do not deny. The power of avarice[7] was so strong in some that they would run any hazard to steal and to plunder; and, particularly in houses where all the families or inhabitants have been dead and carried out, they would break in at all hazards, and, without regard to the danger of infection, take even the clothes off the dead bodies, and the bedclothes from others where they lay dead.

This, I suppose, must be the case of a family in Houndsditch, where a man and his daughter, the rest of the family being, as I suppose, carried away before by the dead-cart, were found stark naked, one in one chamber and one in another, lying dead on the floor, and the clothes of the beds, from whence 'tis supposed they were rolled off by thieves, stolen, and carried quite away.

It is indeed to be observed that the women were, in all this calamity, the most rash, fearless, and desperate creatures; and, as there were vast numbers that went about as nurses to tend those that were sick, they committed a great many petty thieveries in the houses where they were employed; and some of them were publicly whipped for it, when perhaps they ought rather to have been hanged for examples, for numbers of houses were robbed on these occasions; till at length the parish officers were sent to recommend nurses to the sick, and always took an account who it was they sent, so as that they might call them to account if the house had been abused where they were placed.

But these robberies extended chiefly to wearing-clothes, linen, and what rings or money they could come at, when the person died who was under their care, but not to a general plunder of the houses; and I could give you an account of one of these nurses, who several years after, being on her deathbed, confessed with the utmost horror the robberies she had committed at the time of her being a nurse, and by which she had enriched herself to a great degree. But as for murders, I do not find that there was ever any proofs of the fact in the manner as it has been reported, except as above.

The Spread of Horror Stories

They did tell me, indeed, of a nurse in one place that laid a wet cloth upon the face of a dying patient whom she tended, and so put an end to his life, who was just expiring before; and another that smothered a young woman she was looking to, when she was in a fainting fit, and would have come to herself; some that

7. greed

killed them by giving them one thing, some another, and some starved them by giving them nothing at all. But these stories had two marks of suspicion that always attended them, which caused me always to slight them, and to look on them as mere stories that people continually frighted one another with. First—that wherever it was that we heard it, they always placed the scene at the farther end of the town, opposite or most remote from where you were to hear it. If you heard it in Whitechapel, it had happened at St. Giles's, or at Westminster, or Holborn, or that end of the town; if you heard of it at that end of the town, then it was done in Whitechapel, or the Minories, or about Cripplegate Parish; if you heard of it in the city, why, then, it happened in Southwark; and, if you heard of it in Southwark, then it was done in the city, and the like.

In the next place, of what part soever you heard the story, the particulars were always the same, especially that of laying a wet double clout on a dying man's face, and that of smothering a young gentlewoman: so that it was apparent, at least to my judgment, that there was more of tale than of truth in those things.

However, I cannot say, but it had some effect upon the people; and particularly, that, as I said before, they grew more cautious who they took into their houses, and whom they trusted their lives with, and had them always recommended, if they could; and where they could not find such, for they were not very plenty, they applied to the parish officers.

But here again, the misery of that time lay upon the poor, who, being infected, had neither food nor physic: neither physicians nor apothecary[8] to assist them, nor nurse to attend them. Many of those died calling for help, and even for sustenance, out at their windows, in a most miserable and deplorable manner; but it must be added that whenever the cases of such persons or families were represented to my Lord Mayor, they always were relieved.

It is true that in some houses where the people were not very poor, yet, where they had sent perhaps their wives and children away, and if they had any servants, they had been dismissed; I say, it is true, that to save the expenses, many such as these shut themselves in, and, not having help, died alone. . . .

FEMALE HAT THIEVES

I have mentioned above, that notwithstanding this dreadful calamity, yet numbers of thieves were abroad upon all occasions where they had found any prey, and that these were generally women. It was one morning about eleven o'clock, I had walked

8. pharmacist

out to my brother's house in Coleman Street Parish, as I often did, to see that all was safe.

My brother's house had a little court before it, and a brick wall and a gate in it, and, within that, several warehouses, where his goods of several sorts lay. It happened that in one of these warehouses were several packs of women's high-crowned hats, which came out of the country, and were, as I suppose, for exportation, whither I know not.

I was surprised that when I came near my brother's door, which was in a place they called Swan Alley, I met three or four women with high-crowned hats on their heads; and, as I remembered afterwards, one, if not more, had some hats likewise in their hands: but, as I did not see them come out at my brother's door, and not knowing that my brother had any such goods in his warehouse, I did not offer to say anything to them, but went across the way to shun meeting them, as was usual to do at that time, for fear of the plague. But when I came nearer to the gate, I met another woman, with more hats, come out of the gate. "What business, mistress," said I, "have you had there?" "There are more people there," said she; "I have had no more business there than they." I was hasty to get to the gate then, and said no more to her; by which means she got away. But just as I came to the gate, I saw two more coming across the yard, to come out, with hats also on their heads and under their arms; at which I threw the gate to behind me, which, having a spring-lock, fastened itself; and turning to the women, "Forsooth," said I, "what are you doing here?" and seized upon the hats, and took them from them. One of them, who, I confess, did not look like a thief,—"Indeed," says she, "we are wrong; but we were told they were goods that had no owner: be pleased to take them again; and look yonder, there are more such customers as we." She cried, and looked pitifully. . . .

Then I talked a little upon another footing with them, and asked them how they could do such things as these in a time of such general calamity, and, as it were, in the face of God's most dreadful judgments, when the plague was at their very doors, and, it may be, in their very houses, and they did not know but that the dead-cart might stop at their doors in a few hours, to carry them to their graves.

HELP OFFERED BY THE UNDER-SEXTON AND HIS WIFE

I could not perceive that my discourse made much impression upon them all that while, till it happened that there came two men of the neighborhood, hearing of the disturbance, and knowing my brother, for they had been both dependents upon his fam-

During the time of the plague carts were used to transport the dead to the cemetery for burial, often in mass graves.

ily, and they came to my assistance. These being, as I said, neighbors, presently knew three of the women, and told me who they were, and where they lived; and it seems they had given me a true account of themselves before.

This brings these two men to a further remembrance. The name of one was John Hayward, who was at that time undersexton[9] of the parish of St. Stephen, Coleman Street: by undersexton was understood at that time gravedigger and bearer of the dead. This man carried, or assisted to carry, all the dead to their graves, which were buried in that large parish, and who were carried in form, and, after that form of burying was stopped, went with the dead-cart and the bell to fetch the dead bodies from the houses where they lay, and fetched many of them out of the chambers and houses; for the parish was, and is still, remarkable, particularly above all the parishes in London, for a great number of alleys and thoroughfares, very long, into which

9. an employee of a church who is responsible for the upkeep of church property and for digging graves

no carts could come, and where they were obliged to go and fetch the bodies a very long way, which alleys now remain to witness it; such as White's Alley, Cross Key Court, Swan Alley, Bell Alley, White Horse Alley, and many more. Here they went with a kind of handbarrow, and laid the dead bodies on it, and carried them out to the carts; which work he performed, and never had the distemper at all, but lived about twenty years after it, and was sexton of the parish to the time of his death. His wife at the same time was a nurse to infected people, and tended many that died in the parish, being for her honesty recommended by the parish officers; yet she never was infected, neither.

He never used any preservative against the infection other than holding garlic and rue in his mouth, and smoking tobacco. This I also had from his own mouth. And his wife's remedy was washing her head in vinegar, and sprinkling her head-clothes so with vinegar as to keep them always moist; and, if the smell of any of those she waited on was more than ordinarily offensive, she snuffed vinegar up her nose, and sprinkled vinegar upon her head-clothes, and held a handkerchief wetted with vinegar to her mouth.

It must be confessed that though the plague was chiefly among the poor, yet were the poor the most venturous and fearless of it, and went about their employment with a sort of brutal courage; I must call it so, for it was founded neither on religion or prudence. Scarce did they use any caution, but ran into any business which they could get employment in, though it was the most hazardous; such was that of tending the sick, watching houses shut up, carrying infected persons to the pest-house, and, which was still worse, carrying the dead away to their graves.

THE GREAT FIRE OF LONDON

SAMUEL PEPYS

In his diary Samuel Pepys gave his personal account of the fire that swept London in September 1666. Each day he recorded his observations after walking about central London, seeing ordinary people trying to save their possessions and government leaders coping with the disaster. After the fifth day the fire had subsided and Pepys got some needed rest. Samuel Pepys held a variety of government positions over a long public career. He began *The Diary* on January 1, 1660, and in it recorded his observations of London life until May 31, 1669. He is also the author of *Memoirs of the Navy, 1690.*

SEPTEMBER 2 (LORD'S DAY), 1666

Some of our maids sitting up late last night to get things ready against our feast today, Jane called us up about three in the morning, to tell us of a great fire they saw in the City. So I rose and slipped on my nightgown,[1] and went to her window, and thought it to be on the back-side of Marke-lane at the farthest; but, being unused to such fires as followed, I thought it far enough off; and so went to bed again and to sleep. About seven rose again to dress myself, and there looked out at the window, and saw the fire not so much as it was and further off. By and by Jane comes and tells me that she hears that above 300 houses have been burned down tonight by the fire we saw, and that it is now burning down all Fish-street, by London Bridge. So

1. dressing gown.

Excerpted from "The Great Fire of London," by Samuel Pepys, in *The Diary* (London, 1660).

I made myself ready presently, and walked to the Tower,[2] and there got up upon one of the high places, Sir J. Robinson's little son going up with me; and there I did see the houses at that end of the bridge all on fire, and an infinite great fire on this and the other side the end of the bridge; which, among other people, did trouble me for poor little Michell and our Sarah on the bridge. So down, with my heart full of trouble, to the Lieutenant of the Tower, who tells me that it begun [sic] this morning in the King's baker's house in Pudding-lane, and that it hath burned St. Magnus's Church and most part of Fish-street already. So I down to the waterside, and there got a boat and through bridge, and there saw a lamentable fire. Poor Michell's house, as far as the Old Swan, already burned that way, and the fire running further, that in a very little time it got as far as the Steele-yard, while I was there. Everybody endeavoring to remove their goods, and flinging into the river or bringing them into lighters[3] that lay off; poor people staying in their houses as long as till the very fire touched them, and then running into boats, or clambering from one pair of stairs by the water-side to another. And among other things, the poor pigeons, I perceive, were loth to leave their houses, but hovered about the windows and balconys till they were, some of them burned, their wings, and fell down. Having stayed, and in an hour's time seen the fire rage every way, and nobody, to my sight, endeavoring to quench it, but to remove their goods, and leave all to the fire, and having seen it get as far as the Steele-yard, and the wind mighty high and driving it into the City; and every thing, after so long a drought, proving combustible, even the very stones of churches, and among other things the poor steeple by which pretty Mrs. — lives, and whereof my old schoolfellow Elborough is parson, taken fire in the very top, and there burned till it fell down: I to White Hall[4] (with a gentleman with me who desired to go off from the Tower, to see the fire, in my boat); to White Hall, and there up to the King's closet in the Chapel, where people come about me, and I did give them an account dismayed them all, and word was carried in to the King. So I was called for, and did tell the King and Duke of York what I saw, and that unless his Majesty did command houses to be pulled down nothing could stop the fire. They seemed much troubled, and the King commanded me to go to my Lord Mayor from him, and command him to spare no houses, but to pull down before the fire every way. At last met my Lord Mayor in Canning-street, like a man spent, with a handkerchief about his neck. To the King's message he cried, like a fainting woman,

2. London Tower   3. flat-bottomed barges   4. a palace in central London

"Lord, what can I do? I am spent: people will not obey me. I have been pulling down houses; but the fire overtakes us faster than we can do it." People all almost distracted, and no manner of means used to quench the fire. The houses, too, so very thick thereabouts, and full of matter of burning, as pitch and tar, in Thames-street; and warehouses of oil, and wines, and brandy, and other things. And to see the churches all filling with goods by people who themselves should have been quietly there at this time. Met with the King and Duke of York in their barge, and with them to Queenhithe, and there called Sir Richard Browne to them. Their order was only to pull down houses apace, and so below bridge at the water-side; but little was or could be done, the fire coming upon them so fast. River full of lighters and boats taking in goods, and good goods swimming in the water, and only I observed that hardly one lighter or boat in three that had the goods of a house in, but there was a pair of Virginals[5] in it. So near the fire as we could for smoke; and all over the Thames, with one's face in the wind, you were almost burned with a shower of fire-drops. This is very true; so as houses were burned by these drops and flakes of fire, three or four, nay, five or six houses, one from another. When we could endure no more upon the water, we to a little ale-house on the Bankside, over against the Three Cranes, and there stayed till it was dark almost, and saw the fire grow; and, as it grew darker, appeared more and more, and in corners and upon steeples, and between churches and houses, as far as we could see up the hill of the City, in a most horrid malicious bloody flame, not like the fine flame of an ordinary fire. Barbary and her husband away before us. We stayed till, it being darkish, we saw the fire as only one entire arch of fire from this to the other side the bridge, and in a bow up the hill for an arch of above a mile long: it made me weep to see it. The churches, houses, and all on fire and flaming at once; and a horrid noise the flames made, and the cracking of houses at their ruin. So home with a sad heart, and there find every body discoursing and lamenting the fire; and Poor Tom Hater come with some few of his goods saved out of his house, which is burned upon Fish-street Hill. I invited him to lie at my house, and did receive his goods, but was deceived in his lying there, the news coming every moment of the growth of the fire; so as we were forced to begin to pack up our own goods, and prepare for their removal; and did by moonshine (it being brave dry, and moonshine, and warm weather) carry much of my goods into the gar-

5. a small, rectangular spinet without legs, usually spoken of in the plural as a pair of virginals.

den, and Mr. Hater and I did remove my money and iron chests into my cellar, as thinking that the safest place. And got my bags of gold into my office, ready to carry away, and my chief papers of accounts also there, and my tallies into a box by themselves.

SEPTEMBER 3, 1666

About four o'clock in the morning, my Lady Batten sent me a cart to carry away all my money, and plate, and best things, to Sir W. Rider's at Bednall-greene. Which I did, riding myself in my nightgown in the cart; and, Lord! to see how the streets and the highways are crowded with people running and riding, and getting of carts at any rate to fetch away things. The Duke of York come this day by the office, and spoke to us, and did ride with his guard up and down the City to keep all quiet (he being now General, and having the care of all). At night lay down a little upon a quilt of W. Hewer's in the office, all my own things being packed up or gone; and after me my poor wife did the like, we having fed upon the remains of yesterday's dinner, having no fire nor dishes, nor any opportunity of dressing any thing.

SEPTEMBER 4, 1666

Up by break of day to get away the remainder of my things. Sir W. Batten not knowing how to remove his wine, did dig a pit in the garden, and laid it in there; and I took the opportunity of laying all the papers of my office that I could not otherwise dispose of. And in the evening Sir W. Pen and I did dig another, and put our wine in it; and I my Parmazan cheese, as well as my wine and some other things. Only now and then walking into the garden, and saw how horridly the sky looks, all on a fire in the night, was enough to put us out of our wits; and, indeed, it was extremely dreadful, for it looks just as if it was at us, and the whole heaven on fire. I after supper walked in the dark down to Tower-street, and there saw it all on fire, at the Trinity House on that side, and the Dolphin Tavern on this side, which was very near us; and the fire with extraordinary vehemence. Now begins the practice of blowing up of houses in Tower-street, those next the Tower, which at first did frighten people more than any thing; but it stopped the fire where it was done, it bringing down the houses to the ground in the same places they stood, and then it was easy to quench what little fire was in it, though it kindled nothing almost. Paul's[6] is burned, and all Cheap-side. I wrote to my father this night, but the post-house being burned, the letter could not go.

6. St. Paul's Cathedral

SEPTEMBER 5, 1666

About two in the morning my wife calls me up and tells me of new cries of fire, it being come to Barking Church, which is the bottom of our lane. I up, and finding it so, resolved presently to take her away, and did, and took my gold, which was about £2350, W. Hewer, and Jane, down by Proundy's boat to Woolwich; but, Lord! what a sad sight it was by moonlight to see the whole City almost on fire, that you might see it plain at Woolwich, as if you were by it. There, when I come, I find the gates shut, but no guard kept at all, which troubled me, because of discourse now begun, that there is plot in it, and that the French had done it. I got the gates open, and to Mr. Shelden's, where I locked up my gold, and charged my wife and W. Hewer never to leave the room without one of them in it, night or day. So back again, by the way seeing my goods well in the lighters at Deptford, and watched well by people. Home, and whereas I expected to have seen our house on fire, it being now about seven o'clock, it was not. I up to the top of Barking steeple, and there saw the saddest sight of desolation that I ever saw; everywhere great fires, oil-cellars, and brimstone,[7] and other things burning. I became afraid to stay there long, and therefore down again as fast as I could, the fire being spread as far as I could see it; and to Sir W. Pen's, and there eat a piece of cold meat, having eaten nothing since Sunday, but the remains of Sunday's dinner.

SEPTEMBER 6, 1666

It was pretty to see how hard the women did work in the cannells, sweeping of water; but then they would scold for drink, and be as drunk as devils. I saw good butts of sugar broke open in the street, and people go and take handfuls out, and put into beer, and drink it. And now all being pretty well, I took boat, and over to Southwarke, and took boat on the other side the bridge, and so to Westminster, thinking to shift myself,[8] being all in dirt from top to bottom; but could not there find any place to buy a shirt or pair of gloves. A sad sight to see how the River looks; no houses nor church near it, to the Temple, where it stopped.

SEPTEMBER 7, 1666

Up by five o'clock; and, blessed be God! find all well; and by water to Paul's Wharf. Walked thence, and saw all the town burned, and a miserable sight of Paul's church, with all the roofs fallen, and the body of the quire fallen into St. Fayth's; Paul's school also, Ludgate, and Fleet-street, my father's house, and the church,

7. Sulfur   8. to change clothes

and a good part of the Temple the like. This day our Merchants
first met at Gresham College, which, by proclamation, is to be
their Exchange. Strange to hear what is bid for houses all up and
down here; a friend of Sir W. Rider's having £150 for what he
used to let for £40 per annum. Much dispute where the Custom-
house shall be; thereby the growth of the City again to be fore-
seen. I home late to Sir W. Pen's, who did give me a bed; but
without curtains or hangings, all being down. So here I went the
first time into a naked bed, only my drawers on; and did sleep
pretty well: but still both sleeping and waking had a fear of fire
in my heart, that I took little rest. People do all the world over cry
out of the simplicity of my Lord Mayor in general, and more particularly in this business of the fire, laying it all upon him.

The Age of
Reason and
the Arts

CHAPTER 3

MODERN REASON SUPPLANTS MEDIEVAL PHILOSOPHY

FRANCIS BACON AND RENÉ DESCARTES

The seventeenth century launched the modern age of reason. In an excerpt from *Novum Organum* (*New Method*), written in 1620, Francis Bacon explains inductive reasoning—the close study of particular facts in order to draw a logical pattern or conclusion. As Bacon describes this method, he criticizes the old way of thinking that could lead to superstition. In an excerpt from *Discourse on Method*, written in 1637, René Descartes criticizes the logic, geometry, and algebra of the past and establishes new rules for reaching truth. As he applies them, he discovers a true generalization that can be applied deductively to new situations. Francis Bacon (1561–1626), a British intellectual, is the author of *Advancement of Learning* and *History of Henry the Seventh*. René Descartes (1596–1650), a French mathematician and philosopher, is the author of *Traite des Passions*, his chief ethical work.

T here are and can be only two ways of searching into and discovering truth. The one [deduction] flies from the senses and particulars to the most general axioms, and from these principles, the truth of which it takes for settled and immovable, proceeds to judgment and to the discovery of middle axioms [a universally recognized truth]. And this way is now in fashion. The other [induction] derives axioms from the senses and particulars, rising by a gradual and unbroken ascent, so that

Excerpted from *Novum Organum*, by Francis Bacon, 1620. Excerpted from *Discourse on Method* (New York: Liberal Arts Press, 1950) by René Descartes, translated by Laurence J. Lafleur. Copyright © 1950 by The Liberal Arts Press, Inc.

it arrives at the most general axioms last of all. This is the true way, but as yet untried.

Both ways set out from the senses and particulars, and rest in the highest generalities; but the difference between them is infinite. For [deduction] just glances at experiment and particulars in passing, [induction] dwells duly and orderly among them. [Deduction] again, begins at once by establishing certain abstract and useless generalities, [induction] rises by gradual steps to that which is prior and better known in the order of nature.

It cannot be that axioms established by argumentation [deduction] should avail for the discovery of new works; since the subtlety of nature is greater many times over than the subtlety of argument. But axioms duly and orderly formed from particulars [induction] easily discover the way to new particulars, and thus render sciences active.

One method of delivery alone remains to us; which is simply this: We must lead men to the particulars themselves, and their series and order; while men on their side must force themselves for awhile to lay their notions by and begin to familiarise themselves with facts.

DEDUCTION MAY LEAD TO SUPERSTITION

The human understanding when it has once adopted an opinion (either as being the received opinion or as being agreeable to itself) draws all things else to support and agree with it. And though there be a greater number and weight of instances to be found on the other side, yet these it either neglects and despises, or else by some distinction sets aside and rejects; in order that by this great and pernicious predetermination the authority of its former conclusions may remain inviolate. And therefore it was a good answer that was made by one who when they showed him hanging in a temple a picture of those who had paid their vows as having escaped shipwreck, and would have him say whether he did not now acknowledge the power of the gods,—"Aye," asked he again, "but where are they painted that were drowned, after their vows?" And such is the way of all superstition, whether in astrology, dreams, omens, divine judgments, or the like; wherein men, having a delight in such vanities, mark the events where they are fulfilled, but where they fail, though this happen much oftener, neglect and pass them by. But with far more subtlety does this mischief insinuate itself into philosophy and the sciences; in which the first conclusion colours and brings into conformity with itself all that come after, though far sounder and better. Besides, independently of that delight and vanity which I have described, it is the peculiar and perpetual error of human intellect

René Descartes

to be more moved and excited by affirmatives than by negatives; whereas it ought properly to hold itself indifferently disposed towards both alike. Indeed in the establishment of any true axiom, the negative instance is the more forcible of the two.

But not only is a greater abundance of experiments to be sought for and procured, and that too of a different kind from those hitherto tried; an entirely different method, order, and process for carrying on and advancing experience must also be introduced. For experience, when it wanders in its own track, is, as I have already remarked, mere groping in the dark, and confounds men rather than instructs them. But when it shall proceed in accordance with a fixed law, in regular order, and without interruption, then may better things be hoped of knowledge. . . .

Descartes Cites Limitations in Logic, Geometry, and Algebra

Among the branches of philosophy, I had, when younger, studied logic, and among those of mathematics, geometrical analysis and algebra; three arts or sciences which should be able to contribute something to my design. But in examining them I noticed that as far as logic was concerned its syllogisms[1] and most of its other methods serve rather to explain to another what one already knows, or even, as the art of [Spanish philosopher and mystic Raymond] Lully, to speak without judgment of what one does not know, than to learn new things. Although it does contain many true and good precepts, they are interspersed among so many others that are harmful or superfluous that it is almost as difficult to separate them as to bring forth a [Greek goddess] Diana or a Minerva from a block of virgin marble. Then, as far as the [geometrical] analysis of the Greeks and the algebra of the moderns is concerned, besides the fact that they deal with abstractions and appear to have no utility, the first is always so limited to the consideration of figures that it cannot exercise the un-

---

1. a three-part deductive argument with a generalization, a particular instance, and a conclusion. For example: All humans are mortal. Socrates is a human. Therefore, Socrates is mortal.

derstanding without greatly fatiguing the imagination, and the last is so limited to certain rules and certain numbers that it has become a confused and obscure art which perplexes the mind instead of a science which educates it. In consequence I thought that some other method must be found to combine the advantages of these three and to escape their faults. Finally, just as the multitude of laws frequently furnishes an excuse for vice, and a state is much better governed with a few laws which are strictly adhered to, so I thought that instead of the great number of precepts of which logic is composed, I would have enough with the four following ones, provided that I made a firm and unalterable resolution not to violate them even in a single instance.

DESCARTES'S FOUR RULES

The first rule was never to accept anything as true unless I recognized it to be evidently such: that is, carefully to avoid precipitation and prejudgment, and to include nothing in my conclusions unless it presented itself so clearly and distinctly to my mind that there was no occasion to doubt it.

The second was to divide each of the difficulties which I encountered into as many parts as possible, and as might be required for an easier solution.

The third was to think in an orderly fashion, beginning with the things which were simplest and easiest to understand, and gradually and by degrees reaching toward more complex knowledge, even treating as though ordered materials which were not necessarily so.

The last was always to make enumerations so complete, and reviews so general, that I would be certain that nothing was omitted.

What pleased me most about this method was that it enabled me to reason in all things, if not perfectly, at least as well as was in my power. In addition, I felt that in practicing it my mind was gradually becoming accustomed to conceive its objects more clearly and distinctly, and since I had not directed this method to any particular subject matter, I was in hopes of applying it just as usefully to the difficulties of other sciences as I had already to those of algebra. Not that I would dare to undertake to examine at once all the difficulties that presented themselves, for that would have been contrary to the principle of order. But I had observed that all the basic principles of the sciences were taken from philosophy, which itself had no certain ones. It therefore seemed that I should first attempt to establish philosophic principles, and that since this was the most important thing in the world and the place where precipitation and prejudgment were most to be feared, I should not attempt to reach conclusions until I had attained a much more mature age than my then twenty-three years, and had spent much time in preparing for it. This preparation would consist partly in freeing my mind from the false opinions which I had previously acquired, partly in building up a fund of experiences which should serve afterwards as the raw material of my reasoning, and partly in training myself in the method which I had determined upon, so that I should become more and more adept in its use. . . .

DESCARTES DISCOVERS A TRUTH

As our senses deceive us at times, I was ready to suppose that nothing was at all the way our senses represented them to be. As there are men who make mistakes in reasoning even on the simplest topics in geometry, I judged that I was as liable to error as any other, and rejected as false all the reasoning which I had previously accepted as valid demonstration. Finally, as the same precepts which we have when awake may come to us when asleep without their being true, I decided to suppose that nothing that had ever entered my mind was more real than the illusions of my dreams. But I soon noticed that while I thus wished to think everything false, it was necessarily true that I who thought so was something. Since this truth, *I think, therefore I am*, was so firm and assured that all the most extravagant suppositions of the sceptics were unable to shake it, I judged that I could safely accept it as the first principle of the philosophy I was seeking.

I then examined closely what I was, and saw that I could imagine that I had no body, and that there was no world nor any place that I occupied, but that I could not imagine for a moment that I did not exist. On the contrary, from the very fact that I doubted the truth of other things, it followed very evidently and very certainly that I existed. On the other hand, if I had ceased to think while all the rest of what I had ever imagined remained true, I would have had no reason to believe that I existed; therefore I concluded that I was a substance whose whole essence or nature was only to think, and which, to exist, has no need of space nor of any material thing. Thus it follows that this ego, this soul, by which I am what I am, is entirely distinct from the body and is easier to know than the latter, and that even if the body were not, the soul would not cease to be all that it now is.

Next I considered in general what is required of a proposition for it to be true and certain, for since I had just discovered one to be such, I thought I ought also to know of what that certitude consisted. I saw that there was nothing at all in this statement, "I think, therefore I am," to assure me that I was saying the truth, unless it was that I saw very clearly that to think one must exist. So I judged that I could accept as a general rule that the things which we conceive very clearly and very distinctly are always true, but that there may well be some difficulty in deciding which are those which we conceive distinctly.

THE SCIENTIFIC REVOLUTION

FRITJOF CAPRA

Fritjof Capra explains how Galileo Galilei began the scientific revolution when he combined scientific experimentation with mathematics to formulate laws of nature. Capra then explains that Isaac Newton recognized the significance of gravity and, combining ideas of his predecessors, formulated laws of motion that apply to a wide variety of natural phenomena. The discoveries of these two scientists form the basis for modern science. Capra has conducted research in high-energy physics at several European and American universities. He is the author of *The Tao of Physics* and many technical papers.

[N]icolaus] Copernicus was followed by Johannes Kepler, a scientist and mystic who searched for the harmony of the spheres and was able, through painstaking work with astronomical tables, to formulate his celebrated empirical laws of planetary motion, which gave further support to the Copernican system [which proposed that the sun was the center of the universe]. But the real change in scientific opinion was brought about by Galileo Galilei, who was already famous for discovering the laws of falling bodies when he turned his attention to astronomy. Directing the newly invented telescope to the skies and applying his extraordinary gift for scientific observation to celestial phenomena, Galileo was able to discredit the old cosmology beyond any doubt and to establish the Copernican hypothesis as a valid scientific theory.

Excerpted from *The Turning Point*, by Fritjof Capra. Copyright © 1981 by Fritjof Capra. Reprinted with permission from Simon & Schuster, Inc.

GALILEO CREATES A NEW SCIENTIFIC METHOD

The role of Galileo in the Scientific Revolution goes far beyond his achievements in astronomy, although these are most widely known because of his clash with the Church. Galileo was the first to combine scientific experimentation with the use of mathematical language to formulate the laws of nature he discovered, and is therefore considered the father of modern science. "Philosophy [broadly referring to science]," he believed, "is written in that great book which ever lies before our eyes; but we cannot understand it if we do not first learn the language and characters in which it is written. This language is mathematics, and the characters are triangles, circles, and other geometrical figures." The two aspects of Galileo's pioneering work—his empirical approach and his use of a mathematical description of nature— became the dominant features of science in the seventeenth century and have remained important criteria of scientific theories up to the present day.

To make it possible for scientists to describe nature mathematically, Galileo postulated that they should restrict themselves to studying the essential properties of material bodies— shapes, numbers, and movement—which could be measured and quantified. Other properties, like color, sound, taste, or smell, were merely subjective mental projections which should be excluded from the domain of science. Galileo's strategy of directing the scientist's attention to the quantifiable properties of matter has proved extremely successful throughout modern science, but it has also exacted a heavy toll, as the psychiatrist R.D. Laing emphatically reminds us: "Out go sight, sound, taste, touch and smell and along with them has since gone aesthetics and ethical sensibility, values, quality, form; all feelings, motives, intentions, soul, consciousness, spirit. Experience as such is cast out of the realm of scientific discourse." According to Laing, hardly anything has changed our world more during the past four hundred years than the obsession of scientists with measurement and quantification. . . .

NEWTON FORMULATES LAWS OF MOTION

Kepler had derived empirical laws of planetary motion by studying astronomical tables, and Galileo had performed ingenious experiments to discover the laws of falling bodies. Newton combined those two discoveries by formulating the general laws of motion governing all objects in the solar system, from stones to planets.

According to legend, the decisive insight occurred to Newton in a sudden flash of inspiration when he saw an apple fall from a tree. He realized that the apple was pulled toward the earth by the same force that pulled the planets toward the sun, and thus found the key to his grand synthesis. He then used his new mathematical method to formulate the exact laws of motion for all bodies under the influence of the force of gravity. The significance of these laws lay in their universal application. They were found to be valid throughout the solar system and thus seemed to confirm the Cartesian view [referring to René Descartes] of nature. The Newtonian universe was, indeed, one huge mechanical system, operating according to exact mathematical laws.

Newton presented his theory of the world in great detail in his *Mathematical Principles of Natural Philosophy*. The *Principia*, as the work is usually called for short after its original Latin title, comprises a comprehensive system of definitions, propositions, and proofs which scientists regarded as the correct description of nature for more than two hundred years. It also contains an explicit discussion of Newton's experimental method, which he saw as a systematic procedure whereby the mathematical description is based, at every step, on critical evaluation of experimental evidence:

> Whatever is not deduced from the phenomena is to be called a hypothesis; and hypotheses, whether metaphysical or physical, whether of occult qualities or mechanical, have no place in experimental philosophy. In this philosophy, particular propositions are inferred from the phenomena, and afterwards rendered general by induction.

NEWTON CONSIDERS REASON *AND* MAGIC

Before Newton there had been two opposing trends in seventeenth-century science; the empirical, inductive method represented by [Francis] Bacon and the rational, deductive method represented by Descartes. Newton, in his *Principia*, introduced the proper mixture of both methods, emphasizing that neither experiments without systematic interpretation nor deduction from first principles without experimental evidence will lead to a reliable theory. Going beyond Bacon in his systematic experimentation and beyond Descartes in his mathematical analysis, Newton unified the two trends and developed the methodology upon which natural science has been based ever since.

Isaac Newton was a much more complex personality than one would think from a reading of his scientific writings. He excelled not only as a scientist and mathematician but also, at various stages of his life, as a lawyer, historian, and theologian, and he was deeply involved in research into occult and esoteric knowledge. He looked at the world as a riddle and believed that its clues could be found not only through scientific experiments but also in the cryptic revelations of esoteric traditions. Newton was tempted to think, like Descartes, that his powerful mind could unravel all the secrets of the universe, and he applied it with equal intensity to the study of natural and esoteric science. While working at Trinity College, Cambridge, on the *Principia*, he accumulated, during the very same years, voluminous notes on alchemy, apocalyptic texts, unorthodox theological theories, and various occult matters. Most of these esoteric writings have never been published, but what is known of them indicates that Newton, the great genius of the Scientific Revolution, was at the same time the "last of the magicians."

NEWTON'S ABSOLUTE CLOCKWORK UNIVERSE

The stage of the Newtonian universe, on which all physical phenomen took place, was the three-dimensional space of classical Euclidean geometry. It was an absolute space, an empty container that was independent of the physical phenomena occurring in it. In Newton's own words, "Absolute space, in its own nature, without regard to anything external, remains always similar and immovable." All changes in the physical world were described in terms of a separate dimension, time, which again was absolute, having no connection with the material world and flowing smoothly from the past through the present to the future. "Absolute, true, and mathematical time, " wrote Newton, "of itself and by its own nature, flows uniformly, without regard to anything external."

The elements of the Newtonian world which moved in this absolute space and absolute time were material particles; small, solid and indestructible objects out of which all matter was made. The Newtonian model of matter was atomistic, but it differed from the modern notion of atoms in that the Newtonian particles were all thought to be made of the same material substance. Newton assumed matter to be homogeneous; he explained the difference between one type of matter and another not in terms of atoms of different weights or densities but in terms of more or less dense packing of atoms. The basic building blocks of matter could be of different sizes but consisted of the same "stuff," and the total amount of material substance in an object was given by the object's mass.

The motion of the particles was caused by the force of gravity, which, in Newton's view, acted instantaneously over a distance. The material particles and the forces between them were of a fundamentally different nature, the inner constitution of the particles being independent of their mutual interaction. Newton saw both the particles and the force of gravity as created by God and thus not subject to further analysis. In his *Opticks*, Newton gave a clear picture of how he imagined God's creation of the material world:

> It seems probable to me that God in the beginning formed matter in solid, massy, hard, impenetrable, movable particles, of such sizes and figures, and with such other properties, and in such proportion to space, as most conduced to the end for which he formed them; and that these primitive particles being solids, are incomparably harder than any porous bodies compounded of them; even so very hard, as never to wear or break in pieces; no ordinary power being able to divide what God himself made one in the first creation.

THE ROLE OF GOD IN NEWTON'S UNIVERSE

In Newtonian mechanics all physical phenomena are reduced to the motion of material particles, caused by their mutual attraction, that is, by the force of gravity. The effect of this force on a particle or any other material object is described mathematically by Newton's equations of motion, which form the basis of classical mechanics. These were considered fixed laws according to which material objects moved, and were thought to account for all changes observed in the physical world. In the Newtonian view, God created in the beginning the material particles, the forces between them, and the fundamental laws of motion. In this way the whole universe was set in motion, and it has continued to run ever since, like a machine, governed by immutable laws. The mechanistic view of nature is thus closely related to a rigorous determinism, with the giant cosmic machine completely causal and determinate. All that happened had a definite cause and gave rise to a definite effect, and the future of any part of the system could—in principle—be predicted with absolute certainty if its state at any time was known in all details.

This picture of a perfect world-machine implied an external creator; a monarchical god who ruled the world from above by imposing his divine law on it. The physical phenomena themselves were not thought to be divine in any sense, and when science made it more and more difficult to believe in such a god, the divine disappeared completely from the scientific world view, leaving behind the spiritual vacuum that has become characteristic of the mainstream of our culture. The philosophical basis of this secularization of nature was the Cartesian division between spirit and matter. As a consequence of this division, the world was believed to be a mechanical system that could be described objectively, without ever mentioning the human observer, and such an objective description of nature became the ideal of all science.

THE APPLICATION OF NEWTONIAN THEORY

The eighteenth and nineteenth centuries used Newtonian mechanics with tremendous success. The Newtonian theory was able to explain the motion of the planets, moons, and comets down to the smallest details, as well as the flow of the tides and various other phenomena related to gravity. Newton's mathematical system of the world established itself quickly as the correct theory of reality and generated enormous enthusiasm among scientists and the lay public alike. The picture of the world as a perfect machine, which had been introduced by Descartes, was now considered a proved fact and Newton became its symbol. During the last twenty years of his life Sir Isaac Newton reigned in eighteenth-century London as the most famous man of his time, the great white-haired sage of the Scientific Revolution. Accounts of this period of Newton's life sound quite familiar to us because of our memories and photographs of Albert Einstein, who played a very similar role in [the twentieth] century.

Encouraged by the brilliant success of Newtonian mechanics in astronomy, physicists extended it to the continuous motion of fluids and to the vibrations of elastic bodies, and again it worked. Finally, even the theory of heat could be reduced to mechanics when it was realized that heat was the energy generated by a complicated "jiggling" motion of atoms and molecules. Thus many thermal phenomena, such as the evaporation of a liquid, or the temperature and pressure of a gas, could be understood quite well from a purely mechanistic point of view. . . .

Newtonian mechanics was extended far beyond the description of macroscopic bodies. The behavior of solids, liquids, and gases, including the phenomena of heat and sound, was explained successfully in terms of the motion of elementary material particles. For the scientists of the eighteenth and nineteenth centuries this tremendous success of the mechanistic model confirmed their belief that the universe was indeed a huge mechanical system, running according to the Newtonian laws of motion, and that Newton's mechanics was the ultimate theory of natural phenomena.

BACH AND HANDEL: TWO BAROQUE MASTERS

KENNETH CLARK

Kenneth Clark compares the musical styles of Johann Sebastian Bach and George Frideric Handel to architecture. He suggests that Bach's musical structure has qualities of a cathedral built in the Gothic tradition. Handel's music, by contrast, reminds him of an elaborate double staircase with flowing, dramatic movement. Both composers remained true to the baroque musical tradition, which displays long curving lines and controlled elaborations. Kenneth Clark, an art historian, wrote television scripts for a series produced by the British Broadcasting Company and is the author of numerous books, including *Leonardo da Vinci, Landscape in Art,* and *Rembrandt and the Italian Renaissance.*

T he architectural language in which northern Europe became articulate in the eighteenth century was Italian Baroque; and rather the same is true of music. Underlying much of the work of the German composers was the international style of the great Italians, in particular of Alessandro Scarlatti. With its mastery of long curving lines, its controlled elaborations, its perfection of detail, it is remarkably close to the architecture of [Francesco] Borromini. Borromini came from a land of stone-carvers—the Italian lakes that form a boundary with Switzerland—and his style could fit into the craftsman tradition of the Germanic north, a tradition serving a social order that was absolutely the reverse of the centralised bureaucracy of

Excerpted from *Civilization*, by Kenneth Clark. Copyright © 1969 by Kenneth C. Clark. Reprinted with permission from HarperCollins Publishers, Inc.

France. It's true that many of the German princes thought they would like to imitate Versailles [a palace built by Louis XIV]. But the formative element in German art and German music didn't lie there, but in the multiplicity of regions and towns and abbeys—all competing for their architects and their choirmasters; and also relying on the talents of their local organists and plasterers. The creators of the German Baroque—the Assams and the Zimmermanns—were families of craftsmen: *zimmermann* is the German word for carpenter. The finest buildings we shall look at are not palaces, but local pilgrimage churches, deep in the country, like the Vierzehnheiligen—the "Fourteen Saints." And, come to think of it, the Bachs were a family of local musical craftsmen out of which there suddenly emerged one of the great geniuses of Western Europe, Johann Sebastian.

RELIGION INFLUENCES EIGHTEENTH-CENTURY ART

The sound of Bach's music reminds me of a curious fact that people don't always remember when they talk about the eighteenth-century—that the great art of the time was religious art. The thought was anti-religious; the way of life ostentatiously profane; we are right to call the first half of the century the age of reason. But in the arts, what did this emancipated rationalism produce? One adorable painter—[Jean-Antoine] Watteau, some nice domestic architecture, some pretty furniture: but nothing to set beside the *Matthew Passion* or the *Messiah* or the abbeys and pilgrimage churches of Bavaria and Franconia. To some extent Bach's music grew out of the Italian style, just as northern Baroque grew out of Borromini. But there was another musical tradition in Germany which went back to the Reformation. Luther had been a fine musician—he wrote music and sang with (surprisingly enough) a sweet tenor voice. And although the Lutheran reform prohibited many of the arts that civilise our impulses, it encouraged church music. In small Dutch and German towns the choir and the organ became the only means through which men could enter the world of spiritualised emotion; when the Calvinists, in their still more resolute purification of the Christian rite, prohibited organs and destroyed them, they caused more distress than had ever been caused by the destruction of images. Organs have played a variable role in European civilisation. In the nineteenth century they were symbols of newly-won affluence, like billiard tables; but in the seventeenth and eighteenth centuries they were expressions of municipal pride and, independence. They were the work of the leading local craftsmen, often covered with decorative sculpture; and organists were respected members of the community.

Johann Sebastian Bach

Bourgeois democracy, which had provided a background to Dutch painting in the seventeenth century, became partly responsible for German music; and it was a society more earnest and more participating than the Dutch connoisseurs had been. This provincial society was the background of Bach. His universal genius rose out of the high plateau of competitive musical life in the Protestant cities of northern Germany. One can even say that it rose out of a family that had been professional musicians for one hundred years, so that in certain districts the very word "Bach" meant a musician.

And Johann Sebastian's life was that of a conscientious, somewhat obstinate, provincial organist and choirmaster. But he was universal. A great musical critic said of him: "He is the spectator of all musical time and existence, to whom it is not of the smallest importance whether a thing be new or old, so long as it is true."

GERMAN BAROQUE: A COMPLEX PLAN OVERLAID WITH LAVISH ORNAMENT

Baroque elaboration is not the side of Bach that we value most. That severe head belongs equally to the Renaissance or the late Middle Ages; . . . And some of the great moments in Bach's oratorios of the Passion have the solemn simplicity and deep religious feeling of [pre-Renaissance Italian painter and sculptor] Giotto's frescoes. The towering polyphony has the quality of Gothic architecture. But then we remember how closely German Baroque, in its use of controlled space to work on our emotions, follows the traditions of Gothic architecture; and we find that we can illustrate Bach's music by a contemporary building. The pilgrimage church of the Vierzehnheiligen was built by an architect who was only two years younger than Bach. He was called Balthasar Neumann, and although his name is not well known in the English-speaking world, I think he was certainly one of the greatest architects of the eighteenth century. Unlike the other builders of German Baroque, he was not primarily a carver or plasterer, but an engineer. He made his name as a master of town-planning and fortifications. Inside his buildings one is conscious of a complex plan, worked out like the most intricate mathematical problem. But when occasion demanded it, he made use of ornament as lavish and fanciful as that of the most ebullient Bavarian plasterers.

Balthasar Neumann was fortunate in that the painted decorations in his finest interiors were not the work of the amiable local ceiling painters but of the greatest decorator of the age, the Venetian Giovanni Battista Tiepolo; and it is in one of Neumann's great buildings, the Bishop's Palace at Würzburg, that Tiepolo executed his masterpiece, the ceiling that covers the vast area of the staircase. It represents the four continents, a theme for decorative art that had conveniently replaced the once-fashionable allegories of the Christian faith; and, looking at these brilliant inventions, one may happily argue which continent has proved the most inspiring: Africa with its ostriches, camels and disdainful negresses; America with ravishing girls in feathered head-dresses riding on crocodiles; or Asia with its tigers and elephants. Somewhere in the background of Asia is a bare hill with three empty crosses. I wonder if the Bishop ever noticed it. He had more gratifying things to look at, his Residenz being, in fact, about twice the size of Buckingham Palace and filled in every room of the *piano nobile* [quiet elegance] with splendid decoration. One can't help speculating on the tithes and taxes that the peasants of Franconia had to pay in order that their episcopal master should do himself so well. But one must admit that many of these rulers of small German principalities—bishops, dukes, electors—were in fact remarkably cultivated and intelligent men. Their competitive ambitions benefited architecture and music in a way that the democratic obscurity of the Hanoverians in England did not. The Schönborn family, one of whom was responsible for the Residenz, were really great patrons whose name should be remembered with the Medici [Florentine rulers and patrons of the arts].

GEORGE FRIDERIC HANDEL: A CONTRAST TO BACH

I felt some scruples in comparing the music of Bach with a Baroque interior. No such hesitations need prevent me from invoking on the staircase of Würzburg the name of George Frideric Handel. Great men have a curious way of appearing in complementary pairs. This has happened so often in history that I don't think it can have been invented by symmetrically-minded historians, but must represent some need to keep human faculties in balance. However that may be, there is no doubt that the two great musicians of the early eighteenth century, Bach and Handel, fall into this pattern of contrasting and complementary personal-

ities. They were born in the same year—1685; they both went
blind from copying musical scores and were operated on, unsuc-
cessfully, by the same surgeon. But otherwise they were opposites.

In contrast to Bach's timeless universality, Handel was completely of his age. Instead of Bach's frugal, industrious career as
an organist with numerous children, Handel made and lost several fortunes as a theatrical impresario. [Louis-François] Roubil-
lac's statue of him, now in the Victoria and Albert Museum [in
London], was erected by the grateful proprietors of an amuse-
ment park, Vauxhall, in which his music had been one of the at-
tractions. There he sits in unbuttoned mood, one shoe off and one
shoe on, not caring how much he snitched other people's tunes
as long as he produced something effective. In his youth he must
have been charming, because when he went to Rome as an unknown young virtuoso he was immediately taken up by society,
and cardinals wrote libretti for him to set to music. There are remains of remarkable good looks in this head. Later in life, when
he had settled in England and entered the world of operatic production, he became less anxious to please, and is traditionally
said to have held one of his leading ladies out of the window and
threatened to drop her if she did not sing in tune. He remained
faithful throughout his life to the Italian Baroque style. In consequence his music goes well with the decorations of Tiepolo,
which even have the romantic pseudo-historical subjects of his
operas. The extraordinary thing is that this composer of flowing,
florid airs and rousing choruses, when he turned from opera to
oratorio—which was in fact a kind of sacred opera—wrote great
religious music. *Saul, Samson, Israel in Egypt* not only contain
wonderful melodic and polyphonic inventions, but show an understanding of the depths of the human spirit. As for the *Messiah*,
it is, like Michelangelo's *Creation of Adam*, one of those rare works
that appeal immediately to everyone, and yet is indisputably a
masterpiece of the highest order.

Baroque, but Could Be Rococo

I have called Handel a Baroque composer, and referred to the
buildings of Neumann as northern Baroque. I could almost
equally well have called them Rococo—in Würzburg the two
terms overlap: But there is a real difference between them, which
means something in the history of civilisation. Baroque, however
modified in Germany and Austria, was an Italian invention.
Baroque first came into being as religious architecture, and expressed the emotional aspirations of the Catholic Church. Rococo
was to some extent a Parisian invention, and provocatively secular. It was, superficially at any rate, a reaction against the heavy

Classicism of Versailles. Instead of the static orders of antiquity, it drew inspiration from natural objects in which the line wandered freely—shells, flowers, seaweed—especially if it wandered in a double curve. Rococo was a reaction against the academic style; but it was not negative. It represented a real gain in sensibility. It achieved a new freedom of association and captured new and more delicate shades of feeling.

FIVE BAROQUE PAINTERS

MARY ANN FRESE WILL ET AL.

The authors analyze major works of five baroque artists by comparing subject, composition, brush strokes, sources of light, and emotional impact. All of the authors are educators: Mary Ann Frese Will and Charlotte Vestal Brown teach at North Carolina State University at Raleigh; Roberta Ann Dunbar teaches at the University of North Carolina at Chapel Hill; Frank Tirro teaches at Yale University; and Ronald G. Will teaches at Duke University in Durham, North Carolina.

T he rather strange word *baroque* originally meant (from Italian *barocco*) a logical process that was contorted or involuted. In Portuguese, *perola barroca* was a term used by jewelers to designate a rough or irregularly shaped pearl. The French, by the eighteenth century, used the word *baroque* to mean "a painting . . . in which the rules of proportion are not observed and everything is represented according to the artist's whim." All of these meanings were, like "Gothic," originally pejorative. What these definitions share in common is the sense of divergence from an established, accepted ideal. As art history and criticism evolved and the seventeenth century was revalued, *baroque* appeared to be the opposite of *classical*, either in reference to antiquity or to the High Renaissance. In this sense the term suggested art that was naturalistic rather than ideal, and emotional rather than rational. Translated visually, this would produce an art of movement, vitality, and brilliant color, with interest in the realistic rendering of

Excerpted from *The Humanities: Cultural Roots and Continuities,* by Mary Ann Frese Will, Charlotte Vestal Brown, Roberta Ann Dunbar, Frank Tirro, and Ronald G. Witt. Copyright 1985 by D.C. Heath and Co. Reprinted with permission from Houghton Mifflin Company. All rights reserved.

the world and with a powerful emotional impact.

Just as Italian artists had fashioned a new vision of the world that created an artistic revolution in the fifteenth century, so artists came to Rome in the early seventeenth century to renew their sources of creativity. And just as the artists of the fifteenth century had their accomplishments disseminated in a variety of ways, with the work taking on the flavor of its particular artist and country, so the artists who came to Italy in the seventeenth century returned to their own countries and the term *baroque*, which is used to generally characterize their work, took on a flavor peculiar to time, artist, and place. Five painters whose work shows both the diversity and the shared characteristics that are alluded to by the term *baroque* will be considered.

CARAVAGGIO (1573–1610)

Born Michelangelo Merisi, Caravaggio took the name of his home town in Lombardy [a region in northern Italy]. He arrived in Rome during his late teens. There he lived like a rebel, was constantly in trouble for fighting and other violence, killed a man over a tennis match, and fled the city around 1606. His intense anger spilled over into his painting. Caravaggio seems to have deliberately sought to shock people with his art. He produced pictures that seem to dwell on the harsh and brutal reality of daily life—his painting of Christ's mother's corpse portrays a dead, bloated, old woman. But these realities were a means of triggering the intense, internal reality of conflicting feelings that Christ and his message brought to sinful men.

The Calling of St. Matthew (1599–1600), . . . one of three scenes from the apostle's life painted by Caravaggio to decorate the Contarelli Chapel in a church in Rome, demonstrates the psychological reality Caravaggio could draw from a simple scene. The event takes place in a Roman tavern; filtered light falls from the oiled paper in the window onto the bare walls and floor. Another, stronger light slashes across the top third of the canvas. This light reveals the face and uplifted hand of Jesus who, with Peter, steps into the room. Matthew the publican is seated at a table with three somewhat rustic, tacky youths. An older man leans over Matthew's shoulder and Matthew himself, who looks up somewhat surprised, shows with his face and gesture the eternal "Who, me?" even as he draws away from Christ.

What has Caravaggio done to make this such a revolutionary picture? He has located this event in a specific, real setting; a tavern populated with figures who are certainly not idealized in any way. They seem to lounge casually around the table, turning away from the event and the viewer, heightening a sense of irony.

Peter and Christ seem like momentary intruders who bring with them an unexpected, uncomfortable, revealing light. The viewer, who knows more than Matthew, stands very close, indeed, almost in the scene. Nothing really separates the real from the painted and the objects in the painting itself are rendered with hard, firm edges and substantial, varied textures, eliciting a powerful tactile response in the viewer. How could a spiritual event be portrayed with such earthy power? The contrasts reinforce the power of Christ's gesture that makes the earthly divine.

PETER PAUL RUBENS (1577–1640)

Rubens was the son of a wealthy Antwerp Protestant who fled to Germany to avoid persecution by the Catholics seeking control of the Netherlands. After his father's death, his family returned to Antwerp, and Rubens grew up a Catholic. Amiable, handsome, and energetic, he was already a successful painter when he journeyed to Italy in 1600. He remained there until 1608, assimilating the art of the High Renaissance and ancient Rome, and the revolutionary naturalism of Caravaggio. From these sources he created his own distinctive, optimistic, and visually rich view of the world.

When Rubens returned to Flanders, he was made court painter to the Spanish regent, and commissions began to flow into his workshop. He married well and lived in a magnificent townhouse in Antwerp that housed his collections of sculptures, paintings, antique coins and gems, and his personal library. His studio was soon filled with assistants who transferred his sketches onto large canvases. Even when he was absent on diplomatic and professional visits to France, England, or Spain, work was still produced to await his final approval and finishing touches. . . .

Rubens received many important commissions, but surely one of the most important was for a series of twenty-one canvases to celebrate the career of Marie de' Medici, widow of Henry IV and regent of France during the minority of her son, Louis XIII. These canvases transform an inglorious, occasionally unscrupulous, and not too beautiful woman into an object of splendor through the unity of myth, fact, history, and allegory. For example, Marie's arrival at Marseilles shows her greeted by helmeted France, attended by Fame and Neptune, whose court rises from the water to celebrate her safe voyage. Marie, at the center right, is only a part of the rather glorious assemblage, which is beautiful for its rich colors, textures, and vitality of light and movement. We realize that the paintings for Marie were commissioned not only for self-glorification but also for the glorification of the French monarchy and its increasing power. Baroque art could serve to glorify the absolute monarchy as well as the Church Militant.

Rubens was adept at this kind of commission; indeed his portraits of kings and queens, prelates and courtiers depict the brilliant world of the first half of the seventeenth century. But it is important to remember that this great master could render not only memorable scenes of both spiritual and temporal power but also those of his own life and of the world of persons and objects that he loved.

The Garden of Love, painted in 1638 and inspired by Rubens' second marriage, demonstrates the earthly love whose divine counterpart was the impetus for his great paintings of Christian subjects. Rubens and his young wife, Helene, the couple at the far left, are shown in a garden, about to join a group of obviously loving couples—husbands and wives or friends and lovers, it is hardly important. The fantastic fountain house from the artist's garden in Antwerp provides background. A statue of Venus and mischievous cupids complete this vision. The colors are soft and warm, light, gay, ripe, and sensuous. The figures—who stand, sit, lean, talk, and gaze—melt into each other in a soft, flowing rhythm. Velvet and satin, soft skin and hair, sparkling eyes, and rosy lips seduce us with a vision of the joy of life and love that is suspended in this spring garden. The courtly man in the broad-brimmed hat introduces us to a world that will be, more and more, the subject of art—a golden time without pain or anxiety.

REMBRANDT VAN RIJN (1606–1669)

Rubens' was a world of brilliant success. His life, though not without real difficulties and grief, exemplifies the artist who is accepted, adored, and lives to enjoy his fame. His optimism, energy, and success permit us one view of life in the first half of the seventeenth century. Rembrandt, younger than Rubens by almost thirty years, shows us another equally important aspect of that society.

Rembrandt's patrons were not the Catholic monarchy, church, and court but the powerful, successful Lutherans and Calvinists of Holland. The wealthy, individualistic burghers did not decorate their churches nor did they glorify the state, but they memorialized themselves and the infinite variety of objects and experiences that made up their lives.

Seated around a table covered with a magnificent red oriental rug, attended by a servant, the black-coated *Syndics of the Drapers' Guild* discuss the affairs of the guild. Yet the moment is not altogether public, for they seem to have been caught in a quiet conversation. One man rises from his seat to greet someone who has come into the room, and all eyes focus on that person. The intruder is, of course, the viewer, and this is one of the qualities that gives the picture its life. The men, who seem completely un-posed, become the focus of our attention through their glances, their alert faces, the direction of light, and the white collars and broad-brimmed hats. Each is an individual; each face exhibits age, experience, and reserve. The surface textures, contours of form, and the features of faces and hair are all rendered with soft, easily flowing brush strokes. The firm clarity that is present in much of Rubens' work is absent here, but the painting exhibits a softness derived from suffused light more comparable to that in *The Garden of Love*.

Rembrandt's sympathy with his patrons and their view of life grew from his own experience. One can follow his transforma-tion from a pugnacious and witty young man to a mature, intro-spective adult in his many self-portraits. He was never a social success like Rubens, but, like Rubens, he was deeply reliant on his art as the source of meaning in his life, and, like Rubens, he transformed his technique and skills to accommodate his vision of faith and the meaning of love.

Rembrandt's genius, like Rubens', lay in the unity of com-position achieved by light and by the revelation of surface fea-tures, textures, and colors in light. Renaissance painting devel-oped conventions in which light was generally clear, even, and uniformly revealing. . . .

Just as Caravaggio used light in a new way, so, too, did Rubens and Rembrandt, who experimented with and elaborated on the conventions that had defined the way light would be ren-dered in fifteenth- and sixteenth-century painting. Rubens, like Caravaggio, used light dramatically to reveal and focus on ob-jects, but unlike Caravaggio, whose light usually revealed the harsh reality of things, Rubens used light to reveal color and tex-ture and to enliven and enhance objects. Rembrandt used light to create much sharper contrasts between figures and objects in space. In deep shadows and shadowed faces we find that same mystery of life and death, pain and joy. Though these themes were present in Rubens' work, Rembrandt portrays them with-out explosive theatricality. The drama becomes more personal and introspective; it is not something that we witness; it is some-thing that we experience. The contrast is indicative of the differ-ence in emphasis between the theatricality of Counter Reforma-tion Catholicism and the individual piety of the Protestant north.

The Return of the Prodigal Son (ca. 1669) is such a shadowed, al-most soundless picture. The warm light falling on figures and faces reinforces the general warmth of the picture that is derived from gesture as well as from color scheme. The faces that witness this reunion seem observed in light reflected from the two major figures. There is no boisterous welcome but, instead, tender, loving forgiveness. This is earthly love raised to a divine power by the simplicity of composition. The paint itself seems thin except in the figures of father and son, where heavy *impastoed* layers, creating form and shadow, allude to textures. Unlike the uniformly smooth surface of Renaissance pictures, these contrasting layers of paint tell, as they do in Rubens' work, of the expansion of another Renaissance convention.

VERMEER (1632–1675)

The ability to make paint give the illusion of reality has almost no limits. The degree of expansion of that ability was also tested by the third great northern painter, Vermeer of Delft, Holland. The relativity of experience, the limits of reality, and the fragmented perception of the world are denied and confirmed in the ordered visions of Vermeer. The apparently simple subjects—city views and figures in interiors—are chosen in transient moments and rendered permanent. These pictures, all small, are deceptively simple. A maidservant stands before a window pouring milk from a pitcher into a basin. The light from the window is cool and subdued; the colors of her sleeves, apron, and tablecloth are all cool. The pottery, the bread, and the gold of her bodice and red of her skirt challenge the quiet coolness. The gesture endures forever.

What is so remarkable about this painting? The original, more than a reproduction, emits an incredible transparency and glow. It is possible to imagine that, should the light be gone from the room, the painting itself would provide light—so natural and convincing is its revelation of every surface, fold, and wrinkle. The colors themselves vibrate; shadows and folds are not rendered in gray, brown, or black but in thin layers of color itself—deeper blue in her apron, deeper golden red on the basin.

Light, of course, is the most essential and most recalcitrant element in all painting that seeks to render an account of nature as we perceive it. Artists have captured it by conventionalizing its representation. Raphael's even harmonious light, Rubens' dramatic spotlight effects, or Rembrandt's reflected light are some examples of the different ways to render light convincingly without absolute fidelity to light as it is experienced naturally. Vermeer, however, by confining his subjects almost exclusively to figures before windows, proclaims his interest in the transient, cool light that comes from outside and is therefore subject to immediate change. Yet change never occurs, and that is what delights: it is "real" and it is not! We know that *The School of Athens* or *Primavera* are rendered through knowledge of the behavior of light, but there is no attempt to cajole us into thinking that it is "real" or experienced light—not so with Vermeer. Moreover, a woman weighing gold, a girl reading a letter, or a geographer in his study are all intimate revelations of transience where light reveals and suggests the brevity of life and the ephemeral pleasure of things.

As we experience these pictures by Vermeer, we add another layer to our perception of the seventeenth century. Here is a vision very different from that of a Rubens or a Rembrandt. In its realism it is more like Caravaggio, but its order recalls [Italian painters] Piero and Raphael. Above all, however, Vermeer's study of light and delineation of space is uniquely his own, as individual and personally centered as he could make it.

DIEGO RODRÍGUEZ DE SILVA Y VELÁSQUEZ (1599–1660)

It is perhaps curious that of all the acknowledged masters of the seventeenth century a painter at the court of Philip IV, in the period of Spain's decline, could have created a highly original and personal style based on pure sensibility and perceptual experience. During the same years that Rubens executed great religious paintings, and Ribera and Zurbarán, Spanish contemporaries of Velásquez, made deeply moving and powerful religious pictures for Spanish patrons and the Church, the court painter (he had joined the court in 1623, remained there, and was made court chamberlain in 1652) produced a few religious subjects. Rather, his fame grew from his stunning portraits and scenes of classical allegory and myth. Visiting Italy twice provided inspiration but did not essentially alter his manner. Velásquez's manner is most comparable to that of Vermeer. Like Vermeer, he was fascinated by light on objects, the light that reveals and conceals the images the artist sees and reproduces. Thus the actual surfaces of Velásquez's paintings reveal an elegant and systematic brushwork that depicts objects as fragments of light and shade, of colors placed side by each. The edges of objects are slightly indeterminate; the surface is never harsh or crisp but rather seems perpetually modulated by the movement of air and light. The most telling experience is to see a painting by Velásquez, to stalk it silently, in an attempt to discover the precise moment at which the surface dissolves into the fragments, layers, and dots that constitute the source of the painted image. This is very difficult, however, for the moment of dissolution is so close to the moment of seeing the image as a complete whole.

This kind of painting seems to lend itself to speculations about kinds of reality—the reality of image, of surface, of object. Yet like Vermeer's paintings, Velásquez's works do not suggest speculation; rather, they seem truly to depict reality. His most famous work, *Las Meninas* (The Ladies-in-Waiting), painted in 1656, typifies his greatest work.

In the center of the large canvas, near the front edge, stands the five-year-old princess who has come to visit the painter in his studio. To the left stands Velásquez, a very large canvas on his easel. The ladies-in-waiting attend the princess, and to the right are two dwarfs, whose plainness plays against the glitter of royalty. A dog lies quietly in the foreground, a court official enters a lighted doorway at the back of the room. It is then that the viewer sees, or is shown, the images of the King and Queen, reflected by a mirror at the back of the room. They, too, have come to the studio of their painter, who must be working on a painting of the royal family.

The light in this painting seems to fall into the room from an unseen window to the left. It lights the figures, the foreground, and the King and Queen, who stand where the viewer might be. As with Vermeer's painting, it is possible to imagine that one would see into the painting in the dark, because it seems to contain its own light. The surface is fairly smooth, but rich with the paints that so carefully recreate the varying surfaces of hair, skin, fabric, fur, embroidery, jewelry. It is a remarkable achievement; the painting seems to breathe with a life drawn from experienced reality, captured on canvas.

Rubens, Rembrandt, and Caravaggio, each in his own way, explore human emotions with power, drama, and sometimes the rhetoric of experience. Vermeer and Velásquez, on the other hand, seem to explore the experienced world in a direct and candid way, sacrificing nothing to give an account of the essentials of seeing, yet creating an extraordinary series of masterpieces that are, in fact, as carefully considered, composed, and conceptualized as the work of their predecessors or their peers.

LITERATURE IN THE AGE OF REASON

GEORGE K. ANDERSON AND ROBERT WARNOCK

George K. Anderson and Robert Warnock argue that reason drove imagination and emotion from literature in the late seventeenth and early eighteenth centuries. Writers of the period strove to teach readers to act according to reason, not passion. Influenced by Greek and Roman classical writers, French playwrights produced tragedies and satiric comedies, and English writers produced essays on proper living and proper taste. Anderson and Warnock suggest that the invention of the novel was the best contribution of the age. The early novels taught the virtue of living the reasonable moral life.

Anderson, who taught English at Brown University, authored *The Literature of the Anglo-Saxons* and co-edited *The Literature of England*. Warnock taught English at the University of Connecticut.

T he tie between philosophy and literature has never been stronger than in the Age of Enlightenment. All the arts felt the rule of reason and assumed their proper places within the universal system. In this most intellectual of eras they took on a cold, even mathematical character in harmony with the Cartesian [pertaining to philosopher René Descartes] principle. The formal pattern of a Bach fugue and the neat clockwork of a Haydn symphony reflect the rational ordering of music, as of all the arts, in the age of common sense.

Indeed, the philosophy of this period outlawed art of any other kind. In exalting the faculty of reason the rationalists attacked the rival faculty of imagination, which gives us not real-

Excerpted from *The World In Literature*, vol. 2, by George K. Anderson and Robert Warnock. Copyright © 1951 by Scott Foresman and Company. Reprinted with permission from Scott Foresman-Addison Wesley.

ity but irrational dreams. As [French philosopher and mathematician Blaise] Pascal points out in his *Thoughts,* reason shows us things as they are; imagination creates a picture of things as we wish they were or fear they may be. Wishful thinking does not lead to truth; indeed it deliberately evades unpleasant truth. Imagination varies from person to person, as each man dreams his own dreams and sees life irrationally in his own way. But the God-given faculty of reason does not vary; it leads men in China and India, Europe and America to the same timeless truths about the universal system. Hence, imagination is a fraud, in league with the emotions against the true gospel of reason. . . .

FORM AND LANGUAGE IN POETRY

In its attempt to make poetry rational the Age of Reason developed an elaborate theory of poetic diction, a standardized language to distinguish poetry from prose and to give it a special reservoir of pleasant ornaments to be drawn upon at will by the determined poet and poetaster. . . .

The special diction took several forms. First was the abstract circumlocution, by which the poet deliberately avoided mentioning a concrete object, animal, or person by its own name and put it instead into a general class. So fish became "the finny race," sheep "the woolly care," spring flowers "vernal bloom," a telescope "a sight-invigorating tube," a woman "a shining mischief." A second type was personification, which reached its zenith of poetic popularity in this period. "History leaning on her elbow," "Silence on her untroubled throne," "Winter bending o'er his tread," "sable Night descending" everywhere haunt neo-classical verse. Classical gods often provided the same effect. A third type, the latinism, reflects the popularity of ancient classics among the poets and their readers, but also their urge to avoid direct statement about concrete objects. Kings become "the arbiters of this terraqueous swamp"; cattle "ruminate in the contiguous shade"; "the stable yields a stercoraceous heap impregnated with quick fermenting salts." These are some of the devices that implemented the theory of poetic diction. . . .

THE INFLUENCE OF THE ANCIENT CLASSICS

If the classics of Greece and Rome, long so inspiring to the humanists of the Renaissance, were discredited by the rational speculation of the philosophers and the expanding world of the scientists, they nevertheless reached the climax of their literary influence at this time. The critical pronouncements of [Greek philosopher] Aristotle and [Roman poet] Horace hardened into inviolable law. . . .

In both France and England the long century of reason and classicism in literature breaks into two sub-periods around the year 1700. The fifty years that preceded saw the evolution of the rational system and the gradual hardening of the classical ideal. The fifty years that followed saw widespread application of the rational method to all phases of life and the absolute tyranny of the classics in belles-lettres. Beyond 1750 forces of revolt emerged, as rationalism and classicism began a half-century of decline.

From the social point of view, the aristocracy still dominated the literature of the first period, but the middle-class outlook became increasingly militant in the second. In France, belles-lettres flourished during the first period, especially in the drama of [Pierre] Corneille, [Jean] Racine, and Molière, but declined in the second under the intellectual rule of the *Philosophes,* who made literature serve the ends of speculation and social criticism.

A powerful influence toward standardizing literature in the classical mold throughout both periods was the conservative French Academy, the body of forty elected "Immortals," chartered by [the king's adviser Cardinal] Richelieu in 1635. Although it performed a unique service for the French language in compiling its first great dictionary and settling its grammar, it worked against literary experiment in favor of tradition and inflexible rules. Similar academies appeared in Italy, Spain, Holland, and Germany, but none in England. Conformity developed in England under literary dictators in the coffee-houses.

FRENCH TRAGEDY AND COMEDY

The drama of reason, which is the great glory of the age of Louis XIV, had both tragic and comic phases, but both were concerned with showing the unfortunate effects of allowing passion or caprice to assume control of our conduct. The tragic heroes and heroines fight in their minds a battle between reason and emotion, and upon their decision depends the outcome of the play. In Corneille's *Cid,* the first masterpiece of the school, both Rodrigue and Chimène are faced with a choice between love and duty and in accepting the rational claims of duty they avert tragedy for themselves and others. Their long soliloquies take on the character of formal debates between rival urges, and their unfailing renunciation of passion exaggerates the power of will and intelligence in human conduct, and hence falsifies human values. Significantly, the *Cid* appeared in the very year of Descartes's *Discourse on Method* (1636) . His *Treatise on the Passions of the Soul* was later to state the philosophy of the whole school of classical tragedy.

It was Racine who refined this intellectual tragedy into its supreme form, preserving its theme and classical characteristics, but projecting the anguish of passion-wracked men and women with a noble pity and terror. In his *Phaedra* the heroine is torn between a guilty love for her stepson and a sense of duty to her absent husband. All the torture of illicit love appears in her restless writhing. Unlike a heroine of Corneille, she gives in to her guilty desire, declares her passion, and then destroys all three characters in her frantic effort to escape the consequences. In the religious Racine, overweening emotion, whether of love, ambition, pride, or hate, is the mark of original sin in man (or especially woman) living within a world where reason is right. The tragedy of his characters is that they allow passion its ill-fated victory over common sense. . . .

The greatest classical tragedies concentrate on the high point of the conflict and rigidly exclude all intrigue that does not bear directly upon the climax. To this end the dramatic unities of action, place, and time, derived from Aristotle's *Poetics* and a study of ancient tragedies, were universally accepted in France for about two hundred years after the *Cid*. They meant restricting the plot to one moral issue presented by a small group of characters, argued within a single room, and concluded within a time-span of twenty-four hours. There was a similar unity of tone or style in these serious plays; no levity could violate the tragic earnestness of the characters and their intense involvement in the problem that was approaching its climax. To give stature and nobility to the drama, this aristocratic age required that all the leading characters should be of princely rank or of a traditional consequence that amounted to the same thing. Commoners, who were considered incapable of completely rational and civilized behavior, were similarly incapable of tragic feeling or of understanding the conflict of reason and passion. Noble sentiments belonged exclusively to the noble. . . .

More acceptable by far to modern audiences is the rollicking comedy of Molière and his many successful imitators. But the high spirits and frank good humor of the school should not obscure the serious moral purpose of the best comedians, who were making their comment on human nature and society as surely as were the writers of tragedy. In this philosophical century no important kind of literature escaped involvement in the rational system. Indeed, writers of tragedy and comedy had the same philosophy, and their methods were merely reverse sides of the shield.

To Molière a rational society composed of enlightened and cooperative members was the ideal toward which his century was working. Hence any member who ignored the rational laws of conduct and would not collaborate in the common undertaking became an enemy of society. Society has many means of forcing individuals into rational and socially responsible behavior, but the most telling is laughter. Satire, never more popular than in the Age of Reason, is a special weapon for poking fun at irrational actions, fads, and foibles and for bludgeoning offenders back into line. So classical comedy, which gives us a picture of manners in civilized circles, condemns eccentricities but represents the rational norm as well.

Molière's comedies are highly varied; yet through them all runs his fine philosophy. At times, as in *Tartuffe*, the serious purpose almost defeats comedy, but at his best, as in *The Misanthrope*, he makes us laugh as he makes us think. The irrational excesses that he attacks range from the merely foolish affectations of the learned ladies to vicious impositions upon society. He anticipated George Bernard Shaw in his satire of medical quacks who pompously mystify and victimize their public. *Tartuffe* treats religious hypocrisy which masks avarice and carnal desires in mock piety. In *The Misanthrope* Molière exposes those self-righteous ones who carry honesty beyond reason and lose touch with reality in refusing to accept the compromise with virtue by which society operates. . . .

Voltaire, on the other hand, was the all-inclusive man of letters whose works stretch to a hundred volumes. Throughout sixty-five years he never ceased to write in almost every area of literature. His age considered him its greatest poet and playwright, but his poems and tragedies reveal only the low state of these types in the eighteenth century. His histories are still reprinted and studied. But it is his witty little novels, his mordant satires, and his miscellaneous letters, dialogues, and diatribes that are best remembered. They are perennial sources of intellectual stimulation and hilarity. Above all, Voltaire, with his wry smile and mocking laugh, is the enduring symbol of the Enlightenment, the fearless spokesman for free reason in a natural world, who was tolerant of everything but oppression and arrogant authority. This most French of writers is a one-man summary of French classicism in the Age of Reason. . . .

INFLUENTIAL BRITISH WRITERS

[Alexander] Pope was the greatest of Europe's neo-classical poets. All the power and all the weaknesses of "rational" verse shine out from his pages. Accepting the stately and somewhat mechanical heroic couplet as his favorite verse form, he became the spokesman for the poetry of ideas rather than imagination or emotion. His *Essay on Criticism,* derived from Horace and [French critic and poet Nicolas] Boileau, is our clearest and most memorable statement of the classical ideal of literary art and literary criticism. His *Essay on Man* popularized the ideas of rationalism and Deism in scintillating epigrams that have become proverbial. In verse satire, particularly the mock-epic, he was equally brilliant. *The Rape of the Lock* is a completely charming satire of the manners of high society and especially of the frivolous activities of a London belle, while the *Dunciad* bears down on Pope's literary enemies with a full-scale, annihilating attack. As a classicist, he made no pretense of originality: the ideas expressed in his didactic poems are all borrowed; some of his most famous couplets are adapted from older poets. He believed it his role to order and arrange the material that he garnered from others and to give it a more polished and spirited statement than it had ever had before. In this he succeeded beyond any of his contemporaries.

His good friend [Jonathan] Swift, a nobler person but a tragic one, is England's great prose satirist and her most original writer in this period. His originality and his personal tragedy sprang in part from his temperamental opposition to the intellectual trends of the Age of Reason. Aside from frustrated worldly ambitions and emotional needs (which are matters of biography) Swift represents ecclesiastical indignation in the eighteenth century at the rise of pragmatic middle-class government and at the growing attack of science on the substance of religious faith. Although he accepted the rule of reason in a general way, he viewed with alarm the teachings of [philosophers Thomas] Hobbes and [John] Locke and the new science of [Isaac] Newton. When he saw his age veering further from the right course as he conservatively viewed it, Swift's pessimism deepened into full-scale misanthropy and eventual insanity.

His masterpiece, *Gulliver's Travels*, reflects this tendency of his mind: the first two books satirize contemporary government with playful gravity, the third attacks the new science with brilliant but embarrassing savagery, the fourth bitterly excoriates all mankind as less rational and less worthy than the brutes. His method too sinks into coarseness as he dwells upon the ugliness in human nature. Yet ironically, Swift was at heart a humanitarian, outraged at the inhumanity of his time. He was a religious moralist in an age of cocksure philosophers and scientists. Out of step with his era, he became the outspoken pessimist in an age of official optimism. More ironic still, his harshest diatribes can now be read as humorous entertainment, since the issues have grown more remote while the satiric art of Swift remains. . . .

[Essayists Joseph] Addison and [Richard] Steele stand for the genteel tradition in satire, which applies rational criticism to the superficial foibles and eccentricities of men and women but leaves the core of society and human nature largely untouched. They belong to the first generation of middle-class authors, who were still gentlemen who lacked the militant bourgeois outlook of [novelists Daniel] Defoe and [Samuel] Richardson, but pioneered for a literature that would be more popular and more moralistic.

In the periodical essay Steele discovered the ideal medium for his purpose. As a species of journalism it could reach a large audience beyond the intellectual and social uppercrust. Its periodic appearance provided an incessant and cumulative attack on moral laxity and social abuses. And its miscellaneous character made him able to strengthen the virtue of his readers by a variety of entertainments: reflections or "lucubrations," occasional sermons, satiric essays on manners, portraits of social types, and fictitious letters to the editor.

Addison, though actually a more conventional and irreproachable man than his friend, widened the scope of his periodical to make it the mirror of the whole society of their time. Without any serious philosophical purpose, he applied reason to the everyday activities of men and guided the middle class to good taste as well as virtue. Addison's approach is never harsh and seldom austere, often humorous, unfailingly graceful and refined. The periodical essay owed much to the familiar essays of [French essayists Michel Eyquem de] Montaigne and the characters of [Jean de] La Bruyère, but it became a distinct literary type, always at its best in England.

Yet the enduring invention of middle-class authors in eighteenth-century England was the novel. Although it was preceded by various kinds of prose fiction in the Renaissance, the novel became a distinct form on the road to universal popularity in the works of Defoe and Richardson. Daniel Defoe (1661–1731), an unabashed bourgeois who never got beyond the slovenly craftsmanship of journalism, preached the cause of virtue to a large audience through long-winded tales of criminals like Moll Flanders and worthy Englishmen like Robinson Crusoe. In Richardson's interminable novels the moral lesson is combined with sentimentality, and in [Laurence] Sterne the sentimentality becomes an end in itself, something like a parlor philosophy of life. . . .

In retrospect, nothing seems more characteristic of this century than the homogeneity of its point of view. The rational system became a framework upon which every phase of experience took its natural place.

Power Shifts in Asia and Australia

CHAPTER 4

JAPANESE RULERS OUST FOREIGNERS AND ISOLATE THE COUNTRY

G.B. SANSOM

G.B. Sansom explains how and why Japan became an isolated country in the seventeenth century. According to Sansom, the Tokugawa shoguns, who insisted on absolute rule, suspected that Christian missionaries and the Japanese citizens they had converted posed a threat to their control. After the Shimabara uprising in 1637, rulers closed the country entirely and allowed no foreigners in and no Japanese citizens out. G.B. Sansom, a scholar of Japanese history, is the author of *Japan: A Short Cultural History*, three volumes of *A History of Japan*, and *Historical Grammar of Japan*.

T he institutions of Japan under the régime that was firmly established by Ieyasu in 1615 need only a general explanation here. The Tokugawa family had succeeded, after a series of victorious campaigns, in reducing to submission the powerful feudal lords who had opposed them. They thus acquired supreme authority in the land, all other feudal rulers—the daimyo, as they were called—being their vassals. Those who had fought on the Tokugawa side were rewarded with fiefs [estates] commensurate with their services, while the former enemies—known as Tozama or Outside Lords—in return for their submis-

Excerpted from *The Western World and Japan: A Study in the Interaction of European and Asiatic Cultures* (New York: Alfred A. Knopf, 1950) by G.B. Sansom. Copyright © 1949 by G.B. Sansom.

sion were confirmed in their holdings but were not allowed authority beyond their own territories, and in principle could not hold office in the administrative organs set up by the Shogun [commander of the army] for the government of the country as a whole. Each daimyo was left in control of the people and property in his domain, which was in theory not subject to interference by the central government so long as the supreme authority was not endangered. All daimyo were obliged to swear allegiance to each successive Shogun and were then confirmed in their fiefs, but they could be deprived of all or part of their holdings at the will of the Shogun should he deem them guilty of insubordinate conduct or treasonable intentions. These powers were freely exercised by the first three Tokugawa rulers, whose commands were so far-reaching that Japan in their day already exhibited some of the features of a centralized nation state.

THE TOKUGAWA RÉGIME'S FEAR OF REVOLT

The whole of Tokugawa policy was designed to guard against revolt and thus to ensure the permanence of Tokugawa rule. The geographical distribution of fiefs was made with an eye to strategy, hereditary vassals being assigned lands at points that threatened the line of advance of any Outside Lord who might plan an uprising. All daimyo were compelled to spend part of the year in Yedo, the Shogun's capital, and to leave their families behind as hostages when they returned to their provinces. These and many other devices were used to prevent the vassals from plotting mischief, and they did in fact secure for Japan unbroken peace over more than two hundred years. But the Shogunate was never fully at ease with respect to the Outside Lords, who for their part never became reconciled to Tokugawa dominance. Out of easy reach in the north and west of Japan lay powerful and warlike fiefs which had, it is true, been brought to submission but which might alone or in combination with other Outside Lords, or even with disaffected hereditary vassals, rise against the Shogun and plunge the country once more into civil war. Such a prospect the Tokugawa could not face, for they had brought peace to the country by a combination of arms and diplomacy which they could not be sure of repeating.

This fear of domestic uprising has an important bearing upon the policy of seclusion, a policy that was not contemplated in the early years of the seventeenth century but was formed and executed precipitately after 1637. The sudden decision then taken to exclude aliens and to prohibit Japanese from going abroad was closely connected with the presence in Japan of foreign missionaries and traders. Its history is therefore most pertinent to the study of Western influences in Asia and calls for some detailed consideration here.

FOREIGNERS ARE FIRST ACCEPTED, THEN SUSPECTED

It will be remembered that, in describing the progress of Christian missions in Japan after the arrival of [Spanish Jesuit missionary] Francis Xavier in 1549, we stopped at the year 1600, when despite great persecutions the number of converts had risen to 300,000 and promised further increase. At this time Ieyasu had come into power but had not subdued the last of his adversaries. He was much interested in foreign trade, cherishing notions of expanding Japan's merchant fleet and perhaps of making some conquests in the southern seas. He was disposed to be friendly with both Portuguese and Spanish; he even proposed to open harbours in eastern Japan to foreign ships and showed no signs of any intention to diminish, still less to cut off, the foreign intercourse of Japan. He made it known that he would not enforce the anti-Christian edicts, and the work of evangelization went on without interruption, while foreign trade flourished.

But the truce was not to last for long. Though the number of converts steadily increased, there were isolated persecutions in different parts of Japan and hostility towards Christianity grew in high quarters, until after a series of perfunctory orders by Ieyasu, which may be regarded as warnings rather than as definite prohibitions, an edict banning the Christian faith was issued in 1614 and enforced with great severity in some regions, but still mildly elsewhere. By now it was evident that, sooner or later, the partial relaxation would come to an end.

When Ieyasu died in 1616, to be succeeded by the second Shogun, Hidetada, the Tokugawa family were supreme in Japan and determined to permit no activity that might develop into a threat to their primacy in the state. By this time not only the Portuguese and the Spaniards but also the Dutch and the English were competing for trade privileges in Japan, quarrelling with one another and prompt to reveal to the Shogun's officers real or imaginary designs of their rivals upon the safety of the Japanese realm. . . .

Towards 1622 the Shogun discovered evidence that led him to suspect the complicity of the Catholic Church in alleged Spanish plots to invade Japan. Shortly thereafter he re-enacted the anti-Christian edicts and ordered the deportation of all Spaniards, both priests and laymen, while decreeing that no Japanese Christian should leave the country. During this later and more violent phase of repression unspeakable tortures were used in efforts to secure apostasy [abandonment of one's religious faith] and whole families including infants in arms were mercilessly destroyed. Nevertheless the Jesuit documents report a continued enrollment of new converts and an almost joyful acceptance of death by believers of all classes. Their testimony to the bravery of the Japanese Christians is confirmed by a contemporary observer, the English captain Richard Cocks, who was strongly prejudiced against the "papisticall" missionaries. He described the government of Japan as "the greatest and most puissant tyranny that the world has ever known" and, writing of the Shogun's enmity towards Christians, said: "I saw 55 of them martyrized at one time at Miyako. Among them were little children of five or six years, burned alive in the arms of their mothers, who cried `Jesus, receive their souls.' There are many in prison who hourly await death, for very few return to their idolatry."

CHRISTIANS ARE SEVERELY PUNISHED

By 1625 the persecution had reached its peak, and Christianity had been either eradicated or driven underground in most parts of Japan, though martyrdoms continued until as late as 1660. In remote districts, particularly on small islands where official scrutiny was imperfect, it was still practised in stealth and a few missionaries remained to carry out their task in hiding. The culminating tragedy took place in 1638 when a peasant uprising, in which Christians took a leading part, was ruthlessly suppressed by the government with great slaughter. Of about 37,000 peasants with their families and a number of disaffected samurai [professional warriors of the aristocracy], who made a last stand on a headland of the Shimabara peninsula, only one hundred are said to have escaped alive. Even after this attempts were made by missionaries to smuggle themselves into Japan, but so far as is known they were all sooner or later discovered and executed or died in captivity.

The total number of martyrdoms recognized by the Church recorded for the period 1597–1660 is 3,125. This includes only those who were executed or died under torture and leaves out of account those who were stripped of their property, imprisoned, or banished. Many of these died of ill treatment or destitution. The Japanese statesman Arai Hakuseki put the number of Christians who had perished by 1650 at between 200,000 and 300,000. This though no doubt exaggerated may give us some indication of the number of Christians in Japan at its highest. There are no exact data, but only estimates. It is possible that by 1614 the number of Christians was of the order of 500,000, and in view of the drastic enforcement of the edicts after that year it is unlikely that it showed any increase in the next two or three decades. . . .

These calculations are, of course, based upon Jesuit estimates of the numbers of converts at given dates. If those estimates are over-optimistic, then the totals must be reduced.

If Arai Hakuseki was right in saying that as many as 200,000 perished for their faith before 1650 we may (allowing for apostasies) assume that there were left in Japan perhaps as many as 100,000 who practised it in concealment. We know that, even after two hundred years of seclusion, when Japan reopened her doors and the anti-Christian edicts were rescinded, a number of Christians declared themselves, particularly in remote corners of southwestern Japan, where their ancestors had continued to worship secretly. . . .

Several motives combined to create in ruling circles a deep suspicion and hatred of Christianity, but no doubt its chief cause was an unfounded fear of the political power of the Catholic Church, which might, it was supposed, be exercised in Japan with the secular aid of Catholic states—to wit, of Spain and Portugal. Dread of foreign intervention was so firmly fixed in the minds of the Tokugawa rulers that as late as 1673, when the East Indiaman *Return* [a British ship] came to Japan requesting permission to trade, the authorities, at first disposed to allow it, sent the vessel away when they learned that the English King had married a Portuguese princess. This at least was milder treatment than that given to the Portuguese mission that had visited Japan in 1647 for a similar purpose and only narrowly escaped the punishment decreed in the edict of 1640, threatening with death the crew of any Portuguese ship that should enter a Japanese harbour. Probably the Japanese here acted upon hints from the Dutch in Nagasaki, who did nothing to remove suspicions of Christianity from the minds of the Japanese officials. But their apprehensions needed no support from the Dutch, for they were so extreme as to be scarcely rational. The basis of their fears is well revealed in the oaths that apostates were obliged to swear after 1616. In denying the Christian faith each apostate had to repeat reasons for his disbelief in a prescribed formula, which ran: "The [church] fathers, by threats of excommunication and hell fire can do what they like with the people, *and all this is their stratagem to take the countries of others.*" The remainder of the formula is an involuntary tribute to the power of the Christian faith, for the converts, having abjured their religion (generally under duress), were by a curious logic made to swear by the very powers that they had just denied: "By the Father, the Son, and the Holy Ghost, Santa Maria and all the angels . . . if I break this oath may I lose the grace of God forever and fall into the wretched state of Judas Iscariot." By an even further departure from logic all this was followed by an oath to Buddhist and Shinto deities. . . .

RULERS ENACT A STRICT POLICY OF ISOLATIONISM

The action taken by Japan against Christianity cannot be considered separately from the exclusion policy to which it was a prelude. We have seen that the anti-Christian edict of 1616 was inspired in part at least by fear of Spanish intervention in the domestic affairs of Japan. The edict was re-enacted in 1624 because the Shogun had further grounds for suspecting Spain, or at any rate the Spanish in the Philippines, of aggressive designs; and this new edict was accompanied not only by the expulsion of all Spaniards but also by the stoppage of overseas travel by Japanese. The door was gradually being closed to both ingress and egress. The Shimabara rising that began in 1637 evidently caused further misgivings to the Shogunate, for it was followed in 1638 by the expulsion of all Portuguese, whether priests or traders. At the same time the prohibition of foreign travel was strengthened by imposing the death penalty on any Japanese who should attempt to leave the country or, having left it, should return. This embargo was extended to foreign trade by a law that forbade the building of any ship of more than 2,500 bushels' capacity and consequently prevented ocean voyages. Thus Japan deliberately cut herself off from intercourse with other nations rather than face the dangers it involved. In the history of relations between Europe and Asia this was the most decided rejection ever given by an Asiatic people to an approach by the Western world. It was a flat negative, to be supported by force where necessary, as is clear from the execution of Portuguese envoys from Macao who came to Japan in 1640 hoping to persuade the Japanese to change their minds.

From 1641 the only Europeans allowed in Japan were a few Dutch merchants who were confined to a small island (named Deshima) at the head of Nagasaki Bay and allowed to trade under very strict conditions. They and some Chinese traders, also under close surveillance, formed the only channel of communication with foreign countries.

Many different reasons have been suggested for the sudden and drastic exclusionist policy of the Tokugawa shoguns, which was in such striking contrast to the expansive temper of the Japanese only a few decades before. It is at first sight hard to understand why the Asiatic people who gave Europeans the most friendly welcome should have also given them the most violent dismissal. But, granted certain simple assumptions, it does not seem difficult to explain. It was clearly not due to a peculiar distaste for foreign intercourse, since that was resumed with remarkable alacrity once the country was reopened at a later date. It is true that, since the civilization of Japan was self-contained and her economy self-supporting, there was no compelling reason for cultural or commercial exchanges; and conservative sentiment, in Japan as in other countries, was naturally opposed to foreign influences, because to most people what is foreign is also disturbing. But the intense distrust which drove the Tokugawa shoguns to close their doors arose from no ordinary conservatism. They were moved by fear, and fear not of the contamination of national customs (such as had inspired the exclusion policy of the Ming Chinese) but rather of domestic uprising against themselves.

By 1615 Ieyasu, the first Tokugawa Shogun, had after long struggle imposed the authority of his family upon all his feudal rivals. But neither he nor his successors felt entirely secure for several decades, and it was a cardinal feature of their policy to take every possible precaution against rebellion by one or more of the still powerful western feudatories. The legislation of the Tokugawas shows a constant preoccupation with this danger, which was by no means imaginary. The Mori family in 1600 ruled thirteen of the sixty-six provinces, the Shimadzu family were strong in Kyushu, while there were other feudal houses that also chafed under Tokugawa rule. Any of these singly or in combination could have seized a favourable opportunity to revolt, as indeed in the long run they did in 1867 when the Shogunate was overthrown largely by an alliance of the clans of Satsuma (Shimadzu) and Choshu (Mori) with other anti-Tokugawa forces. It is significant that this alliance enjoyed the moral and material support of Western powers.

In 1637 the Tokugawa government had good reason to fear that one or other of these great families might conspire with foreigners—Spanish, Portuguese, or Dutch—trade with them for firearms, get their help in procuring artillery and ships, and even call upon them for military or naval support. The leaders of the ruling house, firmly established as it was, did not feel strong enough to face this risk; and they took steps to remove it by closing the country to foreign influence, so far as that was possible.

THE RISE OF THE CH'ING DYNASTY IN CHINA

FREDERIC WAKEMAN JR.

In 1644 the Manchus from Manchuria overthrew the Ming dynasty, which had ruled China for 276 years, and established the Ch'ing dynasty, which ruled for 268 years. Frederic Wakeman Jr. explains the strategy that three important Manchu leaders used to accomplish this feat. These leaders used marriages to make alliances, reorganized small tribal fighting units into large armies under central command, conquered neighboring tribes and assimilated their warriors, incorporated defecting Chinese soldiers to train tribal warriors, and employed civilian influence to support military might. Wakeman taught Asian Studies at the University of California at Berkeley. He is the author of *Shanghai Sojourners, Conflict and Control in Late Imperial China,* and many other volumes.

The most important concern of Ming frontier officials in Manchuria was to prevent the tribes from confederating under a single khan [ruler] strong enough to attack China. They therefore followed the time-honored policy of divide-and-rule which had been perfected as far back as the Han period and was widely used in central Asia. Each chieftain was placed in a tributary relationship to the Chinese emperor and was supposed to be his vassal. In exchange for acknowledging Chinese suzerainty, the chieftain was given an official Ming title. If any particular leader appeared to be growing too powerful, the Chi-

Excerpted from *The Fall of Imperial China,* by Frederic Wakeman Jr. Copyright © 1975 by The Free Press. Reprinted and edited with permission from The Free Press, a Division of Simon & Schuster, Inc.

nese government took care to favor a rival with higher rank. The Chinese title, which was accompanied by tribute payments from Peking, carried enough prestige to elevate one Manchu chief at the expense of another. By thus inciting jealousy and rivalry Ming frontier commanders usually succeeded in keeping the tribesmen disunited. . . .

By 1583 Nikan Wailan managed to secure enfeoffment [become a ruler of a feudal estate], but only after killing several of his rivals. Two of these were the father and son who commanded a Chien-chou clan called the Aisin Gioro.

Their deaths left the chief's 24-year-old grandson, Nurhaci, in command of the Aisin Gioro. Although indemnified by Li Ch'eng-liang [the Ming general], the young chief was resolved to avenge the murder of his father. With the two leading elders gone, Nurhaci's tribal command was precarious and the loyalty of his kinsmen by no means assured. . . .

Nurhaci now proved to be as judicious as he had earlier been audacious. First he contracted crucial marriage alliances with some of the Hulun clans. Then, by bringing several unruly Yalu River tribes under control, he won both General Li Ch'eng-liang's favor and the Ming title of brigadier general. Partly to defend his earlier gains and partly to ensure continued hegemony over his sub-chiefs, Nurhaci embarked upon further conquests, challenging the Hulun tribes to the north. His great victory at the Battle of Jaka (1593) over a confederation led by the Yehe not only elevated his status in the Ming government's eyes but also strengthened his hold over peers within the Manchu confederation. This was because each new victory brought additional prisoners of war to be distributed as serfs and slaves for the estates of the Manchu *beile* [clan chiefs].

NURHACI AND THE FORMATION OF THE BANNERS

As Nurhaci's following widened through diplomacy and conquest, it became necessary to find some new mode of organization to perpetuate the confederation. In 1601 he divided his troops into three-hundred-men *niru* (arrows, or companies) which were then formed into four permanent banners, identified by the color of their standard. These banners were copied from the Mongol *gūsa* fighting units. Later on, they were given the Chinese name *ch'i* (banner), which was taken from the Ming *wei-so* [border-guard] system. In 1615 the four existing banners were subdivided, forming a permanent total of eight Manchu banners. Each of the *niru* within the banners constituted a single military-civil unit under an hereditary captain. The members of that unit included soldiers and dependents who worked and fought together. The banners themselves were headed by *hošoi beile* (great princes) chosen from among the sons and nephews of Nurhaci.

The formation of the banners marked the transformation of a loosely confederated structure of shifting *niru* into a bureaucratically organized army under the rule of Aisin Gioro nobles. This evolution from a clan federation into a military state was not a novel phenomenon on the frontier, where there had been a long history of tribal and bureaucratic interaction. The Chinese policy of divide-and-rule had already confused tribal leadership with bureaucratic rank: khans and clan elders were both chieftains and officers of the empire, using conferred military titles to endow their temporary authority with permanence. The hybrid forms of government that were thus formed in the frontier zone drew their impetus from both sides of the border, with a marked tendency toward military feudalism characterizing each group. Just as Ming border generals tended to form private armies, so were tribal-bureaucratic leaders likely to become an hereditary aristocracy. . . .

NURHACI GAINS POWER

Nurhaci's own position was not threatened by the powerful *hošoi beile* because he commanded so much personal authority. As khan (a title assumed in 1616), he had openly declared his supremacy over the other Tungusic chieftains of Manchuria—an assertion enforced three years later when Nurhaci's forty thousand bannermen defeated his last major rival, Prince Gintaisi of Yehe. It was in 1616, too, that Nurhaci adopted an even more awesome source of authority by employing his Ju-chen descent to found the Latter Chin Dynasty under the reign title Heavenly Mandate *(T'ien-ming).* As an emperor on the Chinese model, Nurhaci spontaneously generated a large stock of princely titles and bureaucratic ranks to hand out to his Manchu followers. At the same time he also pitted himself against the Ming Dynasty.

Nurhaci had stopped sending tribute to Peking as early as 1609. Now, by taking the name of a barbarian dynasty that had once humiliated the Sung, he was implicitly announcing his intention to attack the Ming—a plan realized in 1618 when he took the imperial garrison at Fu-shun. Three years later he succeeded in capturing the major Ming headquarters of Liaoyang, and from there he drove most of the Ming forces out of the Liaotung peninsula altogether, controlling all the land east of the Sungari River. In February, 1626, however, his troops were repulsed at Ningyuan and eight months later Nurhaci died.

Nurhaci had intended that his heirs, the *beile,* should rule as a council of peers. Before his death he had seen to it that each controlled one of the eight banners and that the four senior *hošoi beile* took turns governing the central administration. One of them would have to be elected khan, but the bearer of that title was supposed to be no more than a *primus inter pares*, a first among equals. Such was not at all the intention of the khan actually selected by the other *beile* when Nurhaci died. The new ruler, Abahai (reigned 1626–1643), was a brilliant military strategist and diplomat who quickly determined to replace feudalism (the domination of many skilled in war) with patrimonialism (the domination of one who uses officials) by curbing the power of his fellow *beile* with the authority he commanded as a Chinese-style emperor. In his capacity as a tribal khan, Abahai was expected to share administrative duties with his brothers. But as an imperial monarch, authority was decreed by him alone. In 1629, therefore, he put an end to the practice of administrative rotation among the *hošoi beile* and began using former Chinese officials to control military appointments within the banner system. By 1633, in fact, he had brought three of the original eight banners under the direct command of the throne.

Abahai also realized how important it was to use Chinese military experts against the Ming forces. The great victories of 1618 and 1621 had placed eastern Manchuria under the Latter Chin's rule. But further expansion down the Liao-hsi coast toward the Great Wall had been blocked by the Ming commander, Yuan Ch'ung-huan, whose Portuguese artillery had repulsed Nurhaci at Ningyuan in 1626. Although the Manchus had excellent cavalry and armored infantry, their line of battle was vulnerable to Chinese firearms. And because they did not understand how to use artillery themselves, they were often forced to retreat from well defended castle walls. Unable to obtain a decisive advantage over Ming forces, Abahai recognized that the stalemate of 1626 would not be broken unless he trusted captured Chinese soldiers to wield firearms and artillery on his behalf.

Chinese elements had joined the Manchu armies as early as 1618 when the Ming commander Li Yung-fang surrendered at Fu-shun. Li was made a banner general, was given gifts of slaves and serfs, and was betrothed to a young woman of the Aisin Gioro clan. Although Li's surrender at the time was exceptional, his integration into the Manchu elite was only the first of many such defections by border generals and their subordinates, who shaved their heads and accepted Manchu customs. It was upon these prisoners, then, that Abahai relied to form new military units to fight their former master, the Ming emperor.

While Abahai proceeded to organize these new units, he also opened diplomatic negotiations with Yuan Ch'ung-huan, thus freeing his own troops for campaigns in Korea and against Mongol enemies. In 1629 Abahai even managed to bypass the Ming defenses facing Manchuria and briefly threatened Peking [today Beijing] from the west, disgracing Yuan and causing his downfall. But because this foray was only a raid, it had no lasting military significance. The military stalemate was really only broken two years later, when Abahai sent his new Chinese artillery force against the walls of the Ming garrison at Ta-ling-ho. There he not only won a decisive battle but proved that the Sino-Manchu forces had finally mastered siege warfare.

The victory of Ta-ling-ho inspired the Manchu emperor to take his people one step nearer the conquest of China by establishing six administrative boards on the Ming model in 1631. Further raids on China were followed in 1636 by Abahai's announcement of a new dynastic title, the Ch'ing, which freed the Manchus' claim on the mandate from any connection with their Chin ancestors. At the same time he solidified his military control over the Amur basin and sent another raiding party across the Great Wall in 1639. But in 1643, one year before his plans for the conquest of China were realized, Abahai's health failed and he died.

DORGON COMBINES CIVIL AND MILITARY SCHEMES

When the *beile* convened to name Abahai's successor, one among them was best equipped to fulfill the dead emperor's plans to defeat the Ming. Abahai's younger brother Dorgon, a *hošoi beile* commanding the Plain White Banner, had early decided that the historical mission of the Manchus was to conquer China. He also recognized that success depended on forming a shadow government and attracting Chinese defectors to its cause. In 1631 he had become president of the Board of Civil Appointments in Abahai's facsimile of the Ming administration, and in that crucial capacity had managed to interview all prominent Chinese captives, diverting the better educated into bureaucratic positions. Civilians were wooed with Confucian deference. Whereas Manchu officials necessarily addressed themselves as "slaves" to the throne, Chinese mandarins were entitled to call themselves "ministers." Such measures reflected Dorgon's realization that a loyal civil bureaucracy and not merely military support would be necessary if the Manchus were ever to occupy Peking. . . .

LI TZU-CH'ENG AND WU SAN-KUEI

Dorgon assumed the regency just as the [Chinese] rebel Li Tzu-ch'eng was making final preparations to attack Peking. Li's victory and the suicide of the Ch'ung-chen Emperor gave the

Manchus the decisive opportunity they had been awaiting. The only force in north China likely to challenge Li Tzu-ch'eng's armies was the Ming border garrison at Ningyuan which guarded the approaches to the Great Wall. Its Chinese commander, Wu San-kuei, was the son of a former border general. Responding to Peking's pleas for aid, Wu decided to abandon Ningyuan and move his army toward the capital, but his progress was too slow to save the dynasty. Five hundred thousand Chinese civilians were said to have joined Wu San-kuei's army on the trek south to the Great Wall at Shan-hai-kuan, and it took 16 days for all of them to pass through the frontier gates. Of course, the moment the last Chinese contingent marched through Shan-hai-kuan that strategic post was promptly occupied by Manchu bannermen following close behind.

Wu's march toward Peking was halted by the news that Li Tzu-ch'eng had taken the capital and that the Ming Dynasty had fallen. Envoys from Li Tzu-ch'eng soon met his column with a promise of forty thousand taels [silver pieces weighing 1.5 ounces] if Wu San-kuei surrendered. In the meantime, Li was leading sixty thousand of his own men towards Shan hai-kuan should Wu refuse the offer. Wu San-kuei could not hope to defeat such a large rebel force alone. Suspecting Li's treachery he contacted Dorgon who urged him to join the Ch'ing cause in exchange for a princely rank and an hereditary fiefdom. The former Ming general hesitated between the regicidal Li and the barbarian invaders who promised to punish the usurper. Then, as the first elements of Li's army drew near, Wu shaved his head and invited Dorgon over the Great Wall.

On May 27, 1644, while the forces of Wu San-kuei and Li Tzu-ch'eng were engaged in battle, the Manchus rode through Shan-hai-kuan under cover of a dust storm. Their intervention was decisive. Li's men were driven back into Peking, pursued by the combined armies of Dorgon and Wu San-kuei. As the Manchus and Ming frontier forces entered the capital from the east, Li's soldiers fled in the opposite direction as rapidly as they had come, strewing looted antiques and jewelry behind them.

DORGAN ESTABLISHES THE CH'ING DYNASTY

Dorgon entered Peking on June 1, 1644. His first decree to the people read:

> In former days our realm wished to have good and harmonious relations with your Ming, [hoping] for perpetual peace. Since we repeatedly sent letters which were not answered, we invaded deep [into your country] four times, until your dynasty showed regret. How

stubborn it was not to comply! Now [the Ming] has been extinguished by roving bandits, and its service [to heaven] is a thing of the past. Let us speak no more [of that]. The empire is not an individual's private property. Whosoever possesses virtue, holds it. The army and the people are not an individual's private property. Whosoever possesses virtue commands them. We now occupy [the empire]. On behalf of your dynasty we took revenge upon the enemies of your ruler-father. We burned our bridges behind us, and we have pledged not to return until every bandit is destroyed. In the counties, districts, and locales that we pass through, all those who are able to shave their heads and surrender, opening their gates to welcome us, will be given rank and reward, retaining their wealth and honor for generations. But if there are those who disobediently resist us when our great armies arrive, then the stones themselves will be set ablaze and all will be massacred. Scholars of resolve will reap the harvest of upright administration, meritorious fame and the opportunity to pursue a vocation [as our officials]. If there are those who lack faith in us, then how are they to serve the empire? Special edict.

Having announced the accession of the Ch'ing Dynasty to the Chinese throne, Dorgon took immediate measures to gather public support. Ming loyalists were mollified by his attention to the burial rites of their last emperor. Civil servants were reassured by offers of amnesty and employment. And the residents of Peking were convinced of the benevolence of the new regime by Dorgon's harsh punishment of Manchu ravishers and looters. The contrast with Li Tzu-ch'eng's rebel government was strikingly clear. By the time Dorgon had sent to Manchuria for the Shun-chih Emperor, none doubted the Manchus meant to stay. Yet few indeed could have predicted that the Ch'ing Dynasty would occupy Peking for the next 268 years.

THE DECLINE OF THE MOGUL EMPIRE IN INDIA

WOODBRIDGE BINGHAM, HILARY CONROY, AND FRANK W. IKLÉ

Woodbridge Bingham, Hilary Conroy, and Frank W. Iklé portray a prosperous Mogul (also known as Mughal) empire in India at the beginning of the 1600s under Shah Akbar. The empire began to decline under Akbar's grandson Shah Jahan and came to ruin under Shah Aurangzeb, Shah Jahan's son. According to the authors, Akbar's descendants taxed India into poverty to support their armies and to build lavish buildings. Moreover, they were Muslims who practiced religious intolerance, even fanaticism, and provoked a Hindu revolt. By 1707 the empire was in shambles, and the anarchy that followed paved the way for British supremacy in India. Bingham, who taught history at the University of California at Berkeley, is the author of *The Founding of the T'ang Dynasty*. Conroy, who taught history at the University of Pennsylvania, is co-editor of *Pearl Harbor Reexamined: Prologue to the Pacific War*. Iklé taught history at the University of New Mexico and at the University of California at Berkeley.

T he Mogul empire had reached its apex under Akbar who died in 1605. A man of exceptional ability, Akbar had a great vision of a truly united India. His governmental machinery had been efficient and during his reign India was the most prosperous and one of the largest empires in the world. However, none of his successors was as able as he had been and after his death came the gradual decline of Mogul power, eventual political an-

Excerpted from pp. 49–58 from *A History of Asia*, vol. 2, by Woodbridge Bingham, Hilary Conroy, and Frank W. Iklé. Copyright © 1965 by Allyn and Bacon, Inc. Reprinted with permission from Pearson Education, Inc.

archy, and the establishment of British supremacy. . . .

Shah Jahan was a capable administrator for most of the years of his reign (1628–1658). But unlike his great predecessors, Shah Jahan was a devout, orthodox, and intolerant Moslem, and he began to abandon the policy of religious toleration with which Akbar had so successfully united the various Indian subjects of his empire. In 1632 Shah Jahan ordered the destruction of all new Hindu temples and the demolition of all Christian churches. He also attacked the declining power of the Portuguese by sending in 1632 a large army against their settlement of Hooghly in Bengal. Although the pretext for this campaign was found in a charge of kidnapping, the real intention of Shah Jahan was to oust the Portuguese and monopolize the trade of Bengal. . . .

After the annexation of the Moslem kingdoms in the Deccan, Shah Jahan appointed his son Aurangzeb viceroy for that region. Aurangzeb, who hated the unorthodox Shi'a [the strictest of the three Muslim sects], had distinguished himself in the campaigns in the Deccan, where he employed European-serviced artillery; he also proved himself a capable ruler over the lands entrusted to him. He reorganized their finances, made a better land survey, and encouraged agriculture and the building of irrigation works. Shah Jahan treated his other three sons, all equally brave, in similar fashion, establishing each as a virtually independent ruler in the provinces which were assigned to them. In 1657, when the emperor's health began to fail, a contest for power among the sons broke out in violent fashion. It was won by Aurangzeb against his father's favorite, Dara Shiko, who had been kept at the court and had been showered with titles, honors, and wealth by Shah Jahan. In this civil war Aurangzeb gained Agra by force and he kept his father captive in the fort of the capital for eight years until Shah Jahan's death in 1666.

In some respects the reign of Shah Jahan was the golden age of the Mogul empire. It was characterized by unexcelled magnificence and the construction of splendid buildings, such as the Taj Mahal at Agra. Shah Jahan was a munificent patron of the arts, who spent immense sums on architecture which made lavish use of marble and precious stones, and on fabulous display, such as the famed Peacock Throne which was built in seven years at the estimated cost of five million dollars in present values. Yet at the same time the economic system of India was nearing collapse, indicated by increasing oppression and poverty. Shah Jahan's building expenditures created a crushing burden, and tax assessments were raised by 50 per cent with the inevitable consequence that agriculture became neglected and fields were abandoned. Terrible and frequent famines also contributed to a decline in production and a weakened economic structure of the state. Officials were more cruel and oppressive than they had been before, and the life of the Indian peasant degenerated into one of abysmal misery. Bernier, a French doctor who travelled in India during this period, gloomily describes the condition of the country:

> The despotic tyranny of local governors was often so excessive as to deprive the peasant and artisan of the necessaries of life, and leave them to die of misery and exhaustion—a tyranny owing to which these wretched people either have no children at all or have them only to endure the agonies of starvation, and to die at a tender age—a tyranny in fine, that drives the cultivator of the soil from his wretched home to some neighboring state, in hopes of finding milder treatment, or to the army, where he becomes the servant of some trooper. The country is ruined by the necessity of defraying the enormous charges required to maintain the splendour of a numerous court, and to pay a large army maintained for the purpose of keeping the people in subjection. No adequate idea can be conveyed of the sufferings of that people. The cudgel and the whip compel them to incessant labor for the benefit of others; and driven to despair by every kind of cruel treatment their revolt or their flight is only prevented by the presence of a military force. Thus do ruin and desolation overspread their land.

THE SUCCESSION STRUGGLE OF THE SONS OF SHAH JAHAN

In the struggle for power the contest was primarily between the oldest son of Shah Jahan, Aurangzeb, and his favorite, Dara Shiko. The great contrast between the two men lent a most dramatic touch to their rivalry. Dara was enlightened, amiable, popular, and of a liberal trend of mind. Influenced by the Sufis [the Muslim sect known for their mysticism], he had shown a marked interest in the religious aspects of Hinduism, and he was somewhat hostile to orthodox Islam. What Dara lacked in military experience, he made up by popular support. Aurangzeb, on the other hand, was cruel, cold, and crafty, a Sunni Moslem who detested his brother with all the hate of a religious bigot. Aurangzeb made use of his other two brothers in the struggle against Dara, and then treacherously betrayed them, executing one and forcing the other to flee. Dara too was betrayed, captured, and then executed in 1658 by Aurangzeb, who was fearful of the support of the masses in favor of his younger brother. Dara's eldest son managed to flee to the Rajputs, but he too eventually was captured and sent to the state prison of Gwalior where he was slowly poisoned to death, by being forced to drink a concoction of opium.

Aurangzeb became Mogul emperor formally in 1659 in a great ceremony conducted at Delhi. The forty-year-old eldest son of Shah Jahan was able and an administrator of wide experience, having served his father as viceroy in the Deccan for many years. Aurangzeb possessed a cool and clear head, he was courageous, energetic, and a scholar in his own right. His personal life was above reproach. He knew the Koran by heart, read it every evening, and spent many nights in the mosque in the company of devout men. He abstained from the slightest overindulgence in food, drink, or dress. Every action of his life was governed by rigid austerity.

Aurangzeb's rule began with great promise. He decreed a series of useful edicts against rapacity and dishonesty in government and took great interest in the encouragement of agriculture. Military campaigns into Assam and the Arakan coast and in the northwest indicated the vigor of his armies. Delhi during the first twenty years of Aurangzeb's reign was the political center of the Moslem world, and attracted embassies from Mecca, Persia, and other Moslem countries as well as from infidel countries such as Abyssinia and Holland.

The reign of Shan Jahan was characterized by the construction of splendid buildings, such as the Taj Mahal at Agra.

AURANGZEB'S RELIGIOUS FANATICISM

But there was one trait of Aurangzeb's personality—his religious attitudes—which undid all his energy, ability, and devotion to government, and which was in a real sense responsible for the rapid collapse of the Mogul empire. He was truly pious, but a fanatic, motivated by grim religious zeal. Precisely because he was not hypocritical, his decision to purify the land of all idolatry and return to the strictest orthodox Islam was a disastrous one. He began his policy of a return to purest Islam by sweeping reforms designed to curtail court pleasure and suppress all vices. Drinking, gambling, and music were outlawed and the great artists of the Mogul court were summarily dismissed. As time went on he also became increasingly distrustful of everyone in his administration. He in turn won universal distrust. Since the emperor attempted to do everything in person and delegated no authority, the administrative system began to break down.

The really fateful step taken by Aurangzeb was the adoption of a policy of religious intolerance. In 1669 he ordered Hindu temples and schools to be desecrated and destroyed, and this order was carried out. Apostates from Islam were executed, while converts to Islam were honored and rewarded. Laws discriminated against Hindus in every aspect of their lives. In 1671 Aurangzeb dismissed all Hindu clerks from his government, a measure which could not be carried out. One-half of them were finally retained in the administration of the state, but no Hindu could expect to occupy high office. The final blow came in 1680 when Aurangzeb reinstated the hated poll tax. This impolitic and very unpopular measure produced the greatest consternation among the Hindus, but to no avail.

These actions of a religious bigot produced disastrous results. In vain did Aurangzeb receive a famous anonymous protest, in which it was pointed out to him that under Akbar Moslems, Christians, Jews, Hindus, Jains, sky-worshippers, and atheists all had lived in harmony. It prophesied the alienation of Aurangzeb's subjects, loss of territory, and a future of devastation and depopulation for the whole of India.

Since the religious fanaticism of Aurangzeb could not be swayed by argument, revolts broke out. There was a peasant rebellion in the Punjab, followed by a revolt of the Rajputs. Aurangzeb, who looked upon the toleration of the Rajputs as an offense against Islam, then made his greatest mistake and alienated his most powerful supporters. Even his own son rebelled when Aurangzeb attempted to annex the Rajput states by force. He sided with the Rajputs, but promptly became a victim to the cunning of his father. Aurangzeb forged a letter in which he made it appear as if his son had joined the Rajputs only to betray them, and he saw to it that this letter fell into Rajput hands. His son had to flee, first into the Deccan, and then to Persia where he died.

AURANGZEB'S VICTORIES TURN HOLLOW

Aurangzeb moved inconclusively against the Rajputs in 1679. He then turned to warfare in the Deccan where he intended finally to annex to his dominions the remaining heretical Moslem states, Bijapur and Golconda. Bijapur, sorely beset by a food shortage, surrendered to the huge Mogul forces in 1686, and the last of the independent states, Golconda, was taken by treachery the following year. By 1690 Aurangzeb had conquered the whole of southern India. The Mogul flag was planted everywhere from Kabul to Cape Comorin; but the victories of Aurangzeb were illusive and hollow for the Mogul empire was on the verge of collapse.

Everywhere in the newly conquered Deccan Aurangzeb's armies encountered fierce guerilla warfare by the Marathas. The Marathas had been organized by a Hindu leader, Shivaji, who had broken off from the state of Bijapur and had founded an independent Hindu state, as part of a general movement of Hindu resistance against the Moguls. His forces, speedy and lightly armed, successfully ambushed the Mogul lines of communications and inflicted defeat after defeat upon the unwieldy Mogul armies. Despite the fact that some Maratha leaders, including Shivaji's son, were captured and executed after the most refined tortures, Maratha resistance did not lessen. Large areas of India were devastated, Aurangzeb's campaigns were a terrible drain upon his treasury, and the emperor himself, absent twenty years from his capital, lost all control over the Mogul government which became rapidly even more inefficient and oppressive. With his wealth and control gone, his troops unpaid, and an ineffective but interminable war continuing against the Marathas and the rebels in the Punjab, the emperor in 1704 appeared a pathetic and even tragic figure to the Italian traveller, Manucci, who was struck by his personality and the stateliness of his appearance, tall, with a flowing white beard, the very figure of a patriarch:

> Most of the time he sits doubled up, his head drooping. When his officers submit a petition, or make report to him of any occurrence, he raises his head and straightens his back. He gives them such an answer as leaves no opening for reply, and still looks after his army in the minutest particulars. But those who are at a distance pay very little attention to his orders. They

make excuses, they raise difficulties; and under cover
of these pretexts, and by giving large sums to the officials at court, they do just what they like. If only he
would abandon his mock sainthood and behead a few
of those in his Empire, there would not be so much disorder, and he would be better obeyed.

But Aurangzeb was no mock saint. He was sincere and with
his sincerity he ruined the Mogul empire. In 1705, still fighting
an endless war in the Deccan, he was attacked by fever. He finally made his retreat to the north, but he died in 1707 at the age
of ninety. As he had requested, his body was shrouded in coarse
cloth and buried in a humble tomb. Aurangzeb was simple, austere, religious. He had wanted to purify India, but he ended by
ruining it.

THE END OF THE MOGUL EMPIRE

After the death of Aurangzeb the Mogul empire almost at once
broke up into separate parts, each ruled by officials who now became hereditary princes in the provinces which they had formerly governed for the Moguls. Oudh was established as a kingdom, the rich province of Bengal became virtually independent,
and in the south, Mysore and Hyderabad also became independent principalities, paying only the most shadowy allegiance to
the nominal Mogul ruler of Delhi. Aurangzeb's death caused a
scramble for power among his sons, from which Bahadur Shah
emerged victor, but he was weak and died in 1712. Bloodshed
and disorder at the capital followed and a series of puppet emperors occupied ruined halls and governed beneath tattered
canopies. Some of these phantom emperors were maltreated,
blinded, or murdered by their subordinates. In 1739 Delhi underwent the ordeal of the foreign invasion of Nadir Shah of Persia, who gave his troops a free hand to massacre and plunder.
When he left the stricken city he carried with him the fabled Peacock Throne, the symbol of former Mogul greatness.

Nevertheless all the powers which struggled for supremacy in
India, even the Hindu Marathas, invoked the imperial Mogul
name and titles and acted under nominal Mogul authority. The series of nominal emperors lasted until the great Indian Mutiny of
1857, when the British deposed the last of these descendants of
Babur [the founder of the Mogul empire], Akbar, and Aurangzeb.

The causes for the downfall of the Mogul empire are many
and complex. Although the Moguls were foreigners to India,
alien both by race and religion, there was at least the possibility
that Akbar's enlightened policy and his great vision of a united
India might have created a more substantial and durable Mogul

dominion. There is certainly no question that Aurangzeb's religious policy had a direct bearing upon the collapse of Mogul power. He alienated the Hindus, ended the Rajput support essential to his government, and caused a Hindu revival, while his long absence proved fatal to effective government. Yet, important as Aurangzeb's reign is, and important as personality was in Indian statecraft, other factors also contributed to the decline of the Moguls.

The Mogul nobility suffered from the losses attendant upon frequent succession struggles to the throne, and was not reinvigorated by new blood. The aristocracy was perhaps more degenerate in the eighteenth century than it had been in the sixteenth. The Mogul armies, too, showed increasing signs of weakness, which was illustrated in their fiasco against the Persians. By the eighteenth century Mogul armies were merely armed rabble and Mogul artillery was of the crudest sort. Another important factor in the decline was the economic degeneration of the empire. The revenue system began to break down after the death of Akbar, and formerly equitable taxes became mere extortion to support the increasing extravagance of the court. At the same time government became more unstable and oppressive.

One factor which did not contribute to the fall of the Mogul empire was outside force. When the empire crashed it did so for internal reasons, much more so than empires of the Ottomans and of the Persians. The Mogul decline preceded the coming of the British; when England appeared, the Indian scene was one of political anarchy in which many powers struggled for political supremacy on equal terms.

THE ENGLISH EAST INDIA COMPANY PREVAILS IN INDIA

J.H. PARRY

By telling the story of the English East India Company in India, J.H. Parry shows how and why trading companies operated. This company first obtained permission to establish a trading depot in Surat, India, and expected protection from local authorities. Competing trading companies from other countries tried to oust the English company, but English sea power prevented a takeover. Parry explains that when India's government declined, the company succeeded in establishing political dominance. Politics, investment, and company structure all worked together to garner profit for the company's shareholders. Parry, who taught history at Harvard University, Cambridge University, and the University College of the West Indies, is the author of *The Spanish Seaborne Empire* and *The Age of Reconnaissance: Discovery, Exploration, and Settlement, 1450–1650*.

The English East India Company's factory at Surat, established with the permission of the local Mughal governor, enjoyed a long and on the whole prosperous career as a depot for cotton, muslin, saltpetre and indigo from the interior of north India. Naturally the ubiquitous Dutch soon appeared to claim a share of the trade; but they could not evict the English by force, nor could the English evict them. A breach of the peace within the Mughal dominions at that time would have led to the eviction of both parties. For the Dutch the trade of the Indian

Excerpted from *The Establishment of the European Hegemony* (New York: Harper & Row, 1961) by J.H. Parry. Reprinted with permission from Taylor & Francis Books, Ltd.

mainland was secondary to the more lucrative trade with the East Indies, and the highhanded methods which they habitually employed against the Indonesian princes would have been mere impertinence in dealing with the Mughal empire. The English, humble through knowledge of their relative weakness, held the trade of Surat against all European rivals. The occasional misfortunes which they suffered were the results either of local famines or of temporary losses of Mughal favour. They were blamed and punished in 1623 for piracies committed by the Dutch against pilgrim ships plying to Mecca; and again in 1636 for the similar piracies of English captains, authorized by Charles I to visit India in contravention of the company's charter. Apart from these interludes the factors at Surat drove a profitable and peaceful trade as long as the Mughal power protected them; and the company's ships made some small return by policing the pilgrim route and by privateering against Dutch and Portuguese, under letters of marque from the Emperor.

THE ENGLISH STRUGGLE TO ESTABLISH A STRONGHOLD IN INDIA

In south-east India Dutch competition was more formidable. The Coromandel coast was more easily accessible for a trade in "white cloth" with the Dutch headquarters in Java. The local rulers on the coast—vassals either of the Muslim kings of Golconda or of the Hindu successors of once great Vijayanagar—were less powerful and less dependable than the Mughal viceroys. The English at Masulipatam and the Dutch at Pulicat, enjoying the favour of different princes, competed and occasionally fought with one another throughout the century. On the whole, the English fared better than the Dutch at the game of Indian politics, largely because of their persistence in securing the protection of great overlords such as the Mughal Emperor or the King of Golconda, instead of relying upon agreements with the petty rajas [chiefs] of the coast. From 1634 the policy of the English company was to maintain a "Continual Residence" at the Golconda court.

In 1639 Francis Day, factor [agent] at Masulipatam, turned the flank of the Dutch by founding a factory at Madras and by securing—despite opposition from his directors—permission from the local raja to build a fort. The Madras grant included not only the factory site, but about six square miles of territory along the coast, including the old Portuguese mission of St. Thomas's Mount. This was the first English acquisition of territory in India. The directors [of the English East India Company] complained bitterly of the expense of fortification and of maintaining a garrison of a hundred men; but the advancement of the company's interests always owed more to individual initiative in India than to the inspiration and support of London. Day's plans went forward on the strength of the approval of the company's officers in India, and Madras grew steadily in importance from its first foundation. The worst enemy of the India trade was famine, and famine visited Madras in 1647; but the factory and garrison were saved from starvation in the midst of a starving country by provisions shipped from Surat—a display of power and resource which so impressed the King of Golconda that he became more than ever the company's friend. He had already, in 1645, confirmed the Madras grant. Gradually the directors in London became aware of the trade possibilities in the Bay of Bengal. In 1658 the company, strengthened and encouraged by [British leader Oliver] Cromwell's charter of the year before, made Madras its headquarters for eastern India.

THE ENGLISH WANT PEACEFUL TRADE AND PROTECTION

1658 was the year of the accession of Aurangzeb, the last great Mughal emperor; a grim and earnest Muslim fanatic. Throughout the first half of the seventeenth century the policy and practice of the English company, as far as the Indians were concerned, was peaceful, unarmed trade. Its resources were at first too small to support a more aggressive policy. It relied upon the great Indian powers for protection, not only against banditry, but to some extent against the intrusion of other Europeans on land. On the high seas its ships could look after themselves. But an armed monopoly was the implied object of the English company, as of most European trading companies, and changes in the political situation in India eventually brought about an overt change in the company's policy. Aurangzeb's religious persecution alienated the [Hindu] Rajput princes, in [Mughal emperor] Akbar's time [1556–1605] the strongest supporters of the empire, and provoked widespread risings among Hindus from the Punjab to the Deccan. The military efficiency of the empire, no longer reinforced by immigrants from central Asia, was declining. In central India a predatory Hindu power, the Maratha confederacy, raided the Mughal provinces and through years of guerrilla warfare resisted or evaded the unwieldy imperial armies.

In 1664 the Marathas raided Surat. They sacked the town but were beaten off by the company's men from the walls of the English factory. For the first time the Mughal had failed to protect his clients, and the company began to look round for means to defend itself. The first requirement was a defensible base, if possible outside the imperial jurisdiction; and such a base lay ready to hand. Bombay had come into Charles II's hands as part of Catherine of Braganza's dowry. His ships had taken possession in 1665, after a protracted dispute with the resident Portuguese, and in 1668, finding the town an expensive liability, he had leased it to the company. It was pestilent but readily defensible, and from 1669 Aungier, the president at Surat, began the work of developing and fortifying the harbour. He established a gunboat squadron as a protection against local pirates and boldly entered into treaty relations with Sivaji, the Maratha chieftain upon whose flank he was entrenched. By 1677, the year of Aungier's death, the trade of Bombay already rivalled that of Surat. The old dependence upon Mughal favour was broken and the company had embarked upon a career of trading sword in hand.

THE ENGLISH EAST INDIA COMPANY CHANGES POLICY

The same growing forces of disorder which had threatened Surat afflicted eastern India also. Madras was threatened by Sivaji in 1677, and a few years later by Aurangzeb himself in the course of his southern campaigns. In Bengal, the small and struggling English factories protested vainly against the exactions of a semi-independent Mughal viceroy, until another local leader, Job Charnock, established a defensible base at Calcutta in the swamps of the Ganges delta. That was in 1686; by that time Charnock's quarrel with the viceroy in Bengal had widened into a general war against the Mughal empire. The policy of unarmed trade had been abandoned and the company was looking to its servants "to establish such a polity of civil and military power, and create and secure such a large revenue as may be the foundation of a large, well-grounded, sure English dominion in India for all time to come." This change of policy was made in conscious imitation of the Dutch; but only ignorance of the forces and the distances involved could have impelled the company to declare war and to send a puny expedition of a few hundred men against an empire which maintained in the field an army of at least a hundred thousand. The English declaration of war, however, if it ever reached Aurangzeb, was for him a matter of small importance; the Emperor was away in south India, fighting the campaigns which destroyed the states of Golconda and Bijapur, but which left intact the real enemy, the power of the Marathas. It was only the company's depredations by sea on the route to Mecca which drew Aurangzeb's attention to this minor war. His officers accordingly seized the company's factories at Surat and Masulipatam and cast its agents into prison. Probably only an appreciation of the English power at sea and the consequent threat to the pilgrim route saved the factors from complete expulsion. As it was, the company sued for peace, and in 1690, obtained a fresh licence to trade at the cost of humble submission and a heavy fine. In the same year Calcutta, abandoned during the war, was reoccupied, this time permanently, and the first buildings of a great city began to appear on the fever-ridden banks of the Ganges.

AN OPPORTUNITY FOR POLITICAL INTERVENTION

Although the Mughal empire was still too strong for the English on land, its power was fast declining. Aurangzeb's reign saw the greatest territorial extension of the Mughal power, and the beginning of its disintegration. During his long absence in south India, he lost much of his control over Delhi and the north. His *subadars* [military officers] became semi-independent feudatories, and his last twenty-five years were a weary and losing battle against growing anarchy. He died in 1707. Under the feeble rule of his successors not only the Mughal viceroys, but Muslim adventurers great and small, some within India and some invaders from Persia and Afghanistan, carved out independent principalities with their swords. Many of these ephemeral kingdoms were in their turn destroyed by the Marathas, who year by year extended the area of their plundering raids. In the anarchy which ensued, peaceful unarmed trade became impossible. The Marathas paved the way for European political intervention in defence of commercial monopolies. The same train of events which had turned Aurangzeb into a wandering soldier, drove the English company in the eighteenth century to political intrigue and military adventure. From being a mere commercial undertaking it was to become a territorial overlord and a gatherer of tribute on a vast scale.

MAJOR RECONSTRUCTION OF THE BRITISH TRADING COMPANY

During all the vicissitudes of the later seventeenth century the company's commerce flourished. Its misfortunes were mainly local ones. While one factory was in trouble another showed a handsome profit. The profits of the company were still made chiefly by exporting bullion, purchasing eastern goods, and selling them in Europe. It exported woollens at a loss, as a concession to mercantile opinion and to conciliate the manufacturing interest; English manufactured goods did not command a ready sale in India until the late eighteenth century. Nevertheless, during the period 1657–91 the average annual dividend was about twenty-five per cent, and in 1683—the peak year—the company's hundred pound shares were being sold for five hundred pounds. Naturally in a period of mounting prosperity the company found increasing difficulty in maintaining its monopoly; the concessions which it made—the opening of the port-to-port trade in India, and the licences granted to ten or twelve "permission ships" to clear for India from England each year—were inadequate to meet the demands of the wealthier interlopers. While the Stuart kings ruled, the danger was small, for Charles II and James II were both shareholders and staunch supporters of the company; but under William III, the fact that the company held a royal and not a parliamentary charter was made the ground of a legal onslaught by the interlopers. In India the company was strong enough to protect itself and to capture many interloping ships; but in London its constitutional position was weakened by the Revolution; and the interlopers soon learned the value of corporate action. They formed themselves into an association in 1690, and began to petition Parliament to throw open the Indian trade. Eventually in 1698 they obtained an Act incorporating them as the New (or English, as distinct from London) East India Company, on condition of a loan of £2,000,000 to the government. The Old Company duly received notice of the termination of its charter; but its members retrieved their parliamentary defeat by subscribing largely to the new loan and so securing a considerable share of the privileges of the New Company. There followed ten years of struggle and competitive bribery. In India the Old Company had all the advantages of established factories and experienced agents and in 1702 its charter was prolonged for a further seven years. By that time the schism and the political struggle were involving both parties in ruinous expense. Finally in 1708–9 the two companies amalgamated. The United Company of Merchants of England trading to the East Indies entered upon a long period of steady advance as a powerful armed monopoly, almost undisturbed by faction at home. In 1715, it opened a new chapter in its history, in a regular trade with China, and Chinese tea eventually became the most important of the commodities which it brought to England.

ELIMINATING COMPETITION

The principal challenge to the growing power of the company in the eighteenth century was to come from other European rivals. The Dutch, it is true, in the face of growing difficulties in India, tended to withdraw more and more to the archipelago where their dominance was now undisputed. The Portuguese retained their capital at Goa, but their power at sea was only a fraction of

what it had once been. The Danes, with a modest factory at Tran-
quebar, concerned themselves mainly with the China trade and
were never dangerous competitors. The chief rivals of the English
were the French. [French finance minister Jean-Baptiste] Colbert's
East India Company of 1664, after a promising beginning, had existed precariously through the long wars against the Dutch and
the English in Europe and America. Its main enemy was unsound
finance; between 1688 and 1713 there was little fighting between
English and French in India, for neither side felt strong enough to
risk a struggle in the presence of formidable native powers. After
the death of Aurangzeb this deterrent was removed. Much of the
history of India in the eighteenth century is the story of the naval
and political struggle between French and English for commercial
mastery. The French, with their single headquarters at Pondicherry,
had the advantage of good relations with the native princes, and
possessed the skill and tact to maintain those relations. The advantage of the English lay in first-class bases—Bombay, Madras,
Calcutta—in widely separated regions. Ultimately the struggle
was decided by the ability of the English to cut communications
between France and India by the use of force at sea.

THE EVOLVING FRENCH INTEREST IN SOUTHEAST ASIA

RICHARD ALLEN

Richard Allen explains how the French began their involvement in Southeast Asia with missionary efforts to spread the Catholic faith in Indochina (Vietnam) and Thailand. Though the French regime never gained power in Thailand, it succeeded in Indochina with the support of the French East India Company. Allen traces European involvement in Vietnamese history from 1663 to the nineteenth century: from missionary work to military and administrative help, and, finally, to the acquisition of Vietnam as a colony. Richard Allen is an Asian studies scholar at Cornell University.

T he French gave serious attention to southern Asia later than the British and, from one aspect, in quite a different manner. As a Catholic power France was known as the "elder daughter of the Church" and a belief in her mission to spread the Catholic faith loomed large in her earlier Asian policies, as it had in those of Portugal and Spain. The Protestant nations such as Holland and Britain were more bluntly materialistic. Proselytizing and conversion were not envisaged as a sacred duty and they had no compunction in seeking an alliance with Muslims to destroy their fellow Christian Catholics, as the Dutch had done in attacking Portuguese Malacca. But the Catholic powers were also . . . in quest of wealth and in 1664 a French East India Company was revived based on Pondicherry in southeastern India,

Excerpted from *A Short Introduction to the History and Politics of Southeast Asia,* by Sir Richard Allen. Copyright © 1968, 1970 by Oxford University Press, Inc. Reprinted with permission from Oxford University Press, Inc.

the efforts of which were to be co-ordinated with France's more spiritual endeavors. This was in the reign of Louis XIV when France had emerged as the leading nation of Europe and her power and prestige were jealously promoted by her royal master. The French secured papal support for their claim to assume authority over Catholic missionary work in the Orient in place of the now feeble Portuguese and appointed French Vicars-Apostolic for various Asian countries. In 1663 the Paris Seminary for Oriental Languages was expanded into the Society for Foreign Missions and a French Bishop was sent out to work in China or alternatively Annam [a region of central Vietnam]. After being shipwrecked in the Gulf of Siam, the bishop returned to Ayuthia [a city of south-central Thailand] and set about making Thailand the headquarters of these Catholic missionary efforts which, from the 1670's, expanded into Cambodia and Vietnam. At the same juncture the Thai King, dissatisfied with the performance of the Dutch and English East India companies in his dominions, encouraged as a counterweight the commercial activities of the French East India Company. The Jesuits, regarding themselves as the elite forces of the Church, were not content to leave the Catholic effort to the Society for Foreign Missions. They had strong influence over the French King and, outbidding their rivals, promoted a plan to establish not only French religious influence but French political hegemony in Thailand. For this purpose they ingratiated themselves with a Greek adventurer, Constantine Phaulkon, who, starting as a cabin boy in the service of the English East India Company, had become first an interpreter at court and eventually controller of Thailand's foreign trade. But the French overplayed their hand. They asked eventually for concessions so sweeping that they aroused Thai suspicion and resentment. In 1688 King Narai, Phaulkon's protector, died. Many were jealous of and hostile to Phaulkon. He was arrested and executed, and from the time of his downfall the Thai rulers were convinced of the danger of intriguing Europeans and isolated their country from most Western contacts for over a hundred and fifty years, until the mid–nineteenth century when King Mongkut welcomed and inaugurated modern reform.

THE FRENCH EAST INDIA COMPANY AND INDOCHINA

Yet even during this period of political isolation from the West the Kings of Thailand permitted the continued if somewhat checkered operation of French Catholic missions which, even more importantly than their East India Company, laid, as we shall see, the foundations for the future French presence in Indochina. Meanwhile, during the same period the Burmese . . . destroyed Ayuthia in 1767 and the Thais subjugated [the Malay ruler, the sultan of] Kedah in 1821 in a drive to reinvigorate their nominal authority in at least the northern half of the Malay peninsula. The isolation of the Thais was in fact never as complete as, say, that of Japan before the arrival of Commodore [Matthew] Perry. Among other things, they continued to appreciate the importance of trade far more keenly than did the Burmese. Hence their decision to place their new capital, Bangkok, nearer to the sea. . . .

EARLY FRENCH EXPANSION INTO INDOCHINA

In Annam and other parts of Indochina the French Catholic missionaries based in Thailand and intermittently supported by their East India Company managed in the seventeenth and eighteenth century to continue the work of the Church. This had been started by the Portuguese Jesuits based on Macao and by other priests forced to leave Japan and China when the rulers of both countries turned against Christianity. In this period one of the pioneers of the French presence in their future colony, Alexander of Rhodes from Avignon, the papal enclave in France, compiled the first map of Vietnam and the first dictionary of Vietnamese. His works were published by the Vatican's missionary organization, the Propaganda Fide, which also encouraged the training of native priests. The French missionary drive in this early period was by no means exclusively nationalist. Exercising France's new pre-eminence in the diffusion of Catholicism in Asia, in 1674 the French Vicar-Apostolic in Thailand appointed a Christian Chinese from the Philippines as Vicar-Apostolic to China. This was resented by the Spanish Dominicans, who had become the dominant religious order there and had acquired in the process some of the largest agricultural plantations. At the time this Franco-Spanish dispute was resolved by the assignment to the Spanish Dominicans in 1693, as a kind of compensation, of the Vicariate-General of Tongking [a city in French Indochina]. Thus the Spaniards from their base in the Philippines became marginally involved in the affairs of Indochina.

THE RIVAL DYNASTIES OF VIETNAM

In the eighteenth century the French missionaries concentrated their efforts mainly in and around Hue, which had become one of the two principal centers of Vietnam. This division was the result of a long triangular civil war following the decline of the dynasty of Le Emperors around 1500. Two out of the three leaders in this struggle emerged as effective rulers of the northern and southern areas of the country, respectively, and set themselves up as kings who still for a time acknowledged the overlordship of a puppet Le Emperor. The two dynasties were those of the Trinh in the north and the Nguyen in the south, and it was the latter whom the French found more receptive to their enterprises. By one of the strange coincidences of history, in the 1630's the Nguyen built two great walls across the narrow waist of the country near Dong Hoi . . . to keep their northern rivals out. It is tempting to conclude from this that there is some basic and fundamental difference between what is once again North and South Vietnam. But this would be quite fallacious. The earlier division resulted simply from a rivalry between rulers of the same race. Both regimes were virtually identical and a truce between them was effective for a hundred years, from 1673 to 1774. But although the northern kingdom had at one time four-fifths of the population of all Vietnam it never succeeded in overcoming the Nguyen and was itself displaced at the end of the eighteenth century. It is paradoxical that this should have occurred, especially in view of the fact that the North favored the Manchu dynasty which was in the ascendant in China, while the South helped refugees from the deposed Ming dynasty [which was deposed by the Manchus in 1644]. The balance of power shifted eventually in favor of the South; partly, it seems, because the economy of the North was static, its trade dead, and corruption widespread. Wealth was concentrated in the hands of a few mandarins, and the country was plagued by peasant rebellions. Another source of strength for the Nguyen was that they were conducting a campaign of colonization which gave them an elastic frontier and permitted the movement of population and economic expansion. Many from the more overcrowded north, hungry for land, flocked southward where there was plenty of it, especially in the rich Mekong delta. In the setting of an ancient rather than a new land the process was not dissimilar to the opening up of the American West. But whereas the latter tended to minimize social differences and democratize the structure of society, in Vietnam tradition and vested interests were too strong. One leading authority suggests that the great landowners did not permit Vietnam's economy to rise above the village level, despite the country's fantastic growth, because they feared that economic undertakings not rooted in the village, such as the creation of a rich merchant class and urban centers of political power, would threaten their position and strengthen that of the central government. They knew that their privileges and power would be more secure if the existing order remained unchanged. Hence Vietnam's continuing semi-feudal, bureaucratic, ideological stagnation and impotence in the struggle against the West. These up-per classes split the country and delayed the development of a unified national community while the central authorities gave them a free hand to exploit the peasants. Yet it was the peasants who achieved territorial expansion and the preservation of na-tional unity. Against this it can be argued that skilled and intelli-gent leadership was fundamental to the development of national greatness—and indeed for all the major measures essential to the agricultural and administrative organization of the new areas—and that this normally emerged among the educated classes. The same author admits that the initially successful peasant rebellion of the late eighteenth century caused no change in the country's social structure.

THE FRENCH EVENTUALLY GAIN A PRESENCE IN VIETNAM

During the truce between the North and the South, in 1749–50, the French East India Company, invigorated by their great empire-builder [Joseph] Dupleix, sent a mission to Hue to con-clude a commercial treaty. Again, however, their forward move-ment failed. The mission incautiously gave offense by abducting an interpreter, and this led to the expulsion of French missionar-ies. Dupleix was recalled, and in 1769 the French East India Com-pany shut down for the second time. Yet a new turn of events soon gave fresh opportunities to the French.

Vietnam's expansion into Cambodia in the 1770's, in competi-tion with Thailand, was checked by a rebellion of three peasant brothers from the village of Tay Son in Cochinchina. While the Nguyen forces were defending Saigon the Trinh forces [of the northern dynasty] marched south and occupied Hue but were dislodged by the Tay Son brothers. Having eliminated the Nguyen in the South and killed off nearly all the family, the rebels invaded the North. They captured Hanoi in 1786 and not only disposed of the Trinh but also terminated the shadowy Le empire which had continued to be recognized as an ultimate symbol of authority. They thus reunited a country which now stretched from the borders of Yunnan [in south-central China] and Kwangsi to the [southern] Ca Mau peninsula. One young prince of sixteen, Nguyen Anh, a nephew of the last southern king, managed to escape from the massacre of his family to an is-land in the Gulf of Siam. A French bishop, Pigneau de Behaine, who had been head of a seminary in Ha Tien province near the Cambodian border, had saved the boy's life by hiding him and helping him to the island. This began a friendship and associa-tion which were to have significant consequences. . . .

French military and administrative help and French supplies were still in time to be of value. With this aid Nguyen Anh was able conclusively to defeat his rivals and unify the whole country. French advisers and technicians then helped to organize the Vietnamese Navy, fortifications and arsenal, and the new administration. . . .

THE FRENCH MAKE VIETNAM A COLONY

France's acquisition of Vietnam and other parts of Indochina was the upshot of varying motives and a rather confused chain of events. The quest for prestige seems to have been the dominant consideration rather than economic profit. Woven into this was the continuing zeal for the promotion of the Catholic religion under the patronage of France, fortified by a strong Catholic revival in Europe.

COOK DISCOVERS EASTERN AUSTRALIA

RODERICK CAMERON

Roderick Cameron explains how British naval officer James Cook, sent to the South Pacific on a scientific mission, also searched for "the Great South Land." Cameron follows Cook's journey around the islands of Tasmania and New Zealand and up the eastern coast of what is now Australia to the point where the Dutch had already explored. Cook's journal and the artists on board recorded plants, animals, and the behavior of the Aborigines. Before leaving, Cook planted British flags, claiming the territory for England. Roderick Cameron, whose father owned a shipping company, lived in many countries and studied their native languages. He is the author of *Equator Farm, Shadow from India, Time of the Mango Flowers*, and several other books.

I t was originally a matter of star-gazing that led James Cook to the shores of Australia. A rare occurrence called the "Transit of Venus" was to take place in 1769. During a transit, Venus passes directly between the earth and the sun and is seen as a small black dot stealing its way across the gassy flames. Important deductions—such as the scale of the solar system and the distance of the earth from the sun—can be made from its passage. Astronomers' charts recorded only two previous transits, the first of which had occurred in 1639. The next had taken place in 1761, but the observation of the 1761 phenomenon had been unsuccessful, and it was therefore of particular importance that the 1769 event be properly charted.

The Royal Society, which was devoted to the cause of natural

Excerpted from *Australia: History and Horizons*, by Roderick Cameron. Copyright © 1971 by Roderick Cameron. Reprinted with permission.

enlightment, took a lively interest in the coming transit and petitioned King George III not to neglect the chance of furthering the fame of British astronomy, "a science," the members pointed out, "on which navigation so much depends." Several European nations, among them Russia, wanted to establish points of observation, and England, the Society argued, should certainly do the same. The Royal Society was considered the world's most distinguished scientific body and its petition carried weight with the King who was particularly interested in science and exploration. Because it was essential that the observers follow the transit from a point south of the equinoxial line [the equator], the recently discovered Island of Tahiti was suggested as a suitable place. The idea of sending an expedition to the Pacific appealed to the King. He promptly gave the project his approval, and the Royal Society approached the Admiralty for a ship and a competent man to sail it. James Cook, a forty-year-old naval officer who had already surveyed the coasts of Newfoundland and Labrador, was chosen to command HMS *Endeavour*.

THE COOK EXPEDITION SAILS FOR THE SOUTH PACIFIC

In 1768 the expedition set out. Sailing with Cook were Charles Green, an astronomer, and various other scientific gentlemen; or simply "the gentlemen" as Cook always referred to Banks and members of his party in his journals. Joseph Banks, later knighted by the King, was a young naturalist of twenty-five with an independent fortune. With him was the slightly older Doctor Daniel Carl Solander, a Swede by origin and [Swedish botanist Carolus] Linnaeus's favourite pupil, also two artists: the twenty-five-year-old Sydney Parkinson and Herman Dietrich Spöring, another Swede, who joined the ship at Cape Town and seems to have acted as Banks's secretary.

The transit of Venus was successfully observed from Tahiti, but it proved to be a task of secondary importance to the expedition, for Cook had been given secret instructions by the Admiralty. After exploring Tahiti and the neighbouring islands, he was to search for the Great South Land, that was believed might somehow still exist.

Cook and Banks between them had an extensive geographical library on board, and amongst the books [French scholar and writer Charles] de Brosses's useful *Histoire des Navigations aux Terres Australes*. Accompanying the text were interesting maps by the celebrated French cartographer, Robert de Vaugondy. In one of the maps, Vaugondy marked out [seaman Abel Janszoon] Tasman's discoveries—the southern part of Van Diemen's Land [Anthony Van Dieman was governor-general of the Dutch East Indies] and the western coasts of New Zealand's North Island. The imaginary eastern coast of New Holland was shown by vague hatchings and was joined by the discoveries of [chief pilot Pedro Fernández de] Quiros, which were displaced westward. Van Diemen's Land, or Tasmania, was also shown connected to the mainland. No accurate chart existed of the straits between New Holland and New Guinea.

These then were the geographical uncertainties which faced the crew of the *Endeavour* as the ship left Tahiti. Possibly New Holland and New Zealand formed the northern humps of the great mythical continent. Cook, however, doubted it. He sailed from the Society Islands in August, and by the end of March of the following year, 1770, he had already charted and had circumnavigated the two islands, thus disproving any continental connection. By April he had turned north-west towards Tasmania, but strong southerly gales drove the *Endeavour* north, so that the English arrived at the south-east corner of Australia itself. Had the weather been fair, Cook would almost certainly have discovered Bass Strait, which separates Australia from Tasmania. On Wednesday, 18 April, certain birds were sighted, a sure sign, Cook noted, of the nearness of land. The following day (20 April

James Cook (pictured) and his crew charted and explored the South Pacific, detailing the plants, animals, and peoples of the region.

by modern computation) Lieutenant Hicks sighted a low hill and
Cook named the point after him, though few maps now carry his
name, their landfall being better known as Cape Everard. Sailing
northwards the *Endeavour* hugged the shore looking for a safe anchorage. "The face of the country is green and woody but the
seashore is all white sand." Dark figures can be distinguished
against the glare. It is a calm, noble landscape with a certain hag-
gard beauty all of its own. Smoke curls up through the dusty
green hanging foliage of the eucalyptus, only to be lost against a
pale sky. At night fires pricked the flat shoreland. One can imagine the intense curiosity of those on board the *Endeavour*. Cook,
Banks, Solander and Tupaia, a Tahitian chief Banks has persuaded to join the expedition, tried to land in a yawl, but were
prevented by the surf. Banks noted the park-like aspect of the
land, the trees separate from each other "without the least un-
derwood." Passing within a quarter of a mile from the shore he
is surprised at the total lack of interest shown by the natives.
Deafened by the surf and concentrated on their occupation, they
did not seem to notice the passing of the yawl; however, an old
woman gathering sticks, followed by three children, "often
looked at the ship but expressed neither surprise nor concern."
It was Sunday 29 April that the *Endeavour* stood into Botany Bay,
anchoring under the south shore.

COOK EXPLORES AND CHARTS THE COAST OF AUSTRALIA

According to traditions in the Cook family, Midshipman Isaac
Smith, Mrs Cook's cousin, afterwards an Admiral of the British
Fleet, was the first to land. Young Isaac, eighteen at the time, later
recalled how Cook, on the point of stepping ashore, said "Isaac,
you shall land first." Cook was forced to fire a musket loaded
with small shot between two natives when a party of them
threatened the explorers with spears.

Cook originally called their anchorage Sting Ray Harbour "occasioned by the great quantity of these sort of fish found in this
place." The prodigious haul of new plants collected by Banks and
Solander later provoked him to change the name to Botany Bay.
The plants were kept fresh in tin chests, wrapped in wet cloths,
while Parkinson and Spöring drew them. (Parkinson worked
with such alacrity that he averaged seven meticulous drawings
a day.) Afterwards, before pressing them, Banks spread the specimens out on sails to dry in the sun.

All the gentlemen remark on the loryquets and cockatoos in
the trees and Banks, generalising, wrote that the Aborigines
"seemed never to be able to muster above fourteen or fifteen

fighting men. . . ." He seemed undecided about their actual colour—"they were so completely covered with dirt, that seemed to have stuck to their bodies from the day of their birth." On one occasion he spat on his fingers and tried to rub it off. His action altered the colour very little, and he judged their skin to be a kind of chocolate.

The *Endeavour* remained in Botany Bay just over a week. On 7 May Cook resumed his voyage and a few miles north passed present-day Sydney. He was aware that the bay or harbour was probably a good anchorage and named it Port Jackson in honour of one of the secretaries of the Admiralty.

Slowly Cook worked his way north, charting the coast. He frequently landed, climbing hills to take his bearings and never sailed very far without sending boats ahead to cast shoreward and seaward.

As they neared the northern end of the island continent, the voyage nearly came to an abrupt end when the ship grounded on a coral reef, twenty miles from the land. Cook's seamanship was, however, equal to the occasion: the *Endeavour* was freed and, much damaged and leaking severely, was guided up the estuary of a small nearby river where she was banked and careened. There the men saw their first kangaroo which Cook described as "an animal something less than a greyhound, of a mouse colour, very slender made and swift of foot." Kangaroo, we learn, is an Aboriginal word. During Cook's stay, natives came to the camp, but they always left their women on the opposite banks of the river. Banks, busy with his glasses, commented on their nudity, noting that they "did not even bother to copy our mother Eve in the fig-leaf."

Although repairs on the ship finally were finished, a strong wind further delayed Cook's departure. Eventually he managed to creep out, and slowly threaded his way through the tortuous mazes of the Great Barrier Reef. Inch by inch, with suppressed anguish, the group advanced to the northern point of Australia which Cook names Cape York in honour of the King's late brother. Sailing west they rediscover Torres Strait, and before departing for Batavia and England they land on a small island (Possession Island) off the coast of Cape York. Cook made no claim regarding the strait, but he did claim the land. Accompanied by Banks and Solander he made for the island and climbed the highest hill from which he saw nothing but islands lying to the north-west.

COOK CLAIMS THE EAST COAST FOR ENGLAND

Cook admitted that to the west he could make no new discoveries "the honour of which belongs to the Dutch navigators; but the east coast I am confident was never seen or visited by any Europeans before us." He had already claimed several places along the coast: now he "once more hoisted the English colours and in the name of His Majesty King George III took possession of the whole eastern coast," christening it New South Wales. Three volleys of small arms were fired, and they were answered by a like number from the ship. Why, one asks, did Cook pick on so improbable a name? It has been suggested that since there already was a New Britain and a Nova Scotia, and since Cook wanted to associate the recent discoveries with his own country, he decided on New South Wales.

Cook had proved that New Zealand was an island group and had closed off Australia's missing coastline. The voyage had also thrust back any southern continent, but it had not proved that one did not exist. A second voyage made in 1772 did, however, settle this question once and for all. In the three years Cook was absent, during this second voyage, he sailed between sixty and seventy thousand miles and made vast sweeps in parts of the Pacific not hitherto explored. He travelled down and up in a giant, irregular zig-zag penetrating as far south as 70°10' latitude, a record not bettered until 1823 by James Weddell in the *Jane of Leith* while on a sealing expedition. During this voyage Cook made numerous major geographical discoveries, one of them being New Caledonia, the largest island in the South Pacific after New Zealand. But ironically it was what he did not discover that was to count as his most important contribution on the second voyage. His conclusive proof that there was no Great South Land put our knowledge of the South Pacific on a sound basis. Indeed the maps of this part of the world still remain essentially as he left them.

European Nations Dominate the Americas

| CHAPTER 5 |

THE ENGLISH
ESTABLISH THE
AMERICAN COLONIES

ALLAN NEVINS AND HENRY STEELE COMMAGER, WITH
JEFFREY MORRIS

Allan Nevins, Henry Steele Commager, and Jeffrey Morris explain that most of the American colonies were financed by a combination of trading companies and proprietary grants, but New York was acquired by conquest. Settlers arrived from England when religious and political events at home jeopardized their freedom and security. According to the authors, most settlers came from the English middle class, and they established representative government from the start. Nevins, a journalist and teacher at Columbia University, is the author of many books, including *The Emergence of Modern America* and a four-volume work entitled *The War for the Union*. Historian Commager, who taught at New York University, is the author of *The Growth of the American Republic* and *The American Mind*. Morris, a lawyer who also taught political science at the University of Pennyslvania, is author of *Federal Justice in the Second Circuit: A History of the United States Courts in New York, Connecticut, and Vermont, 1787–1987*.

T o the raw new continent the first British settlers came in bold groups. The ships that under Christopher Newport sailed into Hampton Roads on the 13th of May, 1607, carried men alone. They laid out Jamestown, with a fort, a church, a storehouse, and a row of little huts. When calamity fell upon them, Captain John Smith showed a nerve, resourcefulness, and

Excerpted from *A Pocket History of the United States*, 9th edition, by Allan Nevins and Henry Steele Commager, with Jeffrey Morris. Copyright © 1986, 1992 by Henry Steele Commager and the Trustees of Columbia University in the City of New York as a beneficiary of Allan Nevins. Reprinted with permission from Simon & Schuster, Inc.

energy that in the second year made him president and practical dictator of the colony. Agriculture was slowly developed; in 1612 John Rolfe began to grow tobacco, and as it brought high prices in the London market everyone took it up, till even the market place was planted with it.

Yet growth was slow. By 1619 Virginia had no more than two thousand people. That year was notable for three events. One was the arrival of a ship from England with ninety "young maidens" who were to be given as wives to those settlers who would pay a hundred and twenty pounds of tobacco for their transportation. This cargo was so joyously welcomed that others like it were soon sent over. Equally important was the initiation of representative government in America. On July 30, in that Jamestown church where John Rolfe several years earlier had cemented a temporary peace with the Indians by marrying Pocahontas, met the first legislative assembly on the continent: a governor, six councilors, and two burgesses each from ten plantations. The third significant event of the year was the arrival in August of a Dutch ship with Negro slaves, twenty of whom were sold to the settlers.

THE PILGRIMS ARRIVE IN MASSACHUSETTS

While Virginia was thus painfully managing to survive and grow, a congregation of English Calvinists who had settled in Holland were making plans to remove to the New World. These "Pilgrims," who had been persecuted because they denied the ecclesiastical supremacy of the king and wished to set up a separate Church of their own, had originally come from the village of Scrooby, in Nottinghamshire. In every way they were a remarkable body. They had three leaders of conspicuous ability: the teacher John Robinson, a learned, broad-minded, generous-hearted graduate of Cambridge University; their sage elder, William Brewster, also a Cambridge man; and William Bradford, shrewd, forcible, and idealistic. The rank and file possessed integrity, industry, and sobriety, as well as courage and fortitude. They had endured popular hostility in England; they had withstood loneliness and harsh toil in Holland. Now, securing a patent to settle in America, a ship called the *Mayflower*, and a store of provisions, they prepared to face the rigors of the wilderness. Sailing from Plymouth one hundred and two in number, the Pilgrims on December 11 (Old Style), 1620, landed on the Massachusetts coast. That winter more than half of them died of cold and scurvy. Well might William Bradford write:

> But here I cannot but stay and maim a pause and stand half amazed at this poor people's present condition. . . .

> Being thus past the vast ocean and a sea of troubles be-
> fore in the preparation . . . they had now no friends to
> welcome them, nor inns to entertain or refresh their
> weatherbeaten bodies, no houses or much less towns
> to repair to, to seek for succor. . . . And for the season,
> it was winter, and those that know the winters of that
> country know them to be sharp and violent and sub-
> ject to cruel and fierce storms, dangerous to travel to
> known places, much more to search an unknown coast.
> Besides what could they see but a hideous and deso-
> late wilderness full of wild beasts and wild men? . . .
> What could now sustain them but the spirit of God and
> His grace?

But the next summer they raised good crops, and in the fall a
ship brought new settlers. Their resolution never faltered. When
the Narraganset chief, Canonicus, sent them a bundle of arrows
in a snakeskin as a challenge to war, Bradford stuffed the skin
with bullets and returned it with a defiant message.

NEW COLONIES EMERGE ALONG THE COAST

Then in rapid succession emerged other English colonies. The
parent hive was ready to send forth its swarms. A May day in
1629 saw the London wharves a scene of bustle and cheery ex-
citement; five ships carrying 400 passengers, 140 head of cattle,
and 40 goats, the largest body thus far sent across the North Atlantic at one time, were sailing for Massachusetts Bay. Before the
end of June they arrived at Salem, where John Endicott and a
small group of associates had planted a town the previous autumn. These people were Puritans—that is, members of the
Church of England who at first wished to reform or purify its
doctrines and who finally withdrew from it—and they opened a
great Puritan exodus. In the spring of 1630 John Winthrop
reached Salem with eleven ships carrying nine hundred settlers,
enough to found eight new towns, including Boston. The Massachusetts Bay colony grew so rapidly that it was soon throwing
off branches to the south and west. Roger Williams, a minister of
Salem who courageously taught the separation of Church and
state, with other radical views, was driven into the Rhode Island
wilderness. Here in 1636 he founded Providence as a place of
perfect religious toleration. In that year, too, the first migration
to Connecticut began under the resolute Reverend Thomas
Hooker, who moved a great part of his congregation from Cambridge westward in a body. Another notable colony sprang into
existence in 1634, when the first settlement was made in Maryland under the guidance of the liberal-minded Cecilius Calvert,

second Baron Baltimore. Most of the gentlemen who first went thither were, like the founder, English Catholics, while most of the common folk were Protestants. Toleration was therefore essential, and Maryland was a home of religious freedom, attracting people of varied faiths. Settlers from Virginia drifted into the Albemarle Sound region of what is now North Carolina as early as the 1650's, but it was not until 1663 that Charles II granted a charter to eight of his favorites for the vast area now embraced by both the Carolinas and Georgia. The proprietors named both the colony and the first city after their royal benefactor, and induced John Locke to draw up for them a Fundamental Constitution which, happily, never went into effect. Settlers drifted down from Virginia and others, including many French Huguenots [Protestants], came directly to the coast from England and the West Indies. Charleston, established in 1670, speedily became the cultural as well as the political capital of the colony.

THE BRITISH CONQUER THE DUTCH TO GAIN NEW YORK

The seat of one rich colony was gained by conquest. The Dutch had sent Henry Hudson, an English mariner, to explore the river which bears his name—a task executed in 1609. Dutch fur traders had followed him, and in 1624 a small settlement was effected on Manhattan Island. The province of New Netherland grew but slowly and failed to develop institutions of self-government, but did leave a permanent mark in the patroon system [whereby a landowner gained proprietary rights to a large tract of land in exchange for bringing fifty new settlers to the colony] of plantations along the Hudson, in architecture, and in "Knickerbocker" families who were to play a leading role in the history of New York and of the nation. Meanwhile, the English never gave up their claim to the entire coast, and the Connecticut settlements were anxious for the seizure of their troublesome neighbor. Why permit this alien element in the very center of British America? Charles II granted the area to his brother, the Duke of York, who took vigorous action. In the summer of 1664 three warships arrived before New Amsterdam. They carried a body of soldiers who were reinforced by Connecticut troops, while forces were promised from Massachusetts and Long Island. Most of the Dutch settlers, sick of despotic rule, made no objection to a change of sovereignty. Although old Peter Stuyvesant declared he would rather be "carried out dead" than surrender, he had no choice. The British flag went up over the town renamed New York and, save for a brief intermission during a subsequent Anglo-Dutch war (1672–1674), it stayed there. Indeed, the British flag now waved from the Kennebec to Florida.

Penn Establishes Pennsylvania and Delaware

Yet one of the most interesting colonies did not take on firm outlines till late in the century. A number of settlers, British, Dutch, and Swedish, had found their way into the area which later became Pennsylvania and Delaware. When the pious and far-sighted William Penn came into control of the region in 1681, he prepared to erect a model commonwealth on the principles of the Quakers—that sect which Voltaire later called the most truly Christian of peoples. In his benevolent fashion, he quieted the Indian title by friendly treaties of purchase. To attract colonists he offered liberal terms, assuring all that they could obtain land, establish thrifty homes, and live in justice and equality with their neighbors. No Christian would suffer from religious discrimination. In civil affairs the laws would rule, and the people would be a party to the laws. He directed the establishment of Philadelphia, his "city of brotherly love," with gardens surrounding each house, so that it would be "a green country town . . . and always be wholesome." In 1682 he came over himself, bringing about a hundred colonists. Pennsylvania throve wonderfully, attracting a great variety of settlers from Britain and the Continent, but keeping its Quaker lineaments.

Trading Companies Finance Colonies

Roughly speaking, two main instruments were used in this work of transferring Britons and others across the seas and founding new states. It was the chartered trading company, organized primarily for profit, which planted Virginia and Massachusetts. The London Company, so-called because organized by stockholders resident in London, had been granted its charter in 1606 to plant a colony between the thirty-fourth and forty-first degrees of latitude. The Plymouth Company, whose stockholders lived in Plymouth, Bristol, and other towns, was chartered that same year to establish a colony between the thirty-eighth and forty-fifth degrees. These companies could distribute lands, operate mines, coin money, and organize the defense of their colonies. The king, who granted the charters, kept ultimate jurisdiction over the colonial governments. After heavy financial losses, the London Company in 1624 saw its charter revoked, the king making Virginia a royal colony. The Plymouth Company promoted various small Northern settlements and fishing stations, but made no money, and after reorganization asked in 1633 for annulment of its charter, calling itself "only a breathless carcass."

Yet if neither the London nor the Plymouth Company was profitable financially, both did an effective work in colonization.

The London Company was in a very real sense the parent of Virginia; the Plymouth Company and its successor, the Council for New England, founded town after town in Maine, New Hampshire, and Massachusetts. And a third corporation, the Massachusetts Bay Company, had a peculiar character and a special destiny. It originated as a body of stockholders, most of them Puritans, who had commercial and patriotic motives. Undaunted by the failure of the earlier companies to pay dividends, they believed that better management would yield profits. Charles I granted a charter early in 1629. Then a strange development took place. When the king and High Church party under Archbishop Laud became masters of the Church of England, many Puritan leaders wished to emigrate. They had property, social position, and an independent spirit. They did not wish to go out to Massachusetts Bay as mere vassals of a company in London. Moreover, they hoped to secure liberty to set up the kind of Church government they liked. Therefore, the principal Puritans of the company simply bought up all its stock, took the charter, and sailed with it to America. A commercial company was thus converted into a self-governing colony—the colony of Massachusetts Bay.

COLONIES ARE FINANCED WITH PROPRIETARY GRANTS

The other principal instrument of colonization was the proprietary grant. The proprietor was a man belonging to the British gentry or nobility, with money at his command, to whom the Crown gave a tract in America as it might have given him an estate at home. The old rule of English law was that all land not otherwise held belonged to the king, and America fell under this rule. Lord Baltimore received Maryland; William Penn, the son of an admiral to whom the king owed money, received Pennsylvania; and a group of royal favorites under Charles II received the Carolinas. All these proprietors were given large powers to devise a government. Lord Baltimore, who had some of the absolutist ideas of the Stuarts, was averse to giving his colonists any lawmaking power, but finally yielded to a popularly created assembly. Penn was wiser. In 1682 he called together an assembly, all of whom were elected by the settlers, and allowed them to enact a constitution, or "Great Charter." This vested many of the powers of government in representatives of the people—and Penn accepted the scheme.

EVENTS IN ENGLAND SPUR MIGRATION

As soon as it was proved that life in America might be prosperous and hopeful, a great spontaneous migration from Europe began. It came by uneven spurts and drew its strength from a variety of impulses. The first two great waves went to Massachusetts and Virginia. From 1628 to 1640 the Puritans in England were in a state of depression and apprehension, suffering much actual persecution. The royal authorities were committed to a revival of old forms in the Church and determined to make it completely dependent on the Crown and the archbishops. Political as well as ecclesiastical turmoil racked the land. The king dissolved Parliament and for ten years got on without it. He imprisoned his chief opponents.

As his party seemed bent on subverting English liberty, many Puritans believed that the best course was to quit the island and build in America a new state. In the great emigration of 1628–1640, some twenty thousand of the sturdiest people of England left home. No fewer than twelve hundred ship voyages were made across the Atlantic with settlers, livestock, and furniture. Boston became one of the important seaports of the world, ministering to an area full of bustle and vitality. . . . One striking characteristic of this movement was the migration of many Puritans not as individuals or families but in whole communities. Certain English towns were half depopulated. The new settlements consisted not of traders and farmers alone, but of doctors, lawyers, schoolteachers, businessmen, craftsmen, and ministers. New England became a microcosm of old England, carrying in extraordinary degree the seeds of future growth.

When the Civil War began in England in 1642 the Puritan exodus slackened; but what may be loosely called the Cavalier exodus began soon afterward. It gained volume in 1649, when Charles was beheaded, and continued vigorously until the Restoration in 1660. As the Puritan migration had lifted the population of New England above thirty thousand, so the Cavalier migration was the main factor in increasing Virginia's population by 1670 to almost forty thousand. And the influx brought a remarkable amount of wealth, for though few of the newcomers were in fact Cavaliers, many were from the prosperous classes. Having capital, they bought and cultivated large estates, and having power or influence, they were often able to enlarge these estates from Royal lands. Virginia, at first predominantly a poor man's colony, became full of the well-to-do. This immigration brought over some of the greatest names in American history. [Robert E.] Lee's ancestors first arrived in Virginia in the 1640's, and [George] Washington's great-grandfather, John Washington, came in 1657. The family traditions of the Marshalls state that their American progenitor had been a captain in the royal forces during the English war and came to Virginia when the royalists were worsted. After the influx we meet in Virginia history such notable families as the Harrisons, the Carys, the Masons, the Carters, the Tylers, the Randolphs, and the Byrds.

MOST SETTLERS ARE FROM THE MIDDLE CLASS

But no real social distinction can be drawn between the settlers of Massachusetts and those of Virginia. The people who made both commonwealths great were drawn from the same large middle-class stratum. In England the Washingtons had been simply country squires, who had a tiny manor called Sulgrave in Northamptonshire; one had been mayor of Northampton. John Marshall's great-grandfather seems to have been a carpenter. The first Randolph in Virginia sprang from a family of Warwickshire squires of no great consequence. None of these Cavaliers was of better birth or more gentility than the Puritan John Winthrop, who came of a well-to-do family which owned the manor of Groton in Suffolk. None was of better origin than Sir Richard Saltonstall, who left many notable descendants in New England, or William Brewster, who as an undersecretary of state had been a man of influence at court. The great majority of the emigrants to both Massachusetts and Virginia before 1660 were yeomen, mechanics, shopkeepers, and clerks of modest means; while many in all parts of America were indentured servants, who paid for their passage by a stated term of labor. Their real wealth lay in their sturdy integrity, self-reliance, and energy.

The Colonial Governor Addresses the Problem of Witchcraft

William Phips

In two letters addressed to British officials, the British-appointed governor William Phips describes the witchcraft trials and pleads for direction from officials on how to bring proper order to the community. Moreover, he describes the procedures he has temporarily taken to prevent false accusations and to offer justice and compassion to those accused of practicing witchcraft. He closes by saying that accusations have subsided since high officials were named as witches. William Phips, born in a Maine village, was a sheep herder and a ship carpenter before he sailed his vessel to the West Indies, where he rescued lost treasure from Spanish galleons. His wealth from this project led to partnerships with British nobles and the appointment as royal governor.

W hen I first arrived I found this Province miserably harrassed with a most Horrible witchcraft or Possession of Devills which had broke in upon severall Townes, some scores of poor people were taken with preternaturall torments some scalded with brimstone some had pins stuck in their flesh others hurried into the fire and water and some dragged out of their houses and carried over the tops of trees and hills for many Miles together; it hath been represented to mee much like

Excerpted from letters written by William Phips to British officials 1692–1693.

that of Sweden about thirty years agoe, and there were many committed to prison upon suspicion of Witchcraft before my arrivall. The loud cries and clamours of the friends of the afflicted people with the advice of the Deputy Governor and many others prevailed with mee to give a Commission of Oyer and Terminer for discovering what witchcraft might be at the bottome or whether it were not a possession. The chief Judge in this Commission was the Deputy Governour and the rest were persons of the best prudence and figure that could then be pitched upon. When the Court came to sitt at Salem in the County of Essex they convicted more than twenty persons of being guilty of witchcraft, some of the convicted were such as confessed their Guilt, the Court as I understand began their proceedings with the accusations of the afflicted and then went upon other humane [human] evidences to strengthen that. I was almost the whole time of the proceeding abroad in the service of Their Majesties in the Eastern part of the Country and depended upon the Judgement of the Court as to a right method of proceeding in cases of Witchcraft but when I came home I found many persons in a strange ferment of dissatisfaction which was increased by some hott Spiritts that blew up the flame,[1] but on enquiring into the matter I found that the Devill had taken upon him the name and shape of severall persons who were doubtless inocent and to my certain knowledge of good reputation for which cause I have now forbidden the committing of any more that shall be accused without unavoydable necessity, and those that have been committed I would shelter from any Proceedings against them wherein there may be the least suspition of any wrong to be done unto the Innocent. I would also wait for any particular directions or commands if their Majesties please to give mee any for the fuller ordering this perplexed affair. I have also put a stop to the printing of any discourses one way or other, that may increase the needless disputes of people upon this occasion, because I saw a likelyhood of kindling an inextinguishable flame if I should admitt any publique and open Contests and I have grieved to see that some who should have done their Majesties and this Province better service have so far taken Councill of Passion as to desire the precipitancy of these matters, these things have been improved by some to give me many interuptions in their Majesties service and in truth none of my vexations have been greater than this, than that their Majesties service has been hereby unhappily clogged, and the Persons who have made soe ill improvement of these matters here are seeking to turne it all upon mee, but I

1. Phips suspects a Baptist preacher circulated a paper criticizing the proceedings.

hereby declare that as soon as I came from fighting against their Majesties Enemyes and understood what danger some of their innocent subjects might be exposed to, if the evidence of the afflicted persons only did prevaile either to the committing or trying any of them, I did before any application was made unto me about it put a stop to the proceedings of the Court and they are now stopt till their Majesties pleasure be known. Sir I beg pardon for giving you all this trouble, the reason is because I know my enemies are seeking to turn it all upon me and I take this liberty because I depend upon your friendship, and desire you will please to give a true understanding of the matter if any thing of this kind be urged or made use of against mee. Because the justnesse of my proceeding herein will bee a sufficient defence. Sir

I am with all imaginable respect
Your most humble Servt

WILLIAM PHIPS.

Dated at Boston
    the 12th of october 1692.
Mem'dm
    That my Lord President be pleased to acquaint his Ma'ty in Councill with the account received from New England from Sir Wm. Phips the Governor there touching Proceedings against severall persons for Witchcraft as appears by the Governor's letter concerning those matters.[2]

Boston in New England Febry 21st, 169⅔.

May it please yor. Lordshp.

By the Capn. of the *Samuell and Henry*[3] I gave an account that att my arrivall here I found the Prisons full of people committed upon suspition of witchcraft and that continuall complaints were made to me that many persons were grievously tormented by witches and that they cryed out upon severall persons by name, as the cause of their torments. The number of these complaints increasing every day, by advice of the Lieut Govr. and the Councill I gave a Commission of Oyer and Terminer to try the suspected witches and at that time the generality of the People represented the matter to me as reall witchcraft and gave very strange instances of the same. The first in Commission was the Lieut. Govr. and the rest persons of the best prudence and figure that could then be pitched upon and I depended upon the Court for a right method of proceeding in cases of witchcraft. At that time I went to command the army at the Eastern part of the

---

2. The letter was addressed to William Blathwayt, clerk of the Privy Council, and it is he who added the memorandum.   3. ship returning to England

William Phips

Province, for the French and Indians had made an attack upon some of our Fronteer Towns. I continued there for some time but when I returned I found people much disatisfied at the proceedings of the Court, for about Twenty persons were condemned and executed of which number some were thought by many persons to be innocent. The Court still proceeded in the same method of trying them, which was by the evidence of the afflicted persons who when they were brought into the Court as soon as the suspected witches looked upon them instantly fell to the ground in strange agonies and grievous torments, but when touched by them upon the arme or some other part of their flesh they immediately revived and came to themselves, upon [which] they made oath that the Prisoner at the Bar did afflict them and that they saw their shape or spectre come from their bodies which put them to such paines and torments: When I enquired into the matter I was enformed by the Judges that they begun with this, but had humane testimony against such as were condemned and undoubted proof of their being witches, but at length I found that the Devill did take upon him the shape of Innocent persons and some were accused of whose innocency I was well assured and many considerable persons of unblameable life and conversation were cried out upon as witches and wizards. The Deputy Govr. notwithstanding persisted vigorously in the same method, to the great disatisfaction and disturbance of the people, untill I put an end to the Court and stopped the proceedings, which I did because I saw many innocent persons might otherwise perish and at that time I thought it my duty to give an account thereof that their Ma'ties pleasure might be signifyed, hoping that for the better ordering thereof the Judges learned in the law in England might give such rules and directions as have been practized in England for proceedings in so difficult and so nice a point; When I put an end to the Court there were at least fifty persons in prison in great misery by reason of the extream cold and their poverty, most of them having only spectre evidence against them, and their mittimusses being defective, I caused some of them to be lett out upon bayle and put the Judges upon considering of a way to reliefe others and prevent them from perishing in prison, upon which some of them were convinced and acknowledged that their former proceedings were too violent and not grounded upon a right foundation but that if they might sit againe, they would proceed after another method, and whereas Mr. Increase Mathew[4] and severall other Divines did give it as their Judgment that the Devill might afflict in the shape of an innocent person and that the look and the touch of the suspected persons was not sufficient proofe against them, these things had not the same stress layd upon them as before, and upon this consideration I permitted a spetiall Superior Court to be held at Salem in the County of Essex on the third day of January, the Lieut Govr. being Chief Judge. Their method of proceeding being altered, all that were brought to tryall to the number of fifety two, were cleared saving three, and I was enformed by the Kings Attorny Generall that some of the cleared and the condemned were under the same circumstances or that there was the same reason to clear the three condemned as the rest according to his Judgment. The Deputy Govr. signed a Warrant for their speedy execucion and also of five others who were condemned at the former Court of Oyer and Terminer, but considering how the matter had been managed I sent a reprieve whereby the execucion was stopped untill their Maj. pleasure be signified and declared. The Lieut. Gov. upon this occasion was inraged and filled with passionate anger and refused to sitt upon

---

4. Mather. Undoubtedly an error of the English copyist. The advice meant was that of the twelve ministers of Boston and vicinity on June 15.

the bench in a Superior Court then held at Charles Towne, and indeed hath from the beginning hurried on these matters with great precipitancy and by his warrant hath caused the estates, goods and chattles of the executed to be seized and disposed of without my knowledge or consent. The stop put to the first method of proceedings hath dissipated the blak cloud that threatened this Province with destruccion; for whereas this delusion of the Devill did spread and its dismall effects touched the lives and estates of many of their Ma'ties Subjects and the reputacion of some of the principall persons here,[5] and indeed unhappily clogged and interrupted their Ma'ties affaires which hath been a great vexation to me, I have no new complaints but peoples minds before divided and distracted by differing opinions concerning this matter are now well composed.

I am

Yor. Lordships most faithfull

humble Servant

WILLIAM PHIPS

[Addressed:] To the Rt. Honble

the Earle of Nottingham

att Whitehall

London

[Indorsed :] R [i. e., received] May 24, 93

abt. Witches

---

5. Members of Council and Justices were accused as well as the wife of Governor Phips.

THE WITCHCRAFT TRIAL OF SUSANNA MARTIN

COTTON MATHER

Cotton Mather provides an account of a typical witchcraft trial, in which testimony of the victims served as the evidence on which the accused was acquitted or convicted. In this trial held in Salem, Massachusetts, on June 29, 1692, John Atkinson, for example, testified that Susanna Martin caused his cow to go berserk and Robert Downer testified that she took the form of a cat and attacked him. Susanna Martin was executed less than a month after this trial. Cotton Mather was a well-educated Puritan minister in New England. He is the author of *The Ecclesiastical History of New England, Essays to do Good,* and *The Christian Philosopher.*

I. Susanna Martin,[1] pleading Not Guilty to the Indictment of Witchcraft brought in against her, there were produced the evidences of many persons very sensibly and grievously Bewitched; who all complaned of the prisoner at the Bar, as the person whom they Believed the cause of their Miseries. And now, as well as in the other Trials, there was an extraordinary endeavour by Witchcrafts, with Cruel and Frequent Fits, to hinder the poor sufferers from giving in their complaints; which the Court was forced with much patience to obtain, by much waiting and watching for it.

1. tried at the Court of Oyer and Terminer at Salem, Massachusetts, on June 29, 1692. She was executed on July 19.

Excerpted from *The Wonders of the Invisible World* (New York, 1692) by Cotton Mather.

II. There was now also an Account given, of what passed at her first examination before the Magistrates. The cast of her eye then striking the Afflicted People to the ground, whether they saw that Cast or no; there were these among other passages between the Magistrates and the Examinate.

Magistrate. Pray, what ails these People?

Martin. I don't know.

Magistrate. But what do you think ails them?

Martin. I don't desire to spend my Judgment upon it.

Magistrate. Don't you think they are Bewitch'd?

Martin. No, I do not think they are.

Magistrate. Tell us your thoughts about them then.

Martin. No, my thoughts are my own when they are in, but when they are out, they are anothers. Their Master——

Magistrate. Their Master? who do you think is their Master?

Martin. If they be dealing in the Black Art, you may know as well as I.

Magistrate. Well, what have you done towards this?

Martin. Nothing at all.

Magistrate. Why, tis you or your Appearance.

Martin. I cannot help it.

Magistrate. Is it not Your Master? How comes your Appearance to hurt these?

Martin. How do I know? He that appeared in the shape of Samuel, a Glorify'd Saint, may Appear in any ones shape.

It was then also noted in her, as in others like her, that if the Afflicted went to approach her, they were flung down to the Ground. And, when she was asked the Reason of it, she said, "I cannot tell; it may be, the Devil bears me more Malice than another."

III. The Court accounted themselves Alarum'd by these things, to Enquire further into the Conversation of the Prisoner; and see what there might occur, to render these Accusations further credible. Whereupon, John Allen, of Salisbury, testify'd, That he refusing, because of the weakness of his Oxen, to Cart some Staves, at the request of this Martin, she was displeased at it; and said, "It had been as good that he had; for his Oxen should never do him much more Service." Whereupon this Deponent said, "Dost thou threaten me, thou old Witch? I'l throw thee into the Brook": Which to avoid, she flew over the Bridge, and escaped. But, as he was going home, one of his Oxen Tired, so that he was forced to Unyoke him, that he might get him home. He then put his Oxen, with many more, upon Salisbury Beach, where Cattle did use to get Flesh. In a few days, all the Oxen upon the Beach were found by their Tracks, to have run unto the mouth of Merrimack-River, and not returned; but the next day they were found come ashore

Witchcraft trials, such as the trial of Susanna Martin, relied on the testimony of victims to judge the guilt or innocence of the accused.

upon Plum-Island. They that sought them used all imaginable gentleness, but they would still run away with a violence that seemed wholly Diabolical, till they came near the mouth of Merrimack-River; when they ran right into the Sea, swimming as far as they could be seen. One of them then swam back again, with a swiftness amazing to the Beholders, who stood ready to receive him, and help up his Tired Carcass: But the Beast ran furiously up into the Island, and from thence, through the Marishes, up into Newbury Town, and so up into the Woods; and there after a while found near Amesbury. So that, of Fourteen good Oxen, there was only this saved: the rest were all cast up, some in one place, and some in another, Drowned.

IV. John Atkinson Testify'd, That he Exchanged a Cow with a Son of Susanna Martins, whereat she muttered, and was unwilling he should have it. Going to Receive this Cow, tho' he Hamstring'd her, and Halter'd her, she of a Tame Creature grew so mad, that they could scarce get her along. She broke all the Ropes that were fastned unto her, and though she were Ty'd fast unto a Tree, yet she made her Escape, and gave them such further Trouble, as they could ascribe to no cause but Witchcraft.

V. Bernard Peache testify'd, That being in Bed on a Lords-day Night, he heard a scrabbling at the Window, whereat he then saw

Susanna Martin come in, and jump down upon the Floor. She took hold of this Deponents Feet, and drawing his Body up into an Heap, she lay upon him near Two Hours; in all which time he could neither speak nor stirr. At length, when he could begin to move, he laid hold on her Hand, and pulling it up to his mouth, he bit three of her Fingers, as he judged, unto the Bone. Whereupon she went from the Chamber, down the Stairs, out at the Door. This Deponent[2] thereupon called unto the people of the House, to advise them of what passed; and he himself did follow her. The people saw her not; but there being a Bucket at the Left-hand of the Door, there was a drop of Blood found on it; and several more drops of Blood upon the Snow newly fallen abroad. There was likewise the print of her two Feet just without the Threshold; but no more sign of any Footing further off.

At another time this Deponent was desired by the Prisoner, to come unto an Husking of Corn, at her House; and she said, If he did not come, it were better that he did! He went not; but the Night following, Susanna Martin, as he judged, and another came towards him. One of them said, "Here he is!" but he having a Quarter-staff, made a Blow at them. The Roof of the Barn broke his Blow; but following them to the Window, he made another Blow at them, and struck them down; yet they got up, and got out, and he saw no more of them.

About this time, there was a Rumour about the Town, that Martin had a Broken Head; but the Deponent could say nothing to that.

The said Peache also testify'd the Bewitching of Cattle to Death, upon Martin's Discontents.

VI. Robert Downer testifyed, That this Prisoner being some years ago prosecuted at Court for a Witch,[3] he then said unto her, He believed she was a Witch. Whereat she being dissatisfied, said, That some Shee-Devil would Shortly fetch him away! Which words were heard by others, as well as himself. The Night following, as he lay in his Bed, there came in at the Window the likeness of a Cat, which Flew upon him, took fast hold of his Throat, lay on him a considerable while, and almost killed him. At length he remembred what Susanna Martin had threatned the Day before; and with much striving he cryed out, "Avoid, thou Shee-Devil! In the Name of God the Father, the Son, and the Holy Ghost, Avoid! " Whereupon it left him, leap'd on the Floor, and Flew out at the Window.

And there also came in several Testimonies, that before ever

---

2. one who testifies   3. in 1669. She was then bound over to the Superior court, but was discharged without trial.

Downer spoke a word of this Accident, Susanna Martin and her Family had related, How this Downer had been Handled!

VII. John Kembal testifyed, that Susanna Martin, upon a Causeless Disgust, had threatned him, about a certain Cow of his, That she should never do him any more Good: and it came to pass accordingly. For soon after the Cow was found stark Dead on the dry Ground, without any Distemper to be discerned upon her. Upon which he was followed with a strange Death upon more of his Cattle, whereof he lost in One Spring to the value of Thirty Pounds. But the said John Kembal had a further Testimony to give in against the Prisoner which was truly admirable.

Being desirous to furnish himself with a Dog, he applied himself to buy one of this Martin, who had a Bitch with Whelps in her House. But she not letting him have his Choice, he said, he would supply himself then at one Blezdels. Having mark'd a puppy which he lik'd at Blezdels, he met George Martin, the Husband of the prisoner, going by, who asked him, Whether he would not have one of his Wives Puppies? and he answered, No. The same Day, one Edmund Eliot, being at Martins House, heard George Martin relate, where this Kembal had been, and what he had said. Whereupon Susanna Martin replyed, "If I live, I'll give him Puppies enough!" Within a few Dayes after, this Kembal coming out of the Woods, there arose a little Black Cloud in the N.W. and Kembal immediately felt a Force upon him, which made him not able to avoid running upon the stumps of Trees, that were before him, albeit he had a broad, plain Cart way, before him; but tho' he had his Ax also on his Shoulder to endanger him in his Falls, he could not forbear going out of his way to tumble over them. When he came below the Meeting-House, there appeared unto him a little thing like a Puppy, of a Darkish Colour; and it shot backwards and forwards between his Legs. He had the Courage to use all possible Endeavours of Cutting it with his Ax; but he could not Hit it; the Puppy gave a jump from him, and went, as to him it seem'd, into the Ground. Going a little further, there appeared unto him a Black Puppy, somewhat bigger than the first, but as Black as a Cole. Its motions were quicker than those of his Ax; it Flew at his Belly, and away; then at his Throat; so, over his Shoulder one way, and then over his Shoulder another way. His heart now began to fail him, and he thought the Dog would have Tore his Throat out. But he recovered himself, and called upon God in his Distress; and Naming the Name of Jesus Christ, it Vanished away at once. The Deponent Spoke not one Word of these Accidents, for fear of affrighting his wife: But the next Morning, Edmond Eliot going into Martins House, this woman asked him where Kembal was? He

Replyed, At home, a bed, for ought he knew. She returned, "They say, he was frighted last Night." Eliot asked, "With what?" She answered, "With Puppies." Eliot asked, Where she heard of it, for he had heard nothing of it? She rejoined, "About the Town." Altho' Kembal had mentioned the Matter to no Creature Living.

VIII. William Brown testify'd, that Heaven having blessed him with a most Pious and prudent wife, this wife of his one day mett with Susanna Martin; but when she approch'd just unto her, Martin vanished out of sight, and left her extremely affrighted. After which time, the said Martin often appear'd unto her, giving her no little trouble; and when she did come, she was visited with Birds that sorely peck't and Prick'd her; and sometimes a Bunch, like a pullets egg, would Rise in her throat, ready to Choak her, till she cry'd out, "Witch, you shan't choak me!" While this good Woman was in this Extremity, the Church appointed a Day of Prayer, on her behalf; whereupon her Trouble ceas'd; she saw not Martin as formerly; and the Church, instead of their Fast, gave Thanks for her Deliverance. But a considerable while after, she being Summoned to give in some Evidence at the Court, against this Martin, quickly thereupon this Martin came behind her, while she was milking her Cow, and said unto her, "For thy defaming me at Court, I'l make thee the miserablest Creature in the World." Soon after which, she fell into a strange kind of Distemper, and became horribly Frantick, and uncapable of any Reasonable Action; the Physicians declaring, that her Distemper was preternatural, and that some Devil had certainly Bewitched her; and in that Condition she now remained.

IX. Sarah Atkinson testify'd, That Susanna Martin came from Amesbury to their House at Newbury, in an extraordinary Season, when it was not fit for any one to Travel. She came (as she said unto Atkinson) all that long way on Foot. She brag'd and show'd how dry she was; nor could it be perceived that so much as the Soles of her Shoes were wet. Atkinson was amazed at it: and professed, that she should her self have been wet up to the knees, if she had then came so far; but Martin reply'd, She scorn'd to be Drabbled! It was noted, that this Testimony upon her Trial cast her in a very singular Confusion.

X. John Pressy testify'd, That being one Evening very unaccountably Bewildred, near a field of Martins, and several times, as one under an Enchantment, returning to the place he had left, at length he saw a marvellous Light, about the Bigness of an Half-Bushel, near two Rod out of the way. He went, and struck at it with a Stick, and laid it on with all his might. He gave it near forty blows; and felt it a palpable substance. But going from it, his Heels were struck up, and he was laid with his Back on the

Ground, Sliding, as he thought, into a Pit; from whence he recover'd, by taking hold on the Bush; altho' afterwards he could
find no such Pit in the place. Having, after his Recovery, gone
five or six Rod, he saw Susanna Martin standing on his Left-
hand, as the Light had done before; but they changed no words
with one another. He could scarce find his House in his Return;
but at length he got home, extreamly affrighted. The next day, it
was upon Enquiry understood, that Martin was in a miserable
condition by pains and hurts that were upon her.

It was further testify'd by this Deponent, That after he had
given in some Evidence against Susanna Martin, many years ago,
she gave him foul words about it; and said, He should never
prosper more; particularly, That he should never have more than
two Cows; that tho' he were never so likely to have more, yet he
should never have them. And that from that very Day to this,
namely for Twenty Years together, he could never exceed that
Number; but some strange thing or other still prevented his having of any more.

XI. Jervis Ring testifyed, that about seven years ago, he was oftentimes and grievously Oppressed in the Night, but saw not
who Troubled him, until at last he, Lying perfectly Awake, plainly
saw Susanna Martin approach him. She came to him, and force-
ably Bit him by the Finger; so that the Print of the Bite is now so
long after to be seen upon him. . . .

Note, This Woman was one of the most Impudent, Scurrilous,
wicked creatures in the world; and she did now throughout her
whole Trial discover herself to be such an one. Yet when she was
asked, what she had to say for her self? her Cheef Plea was, That
she had Led a most virtuous and Holy Life!

AMERICANS RISE AGAINST OPPRESSION

HOWARD ZINN

Howard Zinn analyzes the path that led laboring classes to become a political force poised against British domination. After the Seven Years' War, lower classes took over town meetings to protest their poverty. When leaders from the legal and political community wanted support of the working poor, they aroused the anger of lower-class workers further until it spilled over into violence and house attacks against rich Americans. In 1767 the Stamp Act provided the opportunity to turn the resistance movement away from the American wealthy class toward the British. Howard Zinn, veteran scholar and teacher of American history, is the author of *Disobedience and Democracy, The Politics of History,* and *Postwar America.*

A fter 1763, with England victorious over France in the Seven Years' War (known in America as the French and Indian War), expelling them from North America, ambitious colonial leaders were no longer threatened by the French. They now had only two rivals left: the English and the Indians. The British, wooing the Indians, had declared Indian lands beyond the Appalachians out of bounds to whites (the Proclamation of 1763). Perhaps once the British were out of the way, the Indians could be dealt with. Again, no conscious forethought strategy by the colonial elite, but a growing awareness as events developed.

With the French defeated, the British government could turn its attention to tightening control over the colonies. It needed revenues to pay for the war, and looked to the colonies for that. Also,

Excerpted from *A People's History of the United States,* by Howard Zinn. Copyright © 1980 by Howard Zinn. Reprinted with permission from HarperCollins Publishers, Inc.

the colonial trade had become more and more important to the British economy, and more profitable: it had amounted to about 500,000 pounds in 1700 but by 1770 was worth 2,800,000 pounds.

So, the American leadership was less in need of English rule, the English more in need of the colonists' wealth. The elements were there for conflict.

The war had brought glory for the generals, death to the privates, wealth for the merchants, unemployment for the poor. There were 25,000 people living in New York (there had been 7,000 in 1720) when the French and Indian War ended. A newspaper editor wrote about the growing "Number of Beggers and wandering Poor" in the streets of the city. Letters in the papers questioned the distribution of wealth: "How often have our Streets been covered with Thousands of Barrels of Flour for trade, while our near Neighbors can hardly procure enough to make a Dumplin to satisfy hunger?"

[Historian] Gary Nash's study of city tax lists shows that by the early 1770s, the top 5 percent of Boston's taxpayers controlled 49% of the city's taxable assets. In Philadelphia and New York too, wealth was more and more concentrated. Court-recorded wills showed that by 1750 the wealthiest people in the cities were leaving 20,000 pounds (equivalent to about $2.5 million today).

ORGANIZING AND ACTIVATING THE LOWER CLASSES

In Boston, the lower classes began to use the town meeting to vent their grievances. The governor of Massachusetts had written that in these town meetings "the meanest Inhabitants . . . by their constant Attendance there generally are the majority and outvote the Gentlemen, Merchants, Substantial Traders and all the better part of the Inhabitants."

What seems to have happened in Boston is that certain lawyers, editors, and merchants of the upper classes, but excluded from the ruling circles close to England—men like [politician] James Otis and [lawyer] Samuel Adams—organized a "Boston Caucus" and through their oratory and their writing "molded laboring-class opinion, called the 'mob' into action, and shaped its behaviour." This is Gary Nash's description of Otis, who, he says, "keenly aware of the declining fortunes and the resentment of ordinary townspeople, was mirroring as well as molding popular opinion."

We have here a forecast of the long history of American politics, the mobilization of lower-class energy by upper-class politicians, for their own purposes. This was not purely deception; it involved, in part, a genuine recognition of lower-class grievances, which helps to account for its effectiveness as a tactic over the centuries. As Nash puts it:

> James Otis, Samuel Adams, [lawyers] Royall Tyler, Ox-enbridge Thacher, and a host of other Bostonians, linked to the artisans and laborers through a network of neighborhood taverns, fire companies, and the Cau-cus, espoused a vision of politics that gave credence to laboring-class views and regarded as entirely legiti-mate the participation of artisans and even laborers in the political process.

In 1762, Otis, speaking against the conservative rulers of the Massachusetts colony represented by Thomas Hutchinson, gave an example of the kind of rhetoric that a lawyer could use in mo-bilizing city mechanics and artisans:

> I am forced to get my living by the labour of my hand; and the sweat of my brow, as most of you are and obliged to go thro' good report and evil report, for bit-ter bread, earned under the frowns of some who have no natural or divine right to be above me, and entirely owe their grandeur and honor to grinding the faces of the poor. . . .

GRIEVANCES AGAINST THE RICH LEAD TO VIOLENCE

Boston seems to have been full of class anger in those days. In 1763, in the Boston *Gazette,* someone wrote that "a few persons in power" were promoting political projects "for keeping the people poor in order to make them humble."

This accumulated sense of grievance against the rich in Boston may account for the explosiveness of mob action after the Stamp Act of 1765. Through this Act, the British were taxing the colonial population to pay for the French war, in which colonists had suf-fered to expand the British Empire. That summer, a shoemaker named Ebenezer Macintosh led a mob in destroying the house of a rich Boston merchant named Andrew Oliver. Two weeks later, the crowd turned to the home of Thomas Hutchinson, symbol of the rich elite who ruled the colonies in the name of England. They smashed up his house with axes, drank the wine in his wine cellar, and looted the house of its furniture and other ob-jects. A report by colony officials to England said that this was part of a larger scheme in which the houses of fifteen rich people were to be destroyed, as part of "a War of Plunder, of general lev-elling and taking away the Distinction of rich and poor."

It was one of those moments in which fury against the rich

went further than leaders like Otis wanted. Could class hatred be focused against the pro-British elite, and deflected from the nationalist elite? In New York, that same year of the Boston house attacks, someone wrote to the New York *Gazette*, "Is it equitable that 99, rather 999, should suffer for the Extravagance or Grandeur of one, especially when it is considered that men frequently owe their Wealth to the impoverishment of their Neighbors?" The leaders of the Revolution would worry about keeping such sentiments within limits.

Mechanics were demanding political democracy in the colonial cities: open meetings of representative assemblies, public galleries in the legislative halls, and the publishing of roll-call votes, so that constituents could check on representatives. They wanted open-air meetings where the population could participate in making policy, more equitable taxes, price controls, and the election of mechanics and other ordinary people to government posts. . . .

In the countryside, where most people lived, there was a similar conflict of poor against rich, one which political leaders would use to mobilize the population against England, granting some benefits for the rebellious poor, and many more for themselves in the process. The tenant riots in New Jersey in the 1740s, the New York tenant uprisings of the 1750s and 1760s in the Hudson Valley, and the rebellion in northeastern New York that led to the carving of Vermont out of New York State were all more than sporadic rioting. They were long-lasting social movements, highly organized, involving the creation of countergovernments. They were aimed at a handful of rich landlords, but with the landlords far away, they often had to direct their anger against other, closer farmers who had leased the disputed land from the owners.

Just as the Jersey rebels had broken into jails to free their friends, rioters in the Hudson Valley rescued prisoners from the sheriff and one time took the sheriff himself as prisoner. The tenants were seen as "chiefly the dregs of the People," and the posse that the sheriff of Albany County led to Bennington in 1771 included the privileged top of the local power structure.

LAND RIOTS FROM VERMONT TO NORTH CAROLINA

The land rioters saw their battle as poor against rich. A witness at a rebel leader's trial in New York in 1766 said that the farmers evicted by the landlords "had an equitable Title but could not be defended in a Course of Law because they were poor and . . . poor men were always oppressed by the rich." Ethan Allen's Green Mountain rebels in Vermont described themselves as "a poor people . . . fatigued in settling a wilderness country," and their opponents as "a number of Attorneys and other gentlemen, with all their tackle of ornaments, and compliments, and French finesse."

Land-hungry farmers in the Hudson Valley turned to the British for support against the American landlords; the Green Mountain rebels did the same. But as the conflict with Britain intensified, the colonial leaders of the movement for independence, aware of the tendency of poor tenants to side with the British in their anger against the rich, adopted policies to win over people in the countryside.

In North Carolina, a powerful movement of white farmers was organized against wealthy and corrupt officials in the period from 1766 to 1771, exactly those years when, in the cities of the Northeast, agitation was growing against the British, crowding out class issues. The movement in North Carolina was called the Regulator movement, and it consisted, says Marvin L. Michael Kay, a specialist in the history of that movement, of "classconscious white farmers in the west who attempted to democratize local government in their respective counties." The Regulators referred to themselves as "poor Industrious peasants," as "labourers," "the wretched poor," "oppressed" by "rich and powerful . . . designing Monsters." . . .

TURNING ANGER TOWARD THE BRITISH

Fortunately for the Revolutionary movement, the key battles were being fought in the North, and here, in the cities, the colonial leaders had a divided white population; they could win over the mechanics, who were a kind of middle class, who had a stake in the fight against England, who faced competition from English manufacturers. The biggest problem was to keep the propertyless people, who were unemployed and hungry in the crisis following the French war, under control.

In Boston, the economic grievances of the lowest classes mingled with anger against the British and exploded in mob violence. The leaders of the Independence movement wanted to use that mob energy against England, but also to contain it so that it would not demand too much from them.

When riots against the Stamp Act swept Boston in 1767, they were analyzed by the commander of the British forces in North America, General Thomas Gage, as follows:

> The Boston Mob, raised first by the Instigation of Many of the Principal Inhabitants, Allured by Plunder, rose shortly after of their own Accord, attacked, robbed, and destroyed several Houses, and amongst others, that of the Lieutenant Governor. . . . People then began to be

> terrified at the Spirit they had raised, to perceive that
> popular Fury was not to be guided, and each individual
> feared he might be the next Victim to their Rapacity. The
> same Fears spread thro' the other Provinces, and there
> has been as much Pains taken since, to prevent Insur-
> rections, of the People, as before to excite them.

Gage's comment suggests that leaders of the movement against the Stamp Act had instigated crowd action, but then became frightened by the thought that it might be directed against their wealth, too. At this time, the top 10 percent of Boston's taxpayers held about 66 percent of Boston's taxable wealth, while the lowest 30 percent of the taxpaying population had no taxable property at all. The propertyless could not vote and so (like blacks, women, Indians) could not participate in town meetings. This included sailors, journeymen, apprentices, servants.

Dirk Hoerder, a student of Boston mob actions in the Revolutionary period, calls the Revolutionary leadership "the Sons of Liberty type drawn from the middling interest and well-to-do merchants . . . a hesitant leadership," wanting to spur action against Great Britain, yet worrying about maintaining control over the crowds at home.

REACTION TO THE STAMP ACT

It took the Stamp Act crisis to make this leadership aware of its dilemma. A political group in Boston called the Loyal Nine—merchants, distillers, shipowners, and master craftsmen who opposed the Stamp Act—organized a procession in August 1765 to protest it. They put fifty master craftsmen at the head, but needed to mobilize shipworkers from the North End and mechanics and apprentices from the South End. Two or three thousand were in the procession (Negroes were excluded). They marched to the home of the stampmaster and burned his effigy. But after the "gentlemen" who organized the demonstration left, the crowd went further and destroyed some of the stampmaster's property. These were, as one of the Loyal Nine said, "amazingly inflamed people." The Loyal Nine seemed taken aback by the direct assault on the wealthy furnishings of the stampmaster.

The rich set up armed patrols. Now a town meeting was called and the same leaders who had planned the demonstration denounced the violence and disavowed the actions of the crowd. As more demonstrations were planned for November 1, 1765, when the Stamp Act was to go into effect, and for Pope's Day, November 5, steps were taken to keep things under control; a dinner was given for certain leaders of the rioters to win them over. And when the Stamp Act was repealed, due to overwhelming resistance, the conservative leaders severed their connections with the rioters. They held annual celebrations of the first anti–Stamp Act demonstration, to which they invited, according to Hoerder, not the rioters but "mainly upper and middle-class Bostonians, who traveled in coaches and carriages to Roxbury or Dorchester for opulent feasts."

When the British Parliament turned to its next attempt to tax the colonies, this time by a set of taxes which it hoped would not excite as much opposition, the colonial leaders organized boycotts. But, they stressed, "No Mobs or Tumults, let the Persons and Properties of your most inveterate Enemies be safe." Samuel Adams advised: "No Mobs—No Confusions—No Tumult." And James Otis said that "no possible circumstances, though ever so oppressive, could be supposed sufficient to justify private tumults and disorders. . . ."

QUARTERING OF TROOPS

Impressment and the quartering of troops by the British were directly hurtful to the sailors and other working people. After 1768, two thousand soldiers were quartered in Boston, and friction grew between the crowds and the soldiers. The soldiers began to take the jobs of working people when jobs were scarce. Mechanics and shopkeepers lost work or business because of the colonists' boycott of British goods. In 1769, Boston set up a committee "to Consider of some Suitable Methods of employing the Poor of the Town, whose Numbers and distresses are dayly increasing by the loss of its Trade and Commerce."

On March 5, 1770, grievances of ropemakers against British soldiers taking their jobs led to a fight. A crowd gathered in front of the customhouse and began provoking the soldiers, who fired and killed first Crispus Attucks, a mulatto worker, then others. This became known as the Boston Massacre. Feelings against the British mounted quickly. There was anger at the acquittal of six of the British soldiers (two were punished by having their thumbs branded and were discharged from the army). The crowd at the Massacre was described by John Adams, defense attorney for the British soldiers, as "a motley rabble of saucy boys, negroes, and molattoes, Irish teagues and outlandish jack tarrs [sailors]." Perhaps ten thousand people marched in the funeral procession for the victims of the Massacre, out of a total Boston population of sixteen thousand. This led England to remove the troops from Boston and try to quiet the situation.

TWO PERSPECTIVES ON THE BOSTON MASSACRE

JAMES BOWDOIN, JOSEPH WARREN, SAMUEL PEMBERTON, AND CAPTAIN PRESTON

Quartering British soldiers of the twenty-ninth regiment in Boston created a conflict between the colonists and the soldiers. The conflict intensified until violence erupted on March 5, 1770, and colonists were killed. On March 6 at a Boston town meeting Boston citizens described the events of the previous day and appointed citizens James Bowdoin, Joseph Warren, and Samuel Pemberton to find out who had committed the "murders and massacres" of eleven people, and requested their written report by March 19. Their report, which was reprinted by Frederic Kidder in *History of the Boston Massacre* with modernized punctuation, capitalization, and spelling, includes summaries of several depositions and the authors' interpretation of the information they gathered.

After first publishing the colonists' report of the Boston Massacre, the April 1770 issue of *The Gentleman's Magazine* published the explanation by Captain Preston, the British officer on guard at the time of the event. According to Preston, British soldiers reacted to the colonists' verbal and physical abuse only when they feared their lives were in danger. Preston reports that three colonists were killed.

Excerpted from *History of the Boston Massacre* (Albany: J. Munsell, 1870) by James Bowdoin, Joseph Warren, Samuel Pemberton, and Captain Preston, edited by Frederic Kidder.

Jane Usher declares, that about 9 o'clock on Monday morning the 5th of March current, from a window she saw two persons in the habit of soldiers, one of whom being on horseback appeared to be an officer's servant. The person on the horse first spoke to the other, but what he said, she is not able to say, though the window was open, and she not more than twenty feet distant; the other replied, "he hoped he should see blood enough spilt before morning."

Matthew Adams declares, that on Monday evening the 5th of March instant, between the hours of 7 and 8 o'clock, he went to the house of Corporal Pershall of the 29th regiment, near Quaker lane, where he saw the corporal and his wife, with one of the fifers of said regiment. When he had got what he went for, and was coming away, the corporal called him back, and desired him with great earnestness to go home to his master's house as soon as business was over, and not to be abroad on any account that night in particular, for "the soldiers were determined to be revenged on the ropewalk people; and that much mischief would be done." Upon which the fifer (about eighteen or nineteen years of age), said "he hoped in God they would burn the town down." On this he left the house, and the said corporal called after him again, and begged he would mind what he said to him.

Caleb Swan declares, that on Monday night, the 5th of March instant, at the time of the bells ringing for fire, he heard a woman's voice, whom he knew to be the supposed wife of one Montgomery, a grenadier of the 29th regiment, standing at her door, and heard her say, *"it was not fire; the town was too haughty and too proud; and that many of their arses would be laid low before the morning."*

Margaret Swansborough declares, that a free woman named Black Peg, who has kept much with the soldiers, on hearing the disturbance on Monday evening the 5th instant, said, "the soldiers were not to be trod upon by the inhabitants, but would know before morning, whether they or the inhabitants were to be masters."

Joseph Hooton, jun., declares, that coming from the Southend of Boston on Monday evening the 5th of March instant, against Dr. Sewall's meeting he heard a great noise and tumult, with the cry of murder often repeated. Proceeding towards the Townhouse he was passed by several soldiers running that way, with naked cutlasses and bayonets in their hands. He asked one of them what was the matter, and was answered by him, "by God you shall all know what is the matter soon." Between 9 and 10 o'clock he went into King street, and was present at the tragical scene exhibited near the Custom-house; as particularly set forth in his deposition. . . .

SOLDIERS THREATEN AND PROVOKE LOCAL CITIZENS

By the foregoing depositions it appears very clearly, there was a general combination among the soldiers of the 29th regiment at least, to commit some extraordinary act of violence upon the town; that if the inhabitants attempted to repel it by firing even one gun upon those soldiers, the 14th regiment were ordered to be in readiness to assist them; and that on the late butchery in King street they actually were ready for that purpose, had a single gun been fired on the perpetrators of it.

It appears by a variety of depositions, that on the same evening between the hours of six and half after nine (at which time the firing began), many persons, without the least provocation, were in various parts of the town insulted and abused by parties of armed soldiers patrolling the streets; particularly:

Mr. Robert Pierpont declares, that between the hours of 7 and 8 in the same evening, three armed soldiers passing him, one of them who had a bayonet gave him a back-handed stroke with it. On complaint of this treatment, he said the deponent[1] should soon hear more of it, and threatened him very hard.

Mr. Henry Bass declares, that at 9 o'clock, a party of soldiers came out of Draper's alley, leading to and from Murray's barracks, and they being armed with large naked cutlasses, made at every body coming in their way, cutting and slashing, and that he himself very narrowly escaped receiving a cut from the foremost of them, who pursued him. . . .

Capt. James Kirkwood declares, that about 9 of the clock in the evening of the 5th day of March current, he was going by Murray's barracks: hearing a noise he stopped at Mr. Rhoads's door, opposite the said barracks, where said Rhoads was standing, and stood some time, and saw the soldiers coming out of the yard from the barracks, armed with cutlasses and bayonets, and rushing through Boylston's alley into Cornhill, two officers, namely, Lieuts. Minchin and Dickson, came out of the mess-house, and said to the soldiers, "My lads, come into the barracks and don't hurt the inhabitants," and then retired into the mess-house. Soon after they came to the door again, and found the soldiers in the yard; and directly upon it, Ensign Mall came to the gate of the barrack-yard and said to the soldiers, *"Turn out, and I will stand by you;"* this he repeated frequently, adding, *"Kill them! stick them! knock them down; run your bayonets through them;"* with a great deal of language of like import. Upon which a great number of soldiers came out of the barracks with naked cutlasses, headed

---

1. a person who testifies under oath

by said Mall, and went through the aforesaid alley; that some officers came and got the soldiers into their barracks, and that Mall, with his sword or cutlass drawn in his hand, as often had them out again, but were at last drove into their barracks by the aforesaid Minchin and Dickson. . . .

Samuel Drowne declares that, about nine o'clock of the evening of the fifth of March current, standing at his own door in Cornhill, he saw about fourteen or fifteen soldiers of the 29th regiment, who came from Murray's barracks, armed with naked cutlasses, swords, &c., and came upon the inhabitants of the town, then standing or walking in Cornhill, and abused some, and violently assaulted others as they met them; most of whom were without so much as a stick in their hand to defend themselves, as he very clearly could discern, it being moonlight, and himself being one of the assaulted persons. All or most of the said soldiers he saw go into King street (some of them through Royal Exchange lane), and there followed them, and soon discovered them to be quarrelling and fighting with the people whom they saw there, which he thinks were not more than a dozen, when the soldiers came there first, armed as aforesaid. Of those dozen

Tensions between British soldiers quartered in Boston and the city's residents erupted in violence on March 5, 1770.

people, the most of them were gentlemen, standing together a little below the Town-house, upon the Exchange. At the appearance of those soldiers so armed, the most of the twelve persons went off, some of them being first assaulted.

The violent proceedings of this party, and their going into King street, "quarrelling and fighting with the people whom they saw there" (mentioned in Mr. Drowne's deposition), was immediately introductory to the grand catastrophe.

THE CONFLICT ESCALATES INTO VIOLENCE

These assailants, who issued from Murray's barracks (so called), after attacking and wounding divers persons in Cornhill, as above mentioned, being armed, proceeded (most of them) up the Royal Exchange lane into King street; where, making a short stop, and after assaulting and driving away the few they met there, they brandished their arms and cried out, "Where are the boogers! where are the cowards!" At this time there were very few persons in the street beside themselves. This party in proceeding from Exchange lane into King street, must pass the sentry posted at the westerly corner of the Custom-house, which butts on that lane and fronts on that street. This is needful to be mentioned, as near that spot and in that street the bloody tragedy was acted, and the street actors in it were stationed: their station being but a few feet from the front side of the said Custom-house. The outrageous behavior and the threats of the said party occasioned the ringing of the meeting-house bell near the head of King street, which bell ringing quick, as for fire, it presently brought out a number of the inhabitants, who being soon sensible of the occasion of it, were naturally led to King street, where the said party had made a stop but a little while before, and where their stopping had drawn together a number of boys, round the sentry at the Custom-house. Whether the boys mistook the sentry for one of the said party, and thence took occasion to differ with him, or whether he first affronted them, which is affirmed in several depositions; however that may be, there was much foul language between them, and some of them, in consequence of his pushing at them with his bayonet, threw snowballs at him,[2] which occasioned him to knock hastily at the door of the

---

2. Since writing this narrative, several depositions have appeared, which make it clear that the sentry was first in fault. He overheard a barber's boy saying, that a captain of the 14th (who had just passed by) was so mean a fellow as not to pay his barber for shaving him. Upon this the sentry left his post and followed the boy into the middle of the street, where he told him to show his face. The boy pertly replied, "I am not ashamed to show my face to any man." Upon this the sentry gave him sweeping stroke on the head with his musket, which made him reel and stagger, and cry much.

Custom-house. From hence two persons thereupon proceeded immediately to the mainguard, which was posted (opposite to the State-house) at a small distance, near the head of the said street. The officer on guard was Capt. Preston, who with seven or eight soldiers, with fire-arms and charged bayonets, issued from the guard house, and in great haste posted himself and his soldiers in the front of the Custom-house, near the corner aforesaid. In passing to this station the soldiers pushed several persons with their bayonets, driving through the people in so rough a manner that it appeared they intended to create a disturbance. This occasioned some snowballs to be thrown at them, which seems to have been the only provocation that was given. Mr. Knox (between whom and Capt. Preston there was some conversation on the spot) declares, that while he was talking with Capt. Preston, the soldiers of his detachment had attacked the people with their bayonets; and that there was not the least provocation given to Capt. Preston or his party; the backs of the people being toward them when the people were attacked. He also declares that Capt. Preston seemed to be in great haste and much agitated, and that, according to his opinion, there were not then present in King street above seventy or eighty persons at the extent.

The said party was formed into a half circle; and within a short time after they had been posted at the Custom-house, began to fire upon the people.

Captain Preston is said to have ordered them to fire, and to have repeated that order. One gun was fired first; then others in succession, and with deliberation, till ten or a dozen guns were fired; or till that number of discharges were made from the guns that were fired. By which means eleven persons were killed and wounded, as above represented. . . .

RESTORING ORDER AFTER THE MASSACRE

Soon after the firing, a drum with a party from the main guard went to Murray's and the other barracks, beating an alarm as they went, which, with the firing, had the effect of a signal for action. Whereupon all the soldiers of the 29th regiment, or the main body of them, appeared in King street under arms, and seemed bent on a further massacre of the inhabitants, which was with great difficulty prevented. They were drawn up between the State-house and main guard, their lines extending across the street and facing down King street, where the town-people were assembled. The first line kneeled, and the whole of the first platoon presented their guns ready to fire, as soon as the word should be given. They continued in that posture a considerable time; but by the good providence of God they were restrained from firing. That they then went into King street with such a disposition will appear probable by the two following depositions.

Mrs. Mary Gardner, living in Atkinson street, declares, that on Monday evening the 5th of March current, and before the guns fired in King street, there were a number of soldiers assembled from Green's barracks towards the street, and opposite to her gate; that they stood very still until the guns were fired in King street; then they clapped their hands and gave a cheer, saying, "This is all that we want." They ran to their barrack, and came out again in a few minutes, all with their arms, and ran towards King street.

William Fallass declares, that (after the murder in King street) on the evening of the 5th instant, upon his return home, he had occasion to stop opposite to the lane leading to Green's barracks, and while he stood there, the soldiers rushed by him with their arms, towards King street, saying: "This is our time or chance;" and that he never saw men or dogs so greedy for their prey as those soldiers seemed to be, and the sergeants could hardly keep them in their ranks.

These circumstances, with those already mentioned, amount to a clear proof of a combination among them to commit some outrage upon the town on that evening; and that after the enormous one committed in King street, they intended to add to the horrors of that night by making a further slaughter.

At the time Capt. Preston's party issued from the main guard, there were in King street about two hundred persons, and those were collected there by the ringing of the bell in consequence of the violences of another party, that had been there a very little while before. When Captain Preston had got to the Custom-house, so great a part of the people dispersed at sight of the soldiers, that not more than twenty or thirty then remained in King street, as Mr. Drowne declares, and at the time of the firing not seventy, as Mr. Palmes thinks.

But after the firing, and when the slaughter was known, which occasioned the ringing of all the bells of the town, a large body of the inhabitants soon assembled in King street, and continued there the whole time the 29th regiment was there under arms, and would not retire till that regiment, and all the soldiers that appeared, were ordered, and actually went, to their barracks: after which, having been assured by the Lieutenant-Governor, and a number of the civil magistrates present, that every legal step should be taken to bring the criminals to justice, they gradually dispersed. For some time the appearance of things was dismal. The soldiers outrageous on the one hand, and the inhabitants justly incensed against them on the other; both parties seeming disposed to come to action. In this case the consequences would have been terrible. But by the interposition of his honor, some of his majesty's council, a number of civil magistrates, and other gentlemen of weight and influence, who all endeavored to calm and pacify the people, and by the two principal officers interposing their authority with regard to the soldiers, there was happily no further bloodshed ensued; and by two o'clock the town was restored to a tolerable state of quiet. About that time, Capt Preston, and a few hours after, the party that had fired, were committed to safe custody.

One happy effect has arisen from this melancholy affair, and it is the general voice of the town and province it may be a lasting one—all the troops are removed from the town. They are quartered for the present in the barracks at Castle island; from whence it is hoped they will have a speedy order to remove entirely out of the province, together with those persons who were the occasion of their coming hither.

THE FRENCH FOUND NEW FRANCE IN CANADA

ALFRED LEROY BURT

Alfred Leroy Burt follows the establishment of a French colony in Canada by describing the leadership of four men. He calls Samuel de Champlain "the Father of Canada" because he secured the first colonists in 1632, following a treaty with England. He attributes Jean Talon with an increase in the population of New France, Bishop Laval with the foundation of the Canadian church, and Count Frontenac with protection of the colony until the struggle with the British. Burt taught at the University of Alberta and the University of Minnesota. He is the author of many books, including *The Romance of the Prairie, The Old Province of Quebec,* and *The Romance of Canada.*

Every Canadian today, English as well as French, knows Champlain, for he is the father of their country. Both races revere him, for he was a man above reproach. To this soldier, sailor, explorer, geographer, and author, whom merchants knew as a manager, the king as a loyal friend, and the church as a devout son, Canada owes more than to any other man. He dominated French colonial effort from the time he founded Quebec until he died there. More than once he saved the colony from being abandoned. All seemed lost in 1629 when he was obliged to surrender the little settlement to conquerors from England, and he himself was carried off to England as a prisoner of war. At the end of this, his twenty-fourth voyage across the Atlantic,

Excerpted from *A Short History of Canada for Americans,* 2nd edition, by Alfred Leroy Burt. Copyright © 1942, 1944 by The University Press of Minnesota. Reprinted with permission from The University Press of Minnesota.

he found he was a free man because peace had been signed, and at once he threw all his weight behind French diplomacy to force a recovery of New France.

The treaty of restitution was signed in 1632 and in the following year Champlain returned to the land he had made his own, bringing with him a hundred colonists to join the few he had advised to remain under the conquerors. In 1634 he welcomed forty more from France and established Three Rivers as another trading post and nucleus of settlement. At last his colony was taking root, but he did not live long to see it, for his body had been sadly worn by a life of frequent hardship and incessant toil. In the autumn of 1635 he fell ill, and on Christmas night he died. The spot where he was buried is still a matter of dispute but Canadians have the satisfaction of knowing that his body was laid away somewhere in the heart of the colony that was his only child.

THE ARRIVAL OF THE JESUITS

For almost a generation the governors who followed Champlain were ordinary men who could not begin to fill his shoes. This was a period of neglect when the government of France, distracted by foreign and domestic wars, seemed almost to have forgotten the existence of New France. But the church of France did not slumber, and through it came practically all the strength that New France received from the mother country during this time. Already one of the most glorious chapters in the history of Christian missions had begun in North America.

The principal heroes were the Jesuits, the greatest missionary society in the world. The black-robed priests aspired to convert and civilize the whole continent of red men, to establish the kingdom of heaven in the New World, and they set about their mighty task in a strategic manner. Though not neglecting the nearer but inferior nomadic Algonkins of the St. Lawrence and Ottawa valleys, they put forth their chief effort where it promised to be more effective—among the Hurons. These were a superior agricultural people who lived south of Georgian Bay, about fifty miles north of the present city of Toronto, and were beginning to serve the French trade as middlemen by drawing furs from a widening circle of surrounding tribes. By 1640 the Jesuits had definitely established themselves in this center, and the light was spreading.

Montreal, now the second largest French city in the world, was founded in 1642, a by-product of this missionary endeavor. Over in France the reports of the missionaries were published annually, and these *Jesuit Relations,* as they were called, were eagerly devoured by many readers and inspired a number of pious people to establish some of the best known religious foundations of Canada. . . .

LOUIS XIV SENDS SOLDIERS AND NEW GOVERNING OFFICIALS

Louis XIV, *le roi soleil* [the sun king], took over the colony from the merchants in 1663 and determined to make it strong. Two years later a new set of officials, able men, arrived in Quebec accompanied by the first body of regular soldiers to be sent out from France; and a new day dawned on the St. Lawrence. This Carignan-Salières regiment of six hundred men is by far the most important military unit in Canadian history. It quickly cured the scourge that had been sapping the life of the colony. The Iroquois fled in panic when these troops invaded their country, and from their hiding places they saw their strongly fortified towns, with all their stocks of food, disappear in flames lit by the avenging French. Having learned a great lesson by the light of these fires, a large deputation of chiefs went down to Quebec to beg for peace. And this was only the beginning of what these soldiers did for Canada.

The colony now found its feet under the guidance of three outstanding men. One was Jean Talon, the first and greatest intendant of New France. The office he held, for which there is no English equivalent, is explained by what was happening in France. There the monarchy was becoming more absolute and efficient by undermining the position of the semi-independent provincial governors, relics of the feudal nobility, in favor of career men who, with the title of intendant, were entrusted with much of the business of provincial administration. This development, having proved its value at home, was carried into the French possessions overseas, where, however, the governor retained more power than his namesake in France. The new official was immediately responsible for "justice, police, and finance," while the old official, as the personal representative of the king, had general supervision over the government of New France and was also military commander in chief. As might be expected, there were quarrels between these two functionaries, but there was little friction until after the first intendant had left the country.

Talon straightway saw that the colony's most pressing need, after protection, was more population, for it had barely reached 3,000. If, he had had his way, the French would have greatly outnumbered the English in America, and that would have been quite possible because there were then about four Frenchmen for every Englishman in the world. But settlers would not come voluntarily. . . . As it was, colonists had to be found and sent out by the government, and all Talon's pleadings brought only a few hundred a year. The majority were women, to balance the usual surplus of men found in every new country, and there was a merry marriage market when the ships arrived. What the intendant could not get by ship he sought in the cradle, encouraging early marriages and large families by generous bounties. He also had penalties imposed on recalcitrant bachelors. If they were caught hunting, or fishing, or trading with the Indians, or going into the woods on any pretext whatever—activities that he denied them by law—they were turned over to the courts. From the time Talon arrived until he finally departed in 1672 the population doubled, and thenceforth there was hardly any immigration from France. From such a small number of families are the French Canadian people descended! That is why it is easy for many of them to tell offhand if a French surname is Canadian or not. Here it may also be of interest to note that a genealogical dictionary of all French Canadians from the first settlement until after the British conquest has been published in seven volumes by the Abbé Tanguay.

Talon was interested in more than numbers. Finding that many of the Carignan-Salières regiment were willing to take their discharge in this country, he planted them as a military colony along the Richelieu to bar the gate through which the dreaded Iroquois used to come. The names of various officers of the unit—such as Chambly—are printed on the map of this region, for the places where they settled were called after them. . . .

Before [Talon] came the colony never produced enough food or clothing for its own needs and had to depend upon supplies sent out from France, but before he left, its much larger appetite was fully satisfied by local production and he was able to report "I am now clothed from foot to head with home-made articles."

BISHOP LAVAL ESTABLISHES A CHURCH

A very different man from the intendant was Bishop Laval, the father of the Canadian church. Born of one of the most illustrious noble families in France—his full name was François Xavier de Laval-Montmorency—and endowed with great natural ability, he had a brilliant worldly career before him until he renounced it to follow the Cross. When he first came out, in 1659, he found the colony in a miserable plight, and when he went home for a visit in 1662 he used all his powerful influence with the government to do something for Canada. Many think that he was chiefly responsible for the vital change that began in the following year, when the king took over the colony.

But it is not for this that his name stands out in Canadian history. Every Canadian knows him for the work he had already undertaken very soon after he first set foot in Quebec. Until his arrival the colonists had no clergy of their own apart from the missionaries. Laval resolved to establish a real Canadian church, for which he procured a royal decree in the spring of 1663 on the eve of his return to New France. He was of course the head of the new organization, but the heart and soul of it was the seminary that he founded in Quebec. It was a training college for young Canadians entering the priesthood, and it was much more; it was the home of the clergy. Laval would not allow them to be appointed to parishes permanently but insisted that they return every now and then to live in the seminary for a short while. There, in conversation, reading, and prayer, they rested and gained new life, which was of untold value when they went out to continue their labors; and, instead of being a number of individuals going their own several ways, they were knit together as one family. To support them, the decree just mentioned introduced the tithe. . . . After he resigned his office in 1688 regular parishes were organized with their own priests, but the seminary was still their home. . . .

Count Frontenac Temporarily Secures the Colony

The third great figure of this period was the central hero of Francis Parkman's epic history, Count Frontenac dubbed "The Fighting Governor." At fifteen he entered the army, at twenty-three he was a colonel, and at twenty-six a brigadier general. Shortly afterward the coming of peace turned him into a courtier, but his noble birth was his only qualification for this career. His pride would not let him stoop to please, and it placed such a strain upon his lean purse that he lived above his means and fell into debt. In 1672 he seized the offer of the appointment as governor of New France, and then, though he was past fifty, he entered upon the most active and glorious years of his life. He loved pomp and power, and he knew how to use them; but he could brook no rival. The first to cross his path was François Perrot, the governor of Montreal, who claimed a certain independence in his local command and was a competitor in the fur trade. Frontenac crushed him. The poor fellow was arrested and sent to France, where he spent some little time in the Bastille [prison] before he returned to Montreal a much subdued man. No one else in the colony dared to challenge this high and mighty governor during his first three years. In 1675, however, a ship arrived bringing not only Bishop Laval, who had been in France for four years, but also a successor to Talon, whose office had been left vacant for three years.

At once the colony proved far too small to hold three such big men, but we must not cast upon Frontenac the whole blame for the rows that followed. In the absence of a successor to Talon the home government had allowed the governor to exercise also the authority of the intendant, and Frontenac naturally resented the new appointment, which clipped his wings. The two heads of the Canadian government, who were intended to be a sort of check upon each other, quarreled violently and openly and fined their correspondence home with all manner of mutual accusations. Nor was Frontenac wholly responsible for his quarrel with Laval. The governor belonged to the anti-Jesuit faction in France, whereas the bishop was a firm friend of the Jesuits; and the home government, jealous of ecclesiastical power in the colony, had instructed the governor to keep the church in its place. Naturally the bishop and the intendant worked together to keep the governor in his place. For seven years the strife raged until the home government could stand it no longer, and in 1682 both the governor and the intendant were replaced, while the bishop, who could not be removed in this way, remained and seemed to stand out as the victor. But after another seven years Frontenac returned in triumph because he had already demonstrated how indispensable he was to the colony.

Frontenac's great service to Canada was to give it security. When he first arrived in Quebec it was becoming obvious that the fiery lesson administered to the Iroquois just a few years before was losing its effect. . . .

With the strongest force he could muster he ascended the St. Lawrence to Lake Ontario and there, at Cataraqui, where Kingston now stands, he met the Iroquois, who came in answer to his summons. Then followed many days of talking, feasting, and toiling. The toil was performed by Frontenac's men, who were building a strong fort under the very eyes of the Iroquois envoys and in the midst of the country that they had come to regard as their own. But the Iroquois did not object; there were too many armed Frenchmen. . . .

When his guests went home and the governor departed, the whole face of things had changed. Fort Frontenac, firmly built and strongly garrisoned, stood at the foot of Lake Ontario to keep the stream of furs flowing down the St. Lawrence and to serve as an advance post for further French expansion into the interior. It was also a reminder and a threat; it reminded the Iroquois that the eyes of the great governor were upon them, and it threatened them with the thunder of his wrath if they should dare to provoke it. As long as Frontenac remained in Quebec, they would be no problem.

That he alone could hold them in awe became more and more apparent after his recall in 1682. First one and then another governor came, but neither could hold the Iroquois in check. By the end of seven years Frontenac's work was undone. . . . To make matters worse, war had broken out between France and England. New France was in peril, and old France, engaged in war at home, felt unable to send military aid. But Frontenac was an army in himself, and in the fall of 1689 he returned to save the colony.

Thenceforth the history of New France is more or less overshadowed by the great struggle for empire that ended with the British conquest.

THE FALL OF QUEBEC ENDS THE FRENCH EMPIRE IN CANADA

GUY FRÉGAULT

Before the American Revolution in 1776, North America was composed of the British and the French Empires. The Seven Years' War, fought in Europe from 1756 until 1763, spilled over into a war between the French and English in North America. The fall of Quebec was the turning point of French power. Guy Frégault describes the British euphoria following the victory and analyzes the French military and political practices that caused the French defeat. Finally, he explains British offers to Canadians that persuaded them to be receptive to British rule. Frégault taught history at the University of Montreal in Quebec. He is the author of *Histoire de la Vouvelle France: La grerre de Conquite, 1754–1760* and *Canadian Society in the French Regime*.

Songs of victory echoed throughout the British empire. Britons rejoiced at the fall of Niagara, but it was the capture of Quebec that carried them to the heights of enthusiasm and to the most extravagant expressions of joy. The case of the young Scottish officer [James Abercrombie] who in September 1759 made the following admission in a letter to [Louis-Antoine de] Bougainville was certainly an isolated one: ["My dear confrère, I am of the same opinion as [Voltaire] in Candide that we are fighting for a few acres of snow in that country."] French culture had obviously left its mark on him; he was quite out of tune with the feelings of the British court and people. The

Excerpted from *Canada: The War of the Conquest*, by Guy Frégault, translated by Margaret M. Cameron. Copyright © 1969 by Oxford University Press, Canada. Reprinted with permission from Oxford University Press, Canada.

Russian ambassador to the court of St. James's was at a loss for words "to describe the joy and general enthusiasm" inspired by the capture of Quebec. He added, doubtless echoing what was being said around him, that "it would decide once and for all the American question that has been the cause and origin of this bloody war." Cannon in Hyde Park and at the Tower of London gave the signal for bonfires and fireworks; the whole United Kingdom followed the example set by its capital city, and the king declared 29 November a day of thanksgiving. One London journalist felt overwhelmed by "so stupendous a blessing of Providence" as the conquest of Quebec; it would take time for him to become accustomed to the idea. In a speech couched in a style even more grandiloquent than was his wont, [British political leader William] Pitt lamented the death of the victorious young general at the height of his glory. The prime minister, wrote [British writer and historian Horace] Walpole, "speaking in a low and plaintive voice, pronounced a kind of funeral oration." The speech, although it suggested that Mr. Pitt had done more for Great Britain than any orator for Rome, "was perhaps the worst harangue he ever uttered," but it created the [military leader James] Wolfe legend. The people of England were transported with admiration and enthusiasm. "Carthage may boast of her Hannibal," proclaimed the *Monitor*, "and Rome may decree triumphs to her Scipio, but true courage never appeared more glorious than in the death of the British Wolfe." "Who," asked another admirer, "wrote, like Caesar, from before Quebec?—Who, like Epaminondas, died in glory? . . . Who bequeathed Canada as a triumphant legacy?—Proclaim—'Twas WOLFE." Wolfe would forever be named *"The Conqueror of Canada."* Rejoicing was at least as fervent in the colonies as in the mother country. In Boston "the general joy which appeared on this occasion was perhaps as great as ever known." New Yorkers, for whom "the consequences of such a victory" were happy "in an especial manner," were delirious with joy. Once again the words of [Boston minister] Samuel Cooper speaking from the pulpit struck a deeper note: "God has heard our prayers and those of our progenitors—We behold the day which they desired to see, but saw it not—We have received a salvation from Heaven greater perhaps than any since the foundation of the country—The power of Canada is broken."

THE DETERIORATION OF THE FRENCH MILITARY

At the end of 1759 Canada was no more than a shadow of itself. The deluge had passed, leaving in its wake only a broken stump of country along the St. Lawrence between the rapids and the Jacques-Cartier River. Although the "residue" of military forces holding out inside a circle of ruins could still surprise the victors, in the field of imperial strategy France and Britain judged correctly when they wrote off Canada as a French colony. Its final destruction, as [British military leader Jeffrey] Amherst concluded after a conversation with Major [James] Grant in New York, could not be delayed more than a few months. Grant was more familiar with conditions in Canada than any other Englishman in America. Taken prisoner in 1758 near Fort Du Quesne, he had had occasion to observe the enemy at first hand and to talk frequently to their officers. At the request of his commander-in-chief he wrote a report on what he had learned. The Canadians, according to this report, were all "heartily tired" of the war. Those for whom the war had been an opportunity to amass great fortunes had hastened to place their money in safety in France. The common people were "harassed," and extremely reluctant to go on fighting without pay and almost without rations. Their leaders encouraged them with "the hopes of peace in the spring," and if peace did not come soon most of the population would "wish to fall into the hands of the English." The government was still strong enough to keep the people under arms, but if they were disappointed in their hopes of an early peace and the arrival of a French fleet, Canadian resistance would suddenly crumble. Amherst drew the conclusion that "from the present posts his majesty's army is now in possession of, [even] if no stroke was to be made, Canada must fall or the inhabitants starve."

Grant's report was a good one as far as it went, but it did not go quite far enough, in that it was too narrowly limited to the military aspect of the situation. Even so, it presented a terrifying picture. [French military leader François-Gaston] Lévis counted up the fighting men he would have under his orders when the campaign was resumed in the spring of 1760: a maximum of 3,600 regulars with little or no equipment; the militia from the governments of Montreal and Trois-Rivières, and it would be "difficult to muster them"; about a thousand Indians, provided France sent out a squadron, for "otherwise we shall be lucky if they are not against us." It was absolutely essential that supplies be sent from the mother country. Without supplies, the general foresaw that Canada would be forced "by want" to surrender. This gloomy prospect did not differ from the one that Amherst had evoked. With only 3,600 regulars the high command had to rely more than ever on the militia, and the militiamen were at the end of their tether. Those who had returned to their homes after the "Quebec affair" and who were called back to the colours "reported sick." In most cases, as [Governor-General Pierre de Rigaud] Vaudreuil recognized, this was not a pretext to avoid military service: "There are now in all the parishes more sick than well." The commander of Fort Lévis at the rapids saw his garrison melting away. Although he took great care to grant leave only to those who were "really ill," he had to allow a large number of his men to go: "only a small number of troopers," but "many" Canadians, because the latter, ill-clothed and underfed, "were more subject to illness" than the regulars.

THE DETERIORATION OF CANADIAN MORALE

The morale of the Canadian people was more seriously impaired even than their health. The main action of the tragedy of the conquest took place in the minds of the people. The first blow to their spirit of resistance came from the attitude of France and the French people. The mother country had abandoned Canada in her hour of danger, and British propaganda hastened to make the most of this tactical error. France, proclaimed Wolfe, "unable to support her peoples, abandons their cause in the moment of crisis." Still more serious, statements similar to Wolfe's had been current in Canada for years. One such complaint was made as early as 1752: "It appears that the king is not much concerned for this colony." The reflection was repeated in stronger terms early in 1761: "The court is very ill-disposed towards Canada." Bitter disillusionment did not, however, prevent the people of Canada from rallying from every part of the country to the defence of Quebec.

However, some weeks after the battle of 13 September a British dispatch reported that "the poor remains of the French army (about ten thousand Canadians)" had retired to the Jacques-Cartier River, but that "the Canadians [were] deserting in great numbers every day and coming in to surrender themselves and taking the oath of allegiance to his Britannic Majesty." The form of the oath was explicit: ["I promise and swear solemnly before God, that I will be loyal to His Britannic Majesty, King George the Second, that I will not take up arms against him, and that I will give no information to his enemies that might harm him in any way."] One might have thought the conquest already consummated; if it had not been for the requirement not to furnish information to the French, one might have supposed that Canada had already been ceded to Great Britain. In Quebec, relations between victors and vanquished, though by no means idyllic, were generally good. It did happen that the body of an English soldier who had been mutilated and killed was found in a ditch, and [British military leader James] Murray resorted to punitive expeditions to keep the people in line. But these were normal incidents in a zone occupied by an invading army and contiguous to unoccupied territory. It is nonetheless surprising to see how easily the people of the Quebec government appear to have "reconciled themselves" to the occupying army. A number of individuals returning behind the French lines declared themselves "quite satisfied with their good treatment at the hands of the English." On occasion cordial relationships developed between British soldiers and the local inhabitants. British officers in authority were correct in their dealings with Canadians, and their attitude, though doubtless dictated by reasons of policy, had its effect.

IRRESPONSIBLE AND CORRUPT BEHAVIOR BY FRENCH SOLDIERS

It would be a mistake, however, to attribute to this one cause the rapid and easy pacification of a whole district whose population four or five months earlier had been offering fierce resistance to the invaders. What had happened since then? What had happened was that twice in the course of 13 September the Canadians had seen French battalions turn and run before the enemy. The first flight, from the field of battle, might have been redeemed by a vigorous counter-attack; but the second retreat, which began at ten o'clock at night after mature consideration on the part of the commanding officers, was fatal. This time military units ran as one man, so terrified that the soldiers in retreat "did not dare to pause or blow their noses," even though they were not pursued. Their panic-stricken flight was not forgotten and had far-reaching consequences. When, in mid-November, Murray put the question, "What can you expect from a weak army, hopelessly crushed and beaten?" he was without knowing it echoing the thoughts of the people of Quebec. No later than 15 September François Daine, the civil and criminal lieutenant-general, Jean-Claude Panet, the king's attorney, Jean Tachet, the merchants' syndic, and twenty-two other "bourgeois and citizens" of the capital presented a petition to [French military leader Jean-Baptiste-Nicolas-Roch de] Ramezay requesting him to initiate negotiations for surrender without delay. They represented to him that they had fought to the limit of their strength "until that fatal day" of 13 September, suffered bombardment for two months, supported privations, vigils, "fatiguing service." They had been sustained by the hope of victory and covered by an army. The army had disappeared and the only course open to them was surrender: "Even if three-quarters of their blood were shed, that would not prevent the last quarter [of the people] from falling under the yoke of the enemy." After the sudden collapse of military resistance, the people's resistance also collapsed, the more rapidly since it had already been undermined by two separate factors. The first of these was the nature of the defence organized by [French military leader Louis-Joseph] Montcalm: the policy of passivity that left the besieger free and gave him all the time he wanted to mount his batteries, manoeuvre as if on a parade ground, establish his different camps; a policy that would turn the war into a war of attrition—a type of warfare in which the morale of a people is much more susceptible to deterioration than is that of a professional army such as Wolfe's.

But there was more, infinitely more, than that; the complex nature of the defeat was revealed in the moment of crisis. Here the remark of an eyewitness of the rout of 13 September is particularly revealing: "Most of the Canadians of the Quebec district took advantage of the disorder to return home, caring little to which master they would belong henceforth." Too many Frenchmen considered themselves the "masters" of the Canadians. To come under the yoke of a foreign power was terrifying, but was it such a great misfortune to exchange one servitude for another? The people of the Quebec government were now living in country occupied by the English; they "were satisfied" with the conduct, of the British garrison towards them. Could it be that the enemy troops felt a certain natural sympathy for them? We must not be misled into thinking that the English had established the "country of Love" in the government of Quebec. Let us rather remember the attitude of the French army towards those same people. During the whole campaign Canadians had seen spread out before them the painful and disconcerting spectacle of undisciplined, drunken French soldiers, hungry for loot, giving themselves up to "the most unbridled license." The troopers had taken possession of private property and ravaged the country for several leagues around the places where they were stationed, under the conniving eye of Montcalm, who remained unmoved by the "jeremiads" [bitter laments] of the "dear Canadians." "Nothing," wrote a contemporary, "could equal the damage caused by the troops in every part of the countryside where the army has been encamped." It was even said that on one occasion when an alarm was sounded the general was informed "that he would have 500 fewer soldiers with which to meet the oncoming enemy" if he did not hasten to call his men back from "the depths of Charlebourg . . . where they were busy looting right in the houses." This scandalous conduct was flaunted so shamelessly that it was noticed even by the English. France sent soldiers to Canada, said Wolfe in one of his proclamations, and what good did they do? The answer followed: "They made [Canadians] feel more bitterly the weight of a hand that oppresses instead of helping them." A damning charge!

THE BRITISH OFFER CANADIANS AN ATTRACTIVE ALTERNATIVE

And that was still not all. Even without minimizing their psychological effect, the misdeeds of the French soldiery could be regarded as a passing ill, destined to disappear eventually with the return of more normal conditions. But it was not only by the fact that they were no longer exposed to the force of their arms that Canadians felt themselves drawn towards the English. Messages such as the one that appeared in Murray's declaration of November 1759 struck home: "We earnestly entreat you to have recourse to a free, wise, generous people, ready to offer you help, to free you from a harsh despotism and to share with you the benefits of a just moderate, and equitable government." The "despotism" referred to by the British military commander in Quebec was not embodied in political institutions; it was much more closely related to what is the essential element in any colonial establishment, the economic structure. Lévis, writing almost at the same time as Murray, made the observation that if France lost Canada, it would be "very difficult" for her to win the country back in another war. There were many reasons for this, but in his opinion one was paramount: "The Canadians, judging by what we see of them in Quebec, will not take long to get used to the English government because of the opportunities they will have for trade." The attitude to which Lévis referred was not entirely new. In the eyes of some Canadians a British régime would be a lesser evil than the state of oppression identified with the Great Society [a group of French oligarchs who became rich at the expense of Canadian merchants], whose monopoly reached into every sector of the country's economy. "They write from Quebec," noted Montcalm in the autumn of 1758, "that a large number of families are escaping to France. I say escaping, because they are fleeing from an enemy a thousand times more dangerous than the English." The comparison should be noted. A memorandum drawn up by Bougainville early in 1759 reported rumours current in the colony. "It was said" that the English would allow "freedom of religion," that they would supply traders with trading goods at lower prices than those demanded by the Compagnie des Indes, and that they would pay workmen "generously." These ideas, as the young officer pointed out, were spreading. They were being expressed "by some persons above the common people." Many Canadians were attracted by them, the townspeople especially.

[Great Society leader François] Bigot was furious at the sight of the capital's small merchants clinging for protection to the occupying authorities: "every individual in Quebec is busy advancing his own affairs; they have little thought for the interests of the king or of the colony." The commissary-general, [Joseph] Cadet, sent men to Quebec to carry out a mission in which an earlier team had failed, but the intendant foresaw that no good would come of their efforts: "I think that when they get there they will be bewitched by the English, like the others." It was the small tradesmen in Quebec, not the big businessmen, that fluttered about Murray. The latter stayed with the Canadian government, on which they held enormous credits, in Montreal, now the provisional capital of the country. The men who had been ousted by the all-powerful Franco-Canadian financial aristocracy, the unlucky competitors who for ten years had had to be satisfied with a modest rank in the feudal state set up in the business world by Bigot and his entourage—these were the vassals who paid faithful homage to the new suzerain and who crawled under the table in search of the crumbs to be picked up there. "All the French in Quebec," observed the intendant again, "seek to pay court in order to procure advantages for themselves. I know that because the merchants tell me so themselves." The first social class to lose its vitality, the first to disintegrate, was the class of small tradesmen.

THE SHIFT FROM FRENCH TO BRITISH EMPIRE

Was that American perhaps right, then, who in the autumn of 1759 judged 13 September an unhappy day for Montcalm and his troops, "but happy for Quebec and its inhabitants" since it made it possible for them to "enjoy the liberty to which they have hitherto been strangers"? Here we touch on the most elusive misunderstanding in the history of Canada. The last years of the French régime were painful, its last hours dreadful. The face of France reflected in her government and in many of her representatives in the colony was repulsive. That was true. But in spite of that, so long as France was present in America, Canada existed as a country—even though the royal government detached itself from it, even though it was ill-treated by the agents of that government. France might play her part badly, but it was not a useless part; she might agree to being replaced, but that did not make her replaceable. Admittedly France's policy was disastrous, but the remedy was not to be found in a still greater disaster—the conquest. An empire, let us repeat, is an organic whole. At that stage of its development the Canadian community was still an element in the French empire. Introduced into the British empire, it would be a foreign body that would have to be either dissolved or expelled. The evolution that began in the last months of 1759 announced that it would be dissolved. And already the nascent misunderstanding allowed it to be supposed that the process would be an unconscious one.

SOCIAL COMPLEXITY IN COLONIAL MEXICO

J.I. ISRAEL

Though J.I. Israel focuses on the status of Jews in the Spanish colony of Mexico, he also conveys information about the complex culture that had developed by the seventeenth century—the corruption, prejudices, economic development, and the effect of the Mexican Inquisition, a tribunal of the Catholic Church to suppress heresy. According to Israel, the Jews, by hiding their religion, operated in a variety of merchant and governing roles. In a crackdown in the early 1640s, however, Jews were discovered, arrested, tried, some tortured, and many shipped to Spain. The Jewish conflict is but a manifestation of several broader conflicts, especially those between the colonists and the parent country Spain. J.I. Israel taught history at University College London and the University of Newcastle upon Tyne in England; he is the author of *The Dutch Republic and the Hispanic World, 1606–1661* and *Empires and Entrepots: The Dutch, the Spanish Monarchy, and the Jews.*

T he issue of the foreigners in seventeenth-century Mexico is certainly complicated, indeed inextricably bound up, with the question of crypto-Judaism [Jews hiding their identity as Jews]. It is in fact impossible to determine the position of the non-Spanish white element in Mexican society solely in economic and legal terms, owing to the marked tendency in seventeenth-century Spanish America to confuse Portuguese with Portuguese New Christians and crypto-Jews, to overlook the abhorrence of Portuguese Old Christians for Portuguese New Christians, and to assume that the Portuguese, Jewish and non-Jewish, were

Excerpted from *Race, Class, and Politics in Colonial Mexico: 1610–1670,* by J.I. Israel. Copyright © 1975 by Oxford University Press. Reprinted with permission from Oxford University Press.

united in hatred of the Castilians. Recognition of this brings us to yet another tension in seventeenth-century Mexican society, that arising from religious intolerance and the mutual detestation of Catholic and Jew.

The Mexican Inquisition, it is important to note, though busily engaged against sorcery, bigamy, drug-taking, blasphemy, and solicitation of women by clergy at confession, reserved its chief effort, especially during the first half of the seventeenth century, for the suppression of Judaism. Cases of Mohammedanism and Protestantism were extremely rare, though neither was unknown, and when they did occur aroused the inquisitors' curiosity rather than their wrath. Solicitation of women by clergy employing Latin and the appurtenances of the faith as methods of seduction, though extremely common, was treated leniently and, as a matter of policy, was as far as possible kept from the public view; even the most debauched clergy such as the Jesuit Gaspar de Villenas, arraigned in 1621 for soliciting ninety-seven women from the confessional and actually having illicit relations with more than thirty, some on church premises, were not publicly disgraced and never appeared in *Autos-de-Fe* [inquisition ceremonies or executions]. Judaism alone aroused violent feelings because, of Spain's traditional religious enemies, only the Jews had slipped, by means of disguise, into the mainstream of Spanish life, and only the Jews were evident to any significant extent in seventeenth-century Spanish America. The traditional antipathy to the Jews reappeared in the New World with full force. "New Spain seethed with Jews," wrote the Mexican inquisitor Estrada y Escovedo in 1646, referring to the situation before 1642, "who, concealing their perfidy with constant deception, used to imitate Catholic conduct outwardly; a cruel nation, whose hatred of all the nations of the world is so great, that, if once the mask with which impatiently they conceal it were cast off, the volcano of its virulent hatred would erupt in the most appalling atrocities."

JEWS ARE TRIED AND PUNISHED BY THE INQUISITION

That the vast majority of secretly practising Jews, in seventeenth-century Mexico, were of Portuguese origin is quickly shown by a check through the Mexican Inquisition case books. In the three decades 1620–50, for instance, slightly more than 200 Jews were tried by the inquisitors, the bulk of them in the years 1642–6. Of these 200, slightly less than half had been born in Portugal, mainly at Lisbon and Castelobranco; another thirty-five or so were Mexican-born of Portuguese parents, while a further fifteen or twenty had been born of Portuguese Jewish parents in France,

Italy, and Peru. Of the remainder, most were the offspring of Portuguese crypto-Jews residing in Spain; scarcely a handful even might have been of Spanish origin and some, even of these, had Portuguese wives or mixed with the Portuguese circle. This overwhelming preponderance of Portuguese among the judaizers sentenced in Mexico demonstrates that in general there was no correlation in New Spain, and presumably therefore also in the rest of Spanish America, between New Christians, or Christians of Jewish descent, and crypto-Jews, or Jews only outwardly simulating Christianity. It may be safely assumed, though it can never be proved, that there were many more Spanish New Christians than Portuguese in Mexico, but that the Spanish New Christians had forsaken the old faith to a much greater extent. This is to be explained by the fact that Portuguese Jewry was largely descended from those Spanish Jews who had refused to convert to Catholicism in 1492, and had left Spain, while the Spanish New Christians were mainly descended from those who had converted, and stayed; also, the Portuguese Inquisition had been rather a feeble instrument in comparison with its Spanish counterpart, until the annexation of Portugal, to Spain in 1580, so that the Portuguese crypto-Jews had suffered only a minimum of pressure until a late stage. The preponderance of Portuguese Jews appearing in Mexican *Autos-de-Fe* in the seventeenth century is paralleled by a similar preponderance, though one not quite so complete, in the *Autos-de-Fe* of Spain itself in this period.

JEWISH IMMIGRATION AND WORK HISTORY

Of the role of the Jews in seventeenth-century Mexican society a certain amount can be ascertained. As with the rest of the foreign community, few of them lived in the silver-mining zones, including less than one-eighth of those arrested by the Inquisition. The three main Mexican Jewish centres were Mexico City, where about half of the Jews lived, and Veracruz and Guadalajara which accounted for nearly two-thirds of the remainder. Curiously, scarcely a handful resided in Puebla. The majority of the Jews were shopkeepers, craftsmen, peddlers, and vagabonds; but the élite of the community, men like Simón Váez Sevilla and Matías Rodríguez de Oliveira of Mexico City, and Francisco de Texoso of Veracruz, were wealthy merchants, some of the wealthiest of New Spain. Simón Váez, a native of Castelobranco, whose business contacts ranged from Manila in the Philippines to Pisa in Italy, where part of his family lived, had shops in Mexico City, Zacatecas, and other Mexican towns, and with over 200,000 pesos was of roughly equivalent worth to Manuel Bautista Pérez, who was head of the Jewish community in Peru until his arrest in 1635. Simón Váez presided over Mexican Jewry until the catastrophe of 1642, in company with his relative Captain Antonio Váez de Castelobranco, a merchant and messianic dreamer who had learned his Judaism in Pisa and who, among his various tenets, and much to the indignation of the inquisitors, denied the existence of hell. Most of the Jewish merchants had built up from small beginnings with remarkable speed, and had travelled and fought for a living in an astounding number of places. Mathías Rodríguez de Oliveira, born in Portugal, had lived in Madrid and Seville, obtained Negroes in Angola in person, taken his Negroes to Mexico and sold them, returned to Spain and then Lisbon, and then in 1630 returned to Mexico, where he amassed a considerable fortune and was one of the leaders of the Jewish community until he was seized in 1642 along with Simón Váez and most of his friends and Jewish associates. Julian de Alvarez, merchant and citizen of Cacacuero in Michoacán, had been born in Amsterdam, and had lived in Holland, Italy, and Spain. Francisco López Fonseca, known in Peru as Francisco Méndez, had lived in Coimbra and La Guardia in Portugal, Valladolid, Madrid, and Seville in Spain, Cartagena, Quito, Guayaquil, Riobamba, and Maracaibo in South America, and Veracruz and Mexico City in New Spain. . . . And so the list might be continued. It emerges from the details of the Jews seized by the Mexican Inquisition that the three areas of Mexican commerce with which Jewish entrepreneurs were most closely involved were the slave trade from Africa, the importing of cacao from Venezuela which first became an important element of Mexican commerce in the 1630s, and, most of all, the trade in Chinese, Spanish, northern European, and Mexican textiles.

Wealthy Jews, despite being Portuguese, could and did acquire social standing in Mexico, despite the fact that all, or nearly all of them, including Simón and Antonio Váez, were of very humble origin. The Portuguese were not popular in Mexico, but provided that Judaism was well enough concealed they could rise up the social ladder. Melchor Juarez, who was given away in 1643, escaped the clutches of the Inquisition chiefly because he was then secretary to the visitor-general Bishop Palafox. Jorge de Espinosa, alias Jorge Serrano, who had been in many parts of Spain, Brazil, and the Spanish Indies, was *corregidor* [bishop] of Coatzacoalcos in 1647, despite having been exposed as a Jew by the Peruvian Inquisition and "reconciled" to the Church in the *Auto-de-Fe* at Lima in January 1639. Captain Antonio Váez de Acevedo had commanded an infantry detachment in Mexico City in 1641 and was *corregidor* of Pampanga, in the Philippines, in 1648, when the Inquisition commissioners seized him. His brother, Captain Sebastian Váez de Acevedo, was appointed purveyor-general of the Armada of Barlovento, the Caribbean battle squadron, in 1640 by Viceroy Escalona. Simón Váez and Mathías Rodríguez, though merchants of humble birth, were reputable enough . . . to mix socially with *Audiencia* [court] judges. Simón Enríquez, the Portuguese member of the Mexico City council in the 1620s, despite his certificate purporting to prove that he was a Portuguese *fidalgo* [nobleman] of unsullied Old Christian descent, was very probably of Jewish origin.

JEWISH ATTITUDES

Regarding the attitudes of the Mexican Jews, a little can be said. Spanish suspicions of an inter-continental Jewish political conspiracy had, as far as one can tell, little or no basis in fact; apparently there is little to support Bishop Palafox's assertion that Amsterdam and Lisbon were "the only centres from which the Jews take orders." The Inquisition, despite its eagerness to expose Jewish subversiveness in all its forms, could find nothing more than an occasional indication that the Jews sympathized with the revolt of Portugal against Spain, and indeed with the Portuguese struggle against the Protestant Netherlands, and that Antonio Váez and Luis Núñez Pérez, the two visionaries of Mexican Jewry, had foretold that a great Armada would come from Portugal, conquer Mexico, and save the Jews from the Spaniards. What is abundantly clear is that Jews put their main trust in the Almighty, and if there was any to spare for the Dutch West India Company, it was very little by comparison.

JEWS EXPELLED

That the Jews were contemptuous of the Catholics whom they considered "blind beasts" seems plain enough, and it may also be, as is suggested by an account of Peru left by an anonymous Portuguese Jew in the second decade of the seventeenth century, that they tended to be disdainful of the Creoles, considering them feeble and lethargic, men who "have no wish to take risks or accept danger by land or sea to gain a living." The Indians, according to the anonymous chronicler at least, were the "most cowardly and timid people in the world so that one shout from a Spaniard is enough to make them tremble and a single white man is enough to put a hundred of them to flight." There is no evidence that any Mexican Jews agreed with the Amsterdam Rabbi Manasseh ben Israel, and a number of Spanish friars, who thought that the American Indians were the descendants of the ten lost tribes of Israel. As regards the religious life of the Mexican Jews, it is clear that their knowledge of Hebrew was very limited, but they were much better acquainted with Jewish laws and customs than is sometimes suggested, owing to the circumstance that six or seven of their leaders had lived in Italy as members of orthodox Jewish communities. Most of the prayers and psalms that they recited were in Spanish and Portuguese.

The question why the Jews remained within the territory of the Spanish Monarchy, taking a risk which in the end brought many or most of them to disaster, is not an easy one to answer. It does seem, however, that economic opportunities for Jews in such safe, or relatively safe, areas as France, Italy, or Brazil, were very limited as compared with the opportunities in Spanish-speaking lands, and that the lure of silver-producing, textile-importing colonies with a weak native bourgeoisie was a powerful one. It should also be remembered that from 1601 until the mid-1630s in South America, and until 1642 in Mexico, very few Jews were seized by the Inquisition, and that the risk that Jewish settlers in the Spanish Indies were running in the early seventeenth century must have seemed much less than it appears in retrospect. In Mexico the Inquisition sprang into action suddenly, . . . and, beginning in 1642, seized over 150 Jews in the space of three or four years. These prisoners were tortured until they confessed their Judaism and were then publicly "reconciled" to the Church in a series of *Autos-de-Fe*, beginning in April 1646 when forty Jews were presented, continuing in January 1647 with twenty-one Jews presented, and March 1648 with another forty, and culminating in the famous *Auto General de la Fe* of 11 April 1649, arguably the most costly and grandiose *Auto-de-Fe* ever held outside the Iberian peninsula, when eight Jews were burned and twenty-seven "reconciled." In the years 1650–1 most of those who had been reconciled were deported to Spain, for it was felt that it was better to keep them in Spain than leave them in the Indies where it was so much easier to escape from surveillance. As far as one can tell from Inquisition activity, this deportation seems to have ended the main crypto-Jewish presence in the viceroyalty. Nevertheless, cases of Judaism continued to crop up during the rest of the century and even into the early eighteenth century, and more than thirty judaizers were caught and punished between the expulsions of 1650–1 and the mid-1690s. These included some quite interesting personages, notably Domingo Márquez, *alguacil mayor* [a district police officer] of Tepeaca, tried in 1660, Captain Matías Pereira Lobo, tried in 1662, Doña Teresa de Aguilera y Roche, wife of a governor of New Mexico, sentenced in 1663 (whose husband, Don Bernardo López de Mendizabal, was probably tried in 1662), Captain Agustín Muñoz de Sandoval, sentenced in 1695, and a Jewish friar tried in 1706, Fray Joseph de San Ignacio. . . .

Of the various stresses and strains in Mexican society in the seventeenth century the most important was the conflict between the Spanish colonists on the one hand, in alliance with the bishops and the secular clergy, and the Spanish, Indian, and mendicant bureaucracies on the other, for control, especially economic control, of the Indian population. This is perhaps equivalent to saying that Mexico was subject to much the same sort of battle between officialdom and enterprise as many other European and European-dominated societies in the early modem era. The tension between officers and colonists, however, though the main piece, is by no means the only piece in the framework. The conflict between a powerful, privileged, and well-entrenched administrative and ecclesiastical class and the settlers was also, to a large extent, a conflict between peninsular Spaniards and Creoles with the former occupying a favoured position in respect to offices and dignities in the land colonized by the latter. This situation had its similarities to the friction between Dutch and Boers in eighteenth-century South Africa, or English and English Americans in eighteenth-century New England. In addition, there were a number of subsidiary strains of various kinds, the most significant being that between those, both inside and outside the Mexican bureaucracy, who put loyalty to the Spanish state and the interests of the Spanish state first, especially in such fields as taxation and control of trade, conduct, and consumption, and those who, for their own, usually economic, reasons, preferred lax application of the rules. In allowing for the political relevance of this stress, it should be noted that in the final years of Philip III's reign [1598–1621] and the early years of that of Philip IV [1621–1665], there was much talk of reform in Spain in certain influential quarters, and a strong demand for a new austerity and a crack-down on corruption, proposals which were strongly resisted by bureaucratic elements, both in Mexico and in Spain.

Decline and Unrest in the Middle East and Africa

CHAPTER 6

THE SLAVE TRADE

PAUL BOHANNAN AND PHILIP CURTIN

Paul Bohannan and Philip Curtin explain the slave trade that grew steadily during the 1700s to supply labor for the increasing number of plantations and ranches in the Americas. Because Africans were physically hardier and better workers than Native Americans, traders bought slaves from many sources along the western coast of Africa for a price per slave equal to about six hundred pounds of raw sugar. After first sending women into the fields alongside the men, planters discovered that women could be used primarily to bear children. Paul Bohannan, who has taught history at Princeton, Northwestern University, and the University of Southern California, is author of *How Culture Works*. Philip Curtin taught history at Swarthmore College and Johns Hopkins University. He is the author of *African History, World Migrations and World Cultures* and *The Atlantic Slave Trade: A Census*.

I t is one of the ironies of African history that the end of isolation, made possible through the maritime revolution, should have led in hardly more than two centuries to a new commerce in which Africa's chief export was its own people. Historians have long disputed the causes and consequences of the slave trade—both for Africa and for the world. . . .

THE NEED FOR SLAVE LABOR

In the fourteenth and fifteenth centuries, slavery in southern Europe served three purposes—to furnish domestic service, to provide oarsmen for the galleys that were the principal naval craft, and to concentrate people for new enterprises. Wherever mines or plantations were established in places with an insufficient sup-

Excerpted from *Africa and Africans*, 3rd edition, by Paul Bohannan and Philip Curtin. Copyright © 1988 by Waveland Press, Inc. Reprinted with permission from Waveland Press, Inc., Prospect Heights, IL. All rights reserved.

ply of labor, the institution of slavery was a convenient way of mobilizing labor, especially for sugar plantations on the Mediterranean islands, southern Spain, or Portugal.

Even before the discovery of America, Europeans began to set up similar plantations on Atlantic islands like the Canaries or Madeira. By the early sixteenth century, they had moved as far as São Thomé in the Gulf of Guinea, and these moves were followed later in the century by similar establishments in the Caribbean and Brazil. At each step, the existing population was too small to provide enough workers for a labor-intensive crop like sugar, and the previously isolated populations lived in disease environments that lacked many of the common diseases of Africa and Europe. This meant that the people had no immunities derived from childhood infection or inheritance. With the introduction of Afro-European diseases, they passed through a series of devastating epidemics of diseases like measles, smallpox, typhus, malaria, or yellow fever. The result was a population disaster, sometimes ending in the effective extinction of the original population, especially in the tropical lowlands of the Americas—the region best suited for plantation agriculture. Europeans already had the institution of slavery as a way of forcing labor mobility; they used it in the Atlantic just as they had done in the Mediterranean.

Some form of slavery or forced labor was useful for other reasons as well. The natural conditions of a frontier region, with plenty of land and few people, made for high wage rates, and high labor costs made for labor-extensive use of the land—often pastoralism [raising and herding livestock] or simply hunting wild cattle. It was tempting in these conditions to use force in order to make people work some of the land more intensively. As the Indian populations declined in Mexico and Peru, the Spanish turned increasingly to various forms of peonage [a system by which debtors are bound in servitude to their creditors]. On the eastern frontiers of Europe, the landed class tightened the bonds of serfdom. The solution found for America's tropical lowlands was slavery.

AFRICANS WERE THE BEST SLAVES

But Africans were not the only enforced immigrants to the New World. Convicts, unsuccessful rebels against the government, and indentured workers who bound themselves more or less voluntarily to serve for a period of years were shipped off to the Americas in large numbers. Indians were also enslaved and used for plantation agriculture, especially in Brazil. Of the three sources of labor—Africa, America, and Europe—it was soon clear that the Africans survived best in the tropical American environment. At the time, African superiority in this respect was attributed to some special quality of the Negro race, but modern knowledge of epidemiology shows that early environment rather than race is the true explanation. Europeans died in large numbers in the American tropics, just as they died in even larger numbers in the African tropics. Indians also died on contact with Afro-European diseases, but Africans were comparatively immune both to tropical diseases and to the ordinary range of diseases common on the Afro-Eurasian land mass. Migration from Africa to the Americas brought higher death rates for the first generation, but lower rates than those of Europeans who made the equivalent move.

Given the choice of slavery as a labor system and the fact that Africans were the most efficient workers, the problem of supply remained. A large-scale slave trade would have been impossible if Africa had been truly primitive; European death rates on the coast guaranteed as much. But Africa was not primitive. Developed commercial networks were already in existence before the discovery of America, both in West Africa and the southern savanna. African rulers often enslaved war prisoners, and the prisoners were sold into the slave trade—often for shipment to distant places where escape was less likely. Some were exported across the Sahara to North Africa, and the Portuguese were briefly in the business of buying slaves in one part of Africa and selling them in another, even before the demand from American plantations drew the focus of the slave trade across the Atlantic.

But slavery in Africa was different from slavery on an American plantation. A slave was without rights at the moment of his capture; he could be killed or sold. He continued without rights until he was sold to an ultimate master in Africa—or else to the Europeans for transportation overseas. If he ended up on an American plantation, his rights would be few and he was treated as a mere labor unit. But in Africa, slavery was not mainly an economic institution. The object in buying a slave was to increase the size of one's own group, more often for prestige or military power than for the sake of wealth. Women were therefore more desirable than men, but men and women alike were assimilated into the master's social group. They had rights as well as obligations. In many cases, a second-generation slave could no longer be sold. And slaves belonging to important people could often rise to positions of command over free men.

The Atlantic slave trade thus tapped an existing African slave trade, but in doing so it sent people into a very different kind of slavery. Over the centuries, it diverted increasing numbers to the coast for sale to Europeans. The organization of this trade varied greatly from one part of Africa to the next. In some regions, Europeans built trade forts; twenty-seven were constructed on the Gold Coast over a distance of only about 220 miles. African authorities allowed the Europeans to exercise sovereignty within the forts themselves, but they often charged rent for the land the fort stood on. Other trading posts were nothing more than a few unfortified houses onshore for the storage of trade goods and a tightly fenced yard for slaves awaiting shipment. In that case, the Europeans who stayed onshore between ships' visits did so with the permission of the African ruler, and under his protection. Another form of trade was the "ship trade," in which Europeans sailed down the coast, calling at likely ports, but without leaving European agents permanently stationed onshore.

Whatever the point of trade, elaborate customary procedures had come into existence by the end of the sixteenth century. Trade normally began with a payment to the local authorities, partly a gift to demonstrate good will and partly a tax. Each section of the coast had its own trade currency of account—the "bar" (originally an iron bar), the "ounce" (originally an ounce of gold dust), a form of brass currency called manillas, or cowrie shells from the Indian Ocean. Various European commodities were customarily valued at so many bars or ounces. Bargains were struck in terms of the number of bars or ounces to be paid for a slave and then once more in terms of the "sorting" of different European goods that would be used to make up that value.

The internal trade to the coast was more diverse. In some African kingdoms, such as late-eighteenth-century Dahomey, the slave trade was a royal monopoly, tightly controlled for the profit of the state. Other states, such as Futa Toro on the Senegal River, sold few slaves themselves but charged heavy tolls for the privilege of shipping slaves through the country on the way to the coast. Still other states expanded by conquest in order to be able to control the passage of slaves. The kingdom of Akwamu followed a pattern of expansion in the late seventeenth century, moving to the east and west of the Volta River in present-day Ghana, but some distance back from the coast. After a period of growing strength based on revenue from the flow of trade across the kingdom, Akwamu was able to reach down to the coast itself in the 1680s and dictate terms to the coastal trading states and the European garrisons alike. . . .

African societies south of the tropical forest also adjusted to the trade in slaves. By the late seventeenth century, the Imbangala, who had first appeared as destructive raiders a century earlier, turned to commerce. Their kingdom, inland from the Portuguese post at Luanda, drew slaves from a wide range of central Africa. A little later, the Ovimbundu in the hinterland of Benguela took the same course. Bihé and Mbailundu in particular among the Ovimbundu states became wealthy on the basis of trade routes reaching far into the interior, ultimately as far as the present Shaba province of Zaire. Like Imbangala to the north, the Ovimbundu states were far too strong to be threatened by Portuguese power on the coast. In time, a rough alliance came into existence, in which the Portuguese acquiesced to the trade monopoly of the inland kingdoms for the sake of having a regular and plentiful supply of slaves delivered to the coast. . . .

THE GROWTH AND INCIDENCE OF THE SLAVE TRADE

The European demand for slaves grew slowly and steadily; over many decades African institutions adapted to meet the demand. From an annual average of less than 2,000 slaves imported into the Americas each year in the century before 1600, the trade grew to about 55,000 a year for the eighteenth century as a whole. The peak decade for the whole history of the trade was the 1780s, with an annual average of 88,000 slaves arriving in the Americas each year; deliveries reached more than 100,000 in a few individual years. At least for the crucial period from 1701 to 1809, it is possible to estimate the drain of population from various regions of Africa by taking the combined estimates of the exports carried by the three most important carriers—England, France, and Portugal. (See Fig. 1.) While the map represents the origins of the vast majority of all those carried, it also leaves out some important aspects of the trade. During that century, the sources of the trade shifted dramatically from one part of the coast to another. The Gold Coast, for example, supplied 20 percent of exports in the 1740s, but only about 9 percent in the 1790s. Meanwhile, the Bight of Biafra rose with the development of the Ijo-Aro trade network from about 1 percent of the trade in the 1730s to almost a quarter of the whole in the 1790s. Or again, the exports from central Africa doubled between the 1770s and the 1780s. In short, while the demand for slaves was relatively steady, it was met by rapid shifts from one source of supply to another, depending on African political conditions or the development of new trade routes from the interior.

North Americans, with a view of world history that centers on their own country, often think of the slave trade as a flow of people from Africa to the United States. In fact, about one third of all slaves landed in the Americas went to Brazil; about a half went to the Caribbean islands and mainland; no more than a

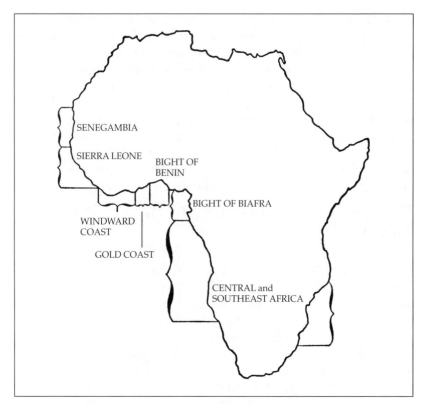

Figure 1. Approximate sources of the eighteenth-century Atlantic slave trade, 1701–1800. (Dutch, British, French, and Portuguese exports.) Totals in thousands.

Region	Slaves Exported	Percent of Total
Senegambia	201	3.6
Sierra Leone	484	8.7
Gold Coast	677	12.3
Bight of Benin	1,279	23.2
Bight of Biafra	814	14.8
Central and Southeast Africa	2,058	37.3
TOTAL	**5,513**	**100.0**

Source: Paul E. Lovejoy, *Transformations in Slavery*, p. 50.

twentieth came to the United States. Yet the Afro-America population of the United States today is one of the largest in the New World. The explanation lies in a sharp and important demographic distinction between North America and the American tropics. While the Negro population of the North American colonies began to grow from natural increase at a very early date, the slave population of the tropical plantations suffered an excess of deaths over births. This meant that the slave trade could not be a one-shot affair, importing a basic population that could then maintain its own numbers. It had to be continuous merely to maintain the existing level of population; any growth of the plantation economy required still more slaves from Africa.

THE ECONOMICS OF THE SLAVE TRADE

Several factors help to account for this demographic peculiarity. Disease environment was important in the first generation, since both morbidity and mortality rates were higher among slaves raised in Africa than they were among the American-born. Planters also imported about two men for every woman, and they worked the women in the fields along with the men, preferring to have their labor rather than creating the kind of social setting in which they would be willing to have children.

The planters may have been correct, on strictly economic grounds, in believing that it was cheaper to import new labor from Africa than to allow the leisure, additional rations, and other privileges that might have encouraged a high birth rate among the slaves. The real cost of slaves was very small indeed before the middle of the eighteenth century. In 1695, for example, a slave could be bought in Jamaica for about £20 currency, or about the same value as six hundred pounds of raw sugar sold on the London market, or the European cost of sixteen trade guns for sale in Africa. All things being equal, a new slave could be expected to add more than six hundred pounds to the plantation's production in a single year. Yet a prime slave on the coast of Africa cost only about eight guns or a half ton of iron in bars— little enough to allow a handsome profit on the slave trade itself.

But the real price of slaves in Africa rose steadily during the eighteenth century. One result was to make planters think twice about their policy of importing slaves, rather than allowing them to breed naturally. By the 1770s, several Caribbean planters began to readjust by balancing the number of men and women on their estates, granting special privileges to child-rearing mothers and time off for child care. It is uncertain how generally these new polities were applied, but some of the older colonies, such as Barbados, began to achieve a self-perpetuating slave population by about 1800. Even where slaves were still imported, the demand tended to drop as the local birth rate rose, and the total number imported dropped in each decade from 1790 to 1820. When the United States, Great Britain, and Denmark abolished their own part of the slave trade in the first decade of the nineteenth century, the planters complained, but the really serious need for continued slave imports was nearing its end—at least in the older plantation areas.

EARLY PETITIONS FOR FREEDOM

ANTHONY PIETERSON, PHILLIP CORVEN, AND PETER VANTRUMP

Before the American Revolution black Americans were able to petition for their freedom. This excerpt contains three such petitions as they were originally written. The first petitioner, an orphan whose parents had been free, was granted freedom as an adult in New York. The second petitioner was a man who was granted freedom in the will of his original owner, but was denied his rights by a Virginia man who had purchased him. The third petitioner was a man who had been brought to North Carolina after being promised passage to Holland, but was denied his freedom.

I ndividual Negroes quite frequently petitioned governmental bodies for freedom prior to the American Revolution. Three examples of such petitions are given below. The first, dated 1661, was in Dutch and was addressed to the colony of New Netherlands (later New York). Its prayer was granted. The second, dated 1675, was the work of a Virginia Negro and what decision was made in regard to it does not appear. The third petition, dated 1726, was addressed to the North Carolina General Court and was denied.

NEW NETHERLANDS PETITION, 1661

To the Noble Right Honorable Director-General and Lords Councillors of New Netherlands

Herewith very respectfully declare Emanuel Pieterson, a free Negro, and Reytory, otherwise Dorothy, Angola, free Negro woman, together husband and wife, the very humble petitioners

---

Excerpted from *The Colonial Records of North Carolina* (Raleigh, 1886) by Anthony Pieterson, Phillip Corven, and Peter Vantrump.

of your noble honors, that she, Reytory, in the year 1643, on the third of August, stood as godparent or witness at the Christian baptism of a little son of one Anthony van Angola, begotten with his own wife named Louise, the which aforementioned Anthony and Louise were both free Negroes; and about four weeks thereafter the aforementioned Louise came to depart this world, leaving behind the aforementioned little son named Anthony, the which child your petitioner out of Christian affection took to herself, and with the fruits of her hands' bitter toil she reared him as her own child, and up to the present supported him, taking all motherly solicitude and care for him, without aid of anyone in the world, not even his father (who likewise died about five years thereafter), to solicit his nourishment; and also your petitioner [i.e., Emanuel] since he was married to Reytory, has done his duty and his very best for the rearing . . . to assist . . . your petitioners . . . very respectfully address themselves to you, noble and right honorable lords, humbly begging that your noble honors consent to grant a stamp in this margin of this [document], or otherwise a document containing the consent and approval of the above-mentioned adoption and nurturing, on the part of your petitioner, in behalf of the aforementioned Anthony with the intent [of declaring] that he himself, being of free parents, reared and brought up without burden or expense of the [West Indian] Company, or of anyone else than your petitioner, in accordance therewith he may be declared by your noble honors to be a free person: this being done, [the document] was signed with the mark of Anthony Pieterson.

Ellipses indicate illegible portions of the document; bracketed words are the editor's.

VIRGINIA PETITION, 1675

To the R^T Honble Sir William Berkeley, Knt., Gover^r and Capt. Genl. of Virg^a, with the Hon. Councell of State.

The Petition of Phillip Corven, a Negro, in all humility showeth: That yor pet^r being a servant^t to Mrs Anny^e Beazley, late of James Citty County, widdow, de^ed. The said Mrs Beazley made her last will & testament in writing, under her hand & seal, bearing date, the 9th day of April, An. Dom. 1664, and, amongst other things, did order, will appoint that yor pe^tr by the then name of Negro boy Phillip, should serve her cousin, Mr. Humphrey Stafford, the terme of eight yeares, then next ensueing, and then should enjoy his freedome & be paid three barrels of corne & a sute of clothes, as by the said will appears. Sonne after the makeing of which will, the said Mrs Beazley departed this life, yon pe^tr did continue & and abide with the said M^r

Stafford, (with whome he was ordered by the said will to live) some yeares, and then the said Mr. Stafford sold the remainder of y^{or} pe^{tr} time to one Mr. Charles Lucas, with whom y^{or} pe^{tr} alsoe continued, doeing true & faithfull service; but the said Mr. Lucas, coveting yo^{r}pe$^{tr's}$ service longer then of right itt was due, did not att the expiracon of the said eight yeares, discharge y^{or} pe^{tr} from his service, but compelled him to serve three years longer than the time set by the said Mrs. Beazley's will, and then not being willing y^{or} pe^{tr} should enjoy his freedome, did, contrary to all honesty and good conscience with threats & a high hand, in the time of y^{or} pe$^{tr's}$ service with him, and by his confederacy with some persons compel yor pe^{tr} to sett his hand to a writeing, which the said Mr Lucas now saith is an Indenture for twenty yeares, and forced yor pe^{tr} to acknowledge the same in the County Court of Warwick.

Now, for that itt please yor Hon^r, yo^{r}pe^{tr}, who all the time of the makeing the said forced writing, in the servicee of the said Mr. Lucas, and never discharged from the same, the said Mr Lucas alwaies unjustly pretending that yor pe^{tr} was to serve him three yeares longer, by an order of Court, w^h is untrue, which pretence of the said Mr. Lucas will appeare to yor hon^s by ye testimony of persons of good creditt.

Yo^r Pe^{tr} therefore most humbly prayeth yor hon^{rs} to order that the said Mr Lucas make him sattisfaction for the said three yeares service above his time, and pay him corne & clothes, with costs of suite.

And yor pe^{tr} (as in duty bound) shall ever pray, &c.

North Carolina Petition, 1726

To the Honoble Christopher Gale Esqr Chief Justice of the General Court February the third one thousand Seven hundred & twenty Six

The Complaint and petition of Peter Vantrump a free Negro Sheweth that yor Complainant being a free Negro and at his own voluntary disposall & hath hired himself to Service Sundry times particularly in New York and other places and being at St Thomas's this Summer past one Captain Mackie in a Brigantine from thence being bound (as he reported) to Europe Your Honors Complainant agreed to go with him in Order to gett to Holland but instead of proceeding the Sayd Voyage the Sayd Mackie came to North Carolina where combining with one Edmund porter of this province and fearing the Sayd Mackie not to be on a lawfull Trade Yor Complainant was desirous to leave him and the Sayd porter by plausible pretences gott Your Complainant to come away from the Sayd Mackie with him although Your Complainant often told the Sayd porter that he was not a Slave but a free man Yet nevertheless the Sayd porter now against all right now pretends Your Complainant to be his Slave and hath held and used him as Such wherefore Your Complainant prays he may be adjudg^d & declar^d free as in Justice he ought to be & Sign^d Peter Vantrump.

THE DUTCH SETTLE SOUTH AFRICA

HARM J. DE BLIJ

Harm J. de Blij explains how the Dutch established a food-supply station at Cape Town, South Africa, and developed it into a permanent settlement. According to de Blij, the first settlers saw opportunities to farm rich land and to graze cattle on the green mountain slopes. After initial conflict with African Hottentots, white settlers made a peaceful agreement, but when the settlers expanded into the valleys, they encountered the less-agreeable Bantu, from the central and southern regions, and the Bushmen. Although Dutch leader Jan van Riebeeck had laid the groundwork for a permanent settlement, support from Holland waned, and the settlement fell to the French in the late 1700s. Harm J. de Blij worked in South Africa as a college lecturer, a government employee, and a concert musician and also taught at Michigan State University and the University of Miami. He is the author of *Mombasa: An African City* and the founder of the *Journal of Geography*.

T he 17th century saw the decline of Portuguese power and the rise of Holland to its "Golden Century." Much of Holland's wealth was based on its merchant navy and its possessions in the East Indies, and the Dutch East India Company was established to coordinate the trade. In 1651, the Company called for the establishment of a revictualling [food-supply] station at the Cape, and late that year, [Jan] van Riebeeck and a party of men boarded the "Drommedaris" and set sail for the southern tip of Africa. In traveling to the Cape, the Dutch ships had to make use of the Canaries Current and the Northeast

Excerpted from *South Africa,* by Harm J. de Blij. Copyright © 1962 by Northwestern University Press. Reprinted with permission from Northwestern University Press.

Tradewinds; they would then cross the Atlantic Ocean to the South American east coast, cross the dangerous Doldrums with the aid of the southward flowing Brazil Current, until, in the general latitude of the Cape, they would begin to be driven eastward again in the Westerly wind belt, thus passing close to the tip of Africa. The tortuous journey from Amsterdam to Cape Town, if it were a fortunate one, might take as long as three or four months, and the total distance traveled might well exceed twice the actual straight-line distance between the two places. A fresh supply of food and water at the Cape would greatly alleviate the lot of the sailors and passengers.

On April 5, 1652, the crew of the "Drommedaris" sighted land, and on April 6 van Riebeeck guided his ship into Table Bay at the foot of magnificent Table Mountain. It must be remembered that the party was under orders to set up a temporary revictualling station and that there were no immediate intentions to set up a Dutch colony here, although there is evidence that the home government was advised to consider this step. As workers in the employ of the Company, the party of settlers was to confine its activities to the setting in motion of the mechanism for revictualling ships; excess production and private trade with the Hottentots was prohibited. The Hottentots were the first Africans with whom the new settlers came into contact, and trouble was not long in coming. With the settlement hardly 18 months old, Hottentots murdered a white guard and drove all cattle into the interior, causing shortages not only for the passing ships but also for the local party itself. However, van Riebeeck had been placed under orders to avoid all conflict with the local inhabitants, and no reprisals were made. Apparently, relations between the Africans and the white settlers improved considerably after the first contact as a result of this policy, and good relations were generally maintained.

THE DUTCH SETTLERS WANT AN INDEPENDENT COLONY

Although the winter rains that year came later than usual at the Cape, and were unusually violent when they did come, washing away many of the vegetable gardens that had been prepared, people soon began to realize the value of the land they had settled and the opportunities for private farming and trade. This fact attests to the great beauty and richness of the Cape, for death and disease were rampant during the early stages of settlement, a period from which the small party was a long time in recovering. As early as April 28, 1655, van Riebeeck wrote home to the governing Council of Seventeen that the settlers would "in due course break altogether with Holland and one day make this place their fatherland." In 1657, indeed, a small number of people resigned from the employment of the Company and settled privately along the slopes of Table Mountain. However, they were not allowed to sell products to any agent other than the Company, and then only at fixed Company prices. These limitations proved unacceptable to these first real colonizers, and they appealed to van Riebeeck to lift them: "We wish to be no Company's slaves."

Labor became a problem as the settlement expanded. "You might as well look for jewels in a hogsty as artisans among this barbarous generation," wrote a disgruntled settler. The first slaves were imported as early as 1658, and thus a new element was added to the heterogeneity of the Cape. The slaves came from both coasts of Africa, west and east, while others came from the islands of the Far East. Some came from Madagascar. While the import of slaves alleviated one problem, the expansion of settlement created another. The Hottentots' pastures were being alienated by the expansion of the white farms. Van Riebeeck attempted at first to prevent aggravation of these difficulties by establishing a boundary beyond which such white settlement was not permitted to expand. This, of course, proved impractical, and the first armed conflict broke out between whites and Africans. As in countless subsequent instances, the cause of friction was land.

VAN RIEBEECK AND DUTCH DOMINATION

When van Riebeeck left the Cape for the Indies in May, 1662, he had laid the groundwork for permanent white settlement at the Cape. Apart from developing an economy, he had also established fortifications, achieved some degree of political advancement for the farmer-settlers, treated the Hottentots with a degree of fairness under the circumstances, fought a successful war against them while insisting that efforts to Christianize them continue, and organized the importation of slaves. Many of his works have some effect today. The slaves have played a significant role in establishing the racial composition of the South African population. Cape Town remains the gateway to Southern Africa. Even the fortifications built by van Riebeeck are in use today by the South African Defense Department.

Van Riebeeck began what was to be some 150 years of Dutch domination of the Cape. During this century and a half, the Cape expanded, though not greatly compared to the expansion of white settlement in such areas as Australia and North America. However limited its expansion, the Cape took on a very definite character. Van Riebeeck had arrived with orders to establish the form of government already in existence in other areas possessed by the Dutch East India Company. Thus, in the beginning, there was a Commander (later Governor) who, appointed by the Company, was responsible for the entire settlement. The Commander was assisted by a Political Council comprised of the most important people at the Cape. In this Council van Riebeeck included two of the settler-farmers who had left the employment of the Company and wished to farm permanently and independently at the Cape. Soon after the departure of van Riebeeck, the Dutch began to recognize the importance of the Cape as a protector of the overseas trade. Immigration to the Cape was encouraged, and a large population there was now seen as an advantage. With the growth of the Cape in population and occupied area, government became a more complex matter. In 1679, during a period of relatively rapid expansion, Simon van der Stel was appointed Commander at the Cape. It was during van der Stel's government that French Huguenot [Protestant] refugees began to arrive at the Cape: in 1688 a party of 200 came, and in 1690 the total white population of the settlement was some 800. The Commander made a policy of scattering these French refugees all over the settlement and prohibiting the use of the French language, but they left a distinctive mark on the colony nonetheless. French contributions to the South African scene include the world-famous Cape vineyards and wines, a nasal twang to the Afrikaans language, and numerous family names in South Africa, some among the most common of all, such as Joubert, Celliers, Marais, Du Toit.

TROUBLE BEGINS WITH EXPANSION

Sporadic border troubles erupted during Simon van der Stel's rule at the Cape, but they were not severe, and they became an accepted consequence of expanding settlement. No contact had been made with the Bantu, and the Hottentots were aware of the reprisals that could occur after excessive resistance to land alienation. Hence the burghers of the Cape were mainly concerned with matters other than friction with the Africans. Simon van der Stel's rule ended in 1699, and his son, Willem Adriaan, succeeded him.

With Willem Adriaan van der Stel began what may be called the dark decades of the history of white settlement in Southern Africa. Though a capable colonizer and excellent farmer, the younger van der Stel proved corrupt and unreliable, and he pursued an unscrupulous campaign of personal gain at the expense of the farmers. In addition, his activities coincided with a reversal of policy on the part of the Company, which wished to reduce the costs of the Colony, which, it considered, was becoming an excessive burden. Faced with hardship, some farmers took to a form of nomadic cattle-herding and trekked into the interior, mainly along the river valleys between the Cape Ranges. Between 1700 and 1730, these people pushed the frontier farther than ever before, they separated themselves from the "civilization" of the Cape, and they removed themselves beyond the limits of effective government. To the north and east they moved, in small numbers but possessed of an individualism that appears to reassert itself at times in the modern Afrikaner.

While the Council continued to sit in Cape Town, the nearby town of Stellenbosch became the center of administration for the areas farther into the hinterland where the free burghers resided. Stellenbosch became the center for the farmers; Cape Town began to attain the characteristics of an urban center, and the population there had entirely different interests. The self-sufficiency of the Cape, the lack of economic stimulus, and the control of the waning Company combined to retard development. In 1781, the French navy occupied Cape Town for a period of four years, providing some stimulus to the place. This was not, however, because France saw the Cape as a desirable colony to possess, but to keep the British from occupying it. With the threat over, the French left in 1784.

CONFLICTS WITH AFRICANS

The events taking place in the interior during the last half of the 18th century are of some importance, for the trekkers who had herded their cattle into these remote parts were coming into contact not only with marauding Bushmen in the north but with Bantu in the east, and a series of conflicts ensued. For some considerable time, the Bushmen had much success in harassing the white farmers, but by the end of the 18th century they were beginning to lose the unequal battle against the well-armed groups of cattlemen. In the east, a series of conflicts with the Bantu occurred, known as the Nine Kaffir Wars. Sporadic contact had been made with the Africans of the east since the early part of the 18th century, but the Company attempted to prevent serious conflict by prohibiting trade between black and white. The African people in question were the Xosa, and, like the whites, they were a cattle people in search of good pastures. While the white cattle-raisers were expanding their holdings toward the east, the Xosa were on their way south and, eventually, west, along the same well-watered slopes of the Cape Ranges. The effectively governed territory of the Company did not extend nearly as far as these areas, and the laws established to prevent friction between the races went unheeded. The major contact took place along the Great Fish River, and efforts were made to name this river the boundary between the conflicting groups and their animals. The Great Fish River runs south-southeast from the Cape Ranges to the Indian Ocean and reaches the sea approximately at the point where the South African coast turns northeast. The river lies in a fertile if limited basin, and it is not a matter for surprise that both races coveted the territory. Cattle raids were common on both sides. In 1778 Governor van Plettenberg attempted to obtain agreements from the African chiefs that the Great Fish River should become the permanent and final boundary and that no crossings should be made by either group for any reason. However, he had only limited success in getting local chiefs to agree to this suggestion, and a major conflict broke out in 1779. Thousands of cattle changed hands in this First Kaffir War, and many people as well as animals were killed.

DUTCH POWER DECLINES

Much of the course of conflict between black and white in the outlying districts of the Cape can be blamed on the failure of the Company to administer the outlying territories or to make an effort to keep them effectively controlled. Outside Cape Town, very few "districts" had been proclaimed: Stellenbosch was first. . . . Only in 1746 was the District of Swellendam established, and the District of Graaff Reinet was not delimited till after the First Kaffir War. Subsequently, Tulbagh was proclaimed to the north of Cape Town, including those areas where most trouble had been encountered with the Bushmen. The frontiersmen felt that the failing Company had done nothing to protect them, and the Districts became the seats of discontent and political agitation. Company officials were defied and even expelled. There was no great dismay, even at Cape Town itself, when the French took possession of the settlement in 1781. Holland's decline and internal division were reflected at the Cape, and after the invasion of Holland by the French in 1794 and the exile to Britain of the Dutch government, the days of Dutch domination of the Cape were numbered.

THE DECLINE OF THE OTTOMAN EMPIRE

ANDREW MANGO

Andrew Mango analyzes the reasons why the Ottoman Empire declined in the eighteenth century. He cites the Turkish failure to seize Vienna and Russia's defeat of Turkey at the end of the seventeenth century, after which European trade and culture penetrated the country and introduced changes. Though the sultan tried to establish reforms, it was too late: A new nationalism was already on the rise, helping to crumble the old order and unity. Andrew Mango, who has lived much of his life in Turkey, is a prominent writer, journalist, and broadcaster of Turkish affairs. He is the author of *Ataturk* and *Turkey Before and After Ataturk: Internal and External Affairs.*

The decline of the Ottoman Empire is usually dated from the Treaty of Carlowitz [following the Ottomans' defeat by czarist Russia] in 1699, and as the decline progressed so European penetration of Turkey increased. European tradesmen—originally Genoese, because they were the rivals of the Ottomans' enemies, the Venetians, and then French, Dutch, English and others—who had been granted privileges and safe-conducts necessary for the pursuit of their activities, grew in importance, displacing local merchants. Their official protectors, the foreign envoys and consuls, tried to create for their nationals enclaves of order in the chaos of decaying oriental despotism, and in so doing began to play an important part in affairs of state. At the same time the Ottoman rulers themselves decided to acquire the learning or magic of their victors.

Excerpted from *Discovering Turkey,* by Andrew Mango. Copyright © 1971 by Andrew Mango. Reprinted with permission from Chrysalis Books.

In the brief period of equilibrium at the beginning of the eighteenth century, European inventions and tastes began to appear in Istanbul. A first printing press was established for Turkish books. French design began to influence the palaces of the rich, which also contained some items of European furniture. Tulips, which had originally come from Asia, were reimported from Holland. A taste for tobacco spread from the west. Turkish envoys were sent to European countries and Europeans began to visit Turkey in greater numbers. In 1720 a Turkish ambassador went to France instructed "to visit fortresses, factories and the works of French civilisation generally and to report on those which might be applicable" in Turkey. At the same time Europeans began to turn up in Turkey with projects of reforms in their pockets. These reforms were at first of a military character, some of the advisers following an old tradition and turning Muslim. Such was the case of the Frenchman Comte de Bonneval (1675–1747) who became known as Humbaraci (Bombardier) Ahmet Pasha. A first western-type institution of learning, a school of military engineering, was opened in 1734 in the Istanbul suburb of Üsküdar (Scutari). Other schools of engineering followed in 1769 and 1776. The prime movers of these first reforms were the French, whose main interest lay in strengthening Turkey's resistance to the encroachment of Russia. Russia acquired nevertheless control of the Black Sea and a privileged position in the Ottoman Empire by the Treaty of Küçük Kaynarca in 1774. After losing yet another war with Russia, the Ottoman Sultan Selim III launched the most ambitious reforms attempted until then. . . .

THE EFFECT OF NATIONALISM

While European ideas were thus being put into practice to save the Ottoman Empire, nationalism, also an idea originating in Europe, had already begun its break-up. The Ottoman Empire, like the Seljuk Sultanate of Rum and the Byzantine Empire before it, was a multi-national state, but the criterion of differentiation among its subjects was religion and not nationality. *Millet*, a word of Arabic origin which in modern Turkish means "nation," was until recently used to describe a religious community. The ruling *millet* was, of course, made up of Muslims regardless of their ethnic origin. But apart from Muslims, the Empire numbered among its subjects many Greeks, Slavs, Roumanians, Christian Albanians, Christian Semites and Jews. . . .

In accordance with existing Muslim precedent, the Greek and Armenian Patriarchs and the Jewish Chief Rabbi were given considerable secular as well as religious authority over members of their communities, for whose loyal behaviour they became answerable to the Sultan. Subsequently, Greeks in the Peloponnese, Cyprus, Crete and elsewhere benefited from the ending of Latin rule. This policy reduced the danger of a large-scale collaboration between the Christian subjects of the Ottoman Empire and its Catholic foes. Nevertheless, attempts at subversion were made and were sometimes successful. . . .

THE THREAT OF RUSSIA

A more dangerous situation developed when an Eastern Orthodox outside power, Russia, began to threaten the Ottoman Empire. As early as 1657, the Greek Patriarch Parthenius III was hanged by the Turks, apparently for engaging in treasonable correspondence with the Czar in Moscow. In 1711 Peter the Great issued a proclamation to the Eastern Orthodox subjects of the Ottoman Empire, inviting them to join his forces and promising them the same privileges that they enjoyed under the Turks. The Russian Empress Catherine II sent agents to stir up the Greeks, and in 1770 the appearance of a Russian fleet off the Peloponnese sparked off a rebellion which was brutally put down by local Muslims, mostly Albanians. However, although subversion based on religious ties continued, the "Greek project" of Catherine the Great and her successors, aiming at the establishment of a Greek kingdom under Russian protection, was thwarted by other European powers. . . .

The rise of nationalism, which both incited and was incited by the Great Powers of Europe to work against the unity and integrity of the Ottoman Empire, and the steady encroachment of Russia, frustrated the efforts of Ottoman reformers.

CHRONOLOGY

1610–1612
Dutch settlements are formed in Guiana and the Amazon region.

1614
Dutch fur traders are active on the Hudson River in New York.

1618
The Thirty Years' War begins.

1619
The first slaves arrive in Virginia.

1620
Plymouth Colony is established; Francis Bacon publishes *Novum Organum.*

1624
The Dutch found New Amsterdam on Manhattan Island.

1628
William Harvey demonstrates the circulation of blood.

1630
The Dutch begin the conquest of Pernambuco in northeast Brazil.

1637
The Shimabara uprising in Japan leads to Japanese isolation; Rene Descartes publishes *Discourse on Method.*

1638
Galileo publishes *Discourse on Two New Sciences;* Peter Paul Rubens paints *The Garden of Love.*

1641
The height of the African slave trade

1642

The civil war in England begins; Claudio Monteverdi completes the opera *The Coronation of Poppea.*

1643–1715

Louis XIV reigns as the king of France.

1644

The Manchus end the Ming dynasty in China and begin the Ch'ing dynasty.

1648

The Peace of Westphalia in Germany ends the Thirty Years' War.

1652

Jan van Riebeeck founds a settlement at Cape Town; the Anglo-Dutch trade wars begin (ending in 1674).

1652–1654

The Portuguese expel the Dutch from northeast Brazil.

1653–1658

Oliver Cromwell rules as lord protector in England.

1655

Sweden and Poland go to war.

1656

Diego Rodríguez de Silva Velazquez paints *Las Meninas.*

1660

The crowning of Charles II restores the English monarchy.

1662

The Royal Society of London is created.

1663

The French begin missionary work in Vietnam and Thailand.

1664

The English take New York City from the Dutch; Johannes Vermeer paints *Woman Holding a Balance.*

1666

Great Fire in London

1667–1713

The balance of power principle evolves.

1668
The Triple alliance of the Dutch Republic, England, and
   Sweden is formed.

1669
The construction of the palace at Versailles begins; Rembrandt
   van Rijn paints *The Return of the Prodigal Son.*

1672–1727
Alawite ruler Maulay Ismail rules in Morocco.

1683
Turks advance to Vienna but are stopped there.

1684
The first fire, life, and marine insurance companies are created.

1685
Johann Sebastian Bach and George Frederick Handel are born.

1687
Isaac Newton publishes *Mathematical Principles.*

1688
Glorious Revolution in England; William III becomes king.

1689
Peter the Great becomes czar in Russia.

1690
The Mogul dynasty in India begins to decline.

1692
The Salem witch trials occur in America.

1694
The Bank of England is formed; French writer Voltaire is born.

1695
Peter the Great leads Russia into war with Turkey.

1697
Peter the Great goes on a mission to the West to promote
   Russia.

1703
Peter the Great founds St. Petersburg.

1706
Benjamin Franklin is born.

1707
The Mogul Empire in India is in ruin.

1713
Treaty of Utrecht

1715
Louis XV becomes king of France.

1720
Financial disasters occur in England and France.

1722
The fall of the Safavids in Iran.

1733
Georgia, the last of the original thirteen colonies, is founded.

1736
The English repeal laws against witchcraft.

1738
The flying shuttle, a device used in weaving, is invented.

1739
Delhi is captured by Nader Shah; the Tokugawa shogun forces all foreign traders, except the Dutch, to leave Japan.

1740–1748
The War of Austrian Succession.

1742
Handel composes his *Messiah.*

1754–1763
The French and Indian War

1756
Wolfgang Amadeus Mozart is born; the Seven Years' War begins in Europe (ending in 1763).

1759
The English take Quebec; canal building begins in England.

1761
The first blast furnace is created.

1762
Catherine the Great becomes czarina in Russia.

1763

The English acquire Canada by the Treaty of Paris.

1764

The spinning jenny, a spinning machine with several spindles, is invented.

1769

James Watt patents the steam engine; James Cook explores eastern Australia and claims it for England.

1770

The Boston Massacre; Ludvig van Beethoven is born.

1774

Louis XVI becomes king of France.

FOR FURTHER RESEARCH

THE WORLD

Isaac Asimov, *Asimov's Chronology of the World*. New York: HarperCollins, 1991.

Bernard Grun, *Timetables of History*. 3rd ed. New York: Simon & Schuster, 1963.

Gerrit P. Judd, *A History of Civilization*. New York: Macmillan, 1966.

EUROPE

Tony Allan et al., eds., *Powers of the Crown: Time Frame A.D. 1600–1700*. Alexandria, VA: Time-Life Books, 1989.

Maurice Ashley, *England in the Seventeenth Century*. Rev. ed. New York: Barnes & Noble, 1980.

Charles Blitzer et al., eds., *Age of Kings*. New York: Time, 1967.

C.R. Boxer, *The Dutch Seaborne Empire: 1600–1800*. New York: Knopf, 1965.

Fritjof Capra, *The Turning Point: Science, Society, and the Rising Culture*. New York: Bantam Books, 1983.

George Clark, *The Seventeenth Century*. Oxford, England: Clarendon Press, 1947.

Kenneth Clark, *Civilisation: A Personal View*. New York: Harper & Row, 1969.

François Crouzet, *The First Industrialists: The Problem of Origins*. Cambridge, England: Cambridge University Press, 1985.

Phyllis Deane, *The First Industrial Revolution*. 2nd ed. Cambridge, England: Cambridge University Press, 1979.

Will Durant and Ariel Durant, *The Age of Louis XIV.* Vol. 8. New York: Simon & Schuster, 1963.

Donald Jay Grout, *A Short History of Opera.* New York: Columbia University Press, 1947.

Robert Edwin Herzstein, *Western Civilization.* Boston: Houghton Mifflin, 1975.

Paul Kennedy, *The Rise and Fall of the Great Powers: Economic Change and Military Conflict from 1500 to 2000.* New York: Random House, 1987.

Andrew Mango, *Discovering Turkey.* New York: Hastings House, 1971.

Frederick L. Nussbaum, *The Triumph of Science and Reason: 1660–1685.* New York: Harper & Brothers, 1953.

J.H. Parry, *The Establishment of the European Hegemony: 1415–1715.* New York: Harper & Row, 1961.

N.J.G. Pounds, *An Historical Geography of Europe.* New York: Cambridge University Press, 1990.

B.H. Sumner, *Peter the Great and the Emergence of Russia.* New York: Collier Books, 1962.

T. Walter Wallbank and Alastair M. Taylor, *Civilization: Past and Present.* Vol. 2. Rev. ed. Chicago: Scott Foresman, 1949.

Leo Weinstein, ed., *The Age of Reason: The Culture of the Seventeenth Century.* New York: George Braziller, 1965.

Mary Ann Frese Witt et al., *The Humanities: Cultural Roots and Continuities.* Vol. 2. 2nd ed. Lexington, MA: D.C. Heath, 1985.

ASIA AND AUSTRALIA

Richard Allen, *A Short Introduction to the History and Politics of Southeast Asia.* New York: Oxford University Press, 1970.

Woodbridge Bingham, Hilary Conroy, and Frank W. Iklé, *A History of Asia. Vol. 2: Old Empires, Western Penetration, and the Rise of New Nations Since 1600.* Boston: Allyn and Bacon, 1965.

Roderick Cameron, *Australia: History and Horizons.* New York: Columbia University Press, 1971.

David Carroll, *The Taj Mahal*. New York: Marshall Cavendish, 1993.

Hugh Finlay and Peter Turner, *Malaysia, Singapore, and Brunei*. Hawthorne, Australia: Lonely Planet, 1994.

Anna C. Hartshorne, *Japan and Her People*. Philadelphia: John C. Winston, 1902.

Valjean McLenighan, *China: A History to 1949*. Chicago: Children's Press, 1949.

David Morgan, *The Mongols*. Oxford, England: Basil Blackwell, 1986.

Richard Lloyd Parry, *Japan*. London: Cadogan Books, 1995.

Edwin O. Reischauer, *The Japanese*. Cambridge, MA: Harvard University Press, 1977.

Edward Rice, *The Ganges: A Personal Encounter*. New York: Four Winds Press, 1974.

Carl Robinson, *Australia*. Lincolnwood, IL: Passport Books, 1990.

G.B. Sansom, *The Western World and Japan: A Study in the Interaction of European and Asiatic Cultures*. New York: Knopf, 1950.

Jonathan D. Spence, *Emperor of China: Self-Portrait of K'ang-his*. New York: Knopf, 1974.

Frederic Wakeman Jr., *The Fall of Imperial China*. New York: Free Press, 1975.

THE AMERICAS

Hubert Howe Bancroft, *History of Mexico: 1600–1803*. Vol. 3. San Francisco: A.L. Bancroft, 1883.

Alfred Leroy Burt, *A Short History of Canada for Americans*. 2nd ed. Minneapolis: University of Minnesota Press, 1944.

Marshall C. Eakin, *Brazil: The Once and Future Country*. New York: St. Martin's Press, 1997.

Guy Frégault, *Canada: The War of Conquest*. Trans. Margaret M. Cameron. Toronto: Oxford University Press, 1969.

J.I. Israel, *Race, Class, and Politics in Colonial Mexico, 1610–1670*. London: Oxford University Press, 1975.

Desmond Morton, *A Short History of Canada.* 3rd ed. Toronto: McClelland & Stewart, 1997.

Allan Nevins and Henry Steele Commager, with Jeffrey Morris, *A Pocket History of the United States.* 9th ed. New York: Pocket Books, 1992.

Rollie E. Poppino, *Brazil: The Land and People.* 2nd ed. New York: Oxford University Press, 1973.

Selden Rodman, *A Short History of Mexico.* New York: Stein and Day, 1982.

James D. Rudolph, ed., *Argentina: A Country Study.* Washington, DC: U.S. Government Printing Office, 1985.

James R. Scobie, *Argentina: A City and a Nation.* New York: Oxford University Press, 1964.

Conrad Stein, *Mexico.* Chicago: Children's Press, 1984.

George Woodcock, *The Canadians.* Cambridge, MA: Harvard University Press, 1979.

THE MIDDLE EAST AND AFRICA

Yahya Armajani, *Middle East Past and Present.* Englewood Cliffs, NJ: Prentice-Hall, 1970.

Nevill Barbour, *Morocco.* New York: Walker, 1965.

Harm J. de Blij, *South Africa.* Evanston, IL: Northwestern University Press, 1962.

Paul Bohannan and Philip Curtin, *Africa and Africans.* 3rd ed. Prospect Heights, IL: Waveland Press, 1988.

Arthur Goldschmidt, *A Concise History of the Middle East.* 4th ed. Boulder, CO: Westview Press, 1991.

Robert Lacour-Gayet, *A History of South Africa.* Trans. Stephen Hardman. New York: Hastings House, 1977.

William D. Piersen, *From Africa to America: African American History from the Colonial Era to the Early Republic, 1526–1790.* New York: Twayne, 1996.

Leonard Thompson, *A History of South Africa.* New Haven, CT: Yale University Press, 1990.

INDEX

Abahai, 160–61
absolutism. *See* monarchy
Adams, Matthew, 221
Adams, Samuel, 219
Addison, Joseph, 147–48
Adriaan, Willem, 265
Africa
  Dutch East India Company's journey
    to, 262–63
  slaves from, 252–55
  see also South Africa
African Company, 82, 85
Age of Kings, 16
Age of Reason, 147
Aguilera y Roche, Doña Teresa de, 248
Ahmed, Kuprili, II, 51
Akbar (shah of India), 164–65
Akwamu kingdom, 254
Albert of Wallenstein, 31, 34
Alexander of Rhodes, 181
algebra, 118–19
Allen, Richard, 179
Alvarez, Julian de, 246
America
  anger toward British in, 217
  arrival of Pilgrims in, 193–94
  British in need of, 213–14
  colonies in, 194–97
  early government in, 193
  exports from, 19
  first British settlers in, 192–93
  land riots in, 216–17
  lower-class grievances against the rich
    in, 214–16
  migration to, 197–98
  settlers of, 198–99
  Stamp Act in, reaction to, 217–19
  see also Boston Massacre; slavery
Anderson, George K., 17, 24, 142
architecture, 25
  and Bach's music, 130–31
  and German music, 128–29
  Indian, under Shah Jahan, 165
art, 24
  reason vs. imagination in, 142–43
  Rococo style, 132–33

see also architecture; baroque style
Attucks, Crispus, 219
Augsburg settlement of 1555, 35
Aurangzeb, 165, 166
  death of, 170
  and decline of Mogul empire, 171
  and English East India Company, 174,
    175–76
  religious attitudes of, 168
  revolts against, 168–69
  rule by, 167
  warfare under, 169
Australia, 18
  see also Cook, James
Austria, 17
Avenant, Richard, 95

Bach, Johann Sebastian, 26
  and baroque architecture, 130–31
  and Handel, 131–32
  and religion, 129
Backbarrow Company, 95–96
Bacon, Francis, 116
Balkans, 55
Baltic, 59–60
banking, 19, 21
Bank of England, 19, 83, 91
Banks, Joseph, 186, 189
Baron of Tilly, 30–31, 32
baroque style
  architecture, 25
  defined, 24, 134
  music, 26, 130–31, 132
  painting, 66, 135–41
Baskerville, John, 97
Bass, Henry, 222
Bautista Pérez, Manuel, 245–46
Bigot, Francois, 241–42
Bill of Rights (English), 46–47
Bingham, Woodbridge, 164
Blinding of Samson, The (Rembrandt), 26
Bohannan, Paul, 251
Bohemia, 30–31
Bonneval, Comte de, 269
Borromini, Francesco, 128
Boston Massacre, 219

restoring order after, 225–27
soldiers provoking citizens for, 222–24
violence in, 224–25
witness reports on, 221–22
Botany Bay, 189
Boulton, Matthew, 97
Bourbon family, 17
Bowdoin, James, 220
Boyle, Robert, 23–24
Bradford, William, 193–94
Brazil, 255
brewing industry, 96
Brewster, William, 193
Briggs, Asa, 78
Burma, 181
Burt, Alfred Leroy, 228

Calling of St. Matthew, The (Caravaggio),
    135–36
Calvert, Cecilius, 194–95
Calvert, Sir William, 96–97
Calvinists, 30, 193
Cambodia, 183
Cameron, Roderick, 185
Canada. See New France
canals, 22, 75–80
Cape York, 189
Capra, Fritjof, 122
Caravaggio, 135–36, 138
Caribbean islands, 255
Caspian Front, 57–58
Catholic Church
    hopes of restoring in England, 42–43
    missionaries, in India, 179–80
    see also Thirty Years' War
Cavalier exodus, 198
Chaloner, W.H., 98
Chapman, S.D., 98
Charles I (king of England)
    Anglican church under, 37–38
    death of, 40
    and Parliament, 36–37, 38–40
    relationship with people of England,
        36
    Scottish rebellion against, 38
Charles II (king of England), 41
    and American colonization, 195
    and English East India Trading
        Company, 175, 176
Charles of Lorraine, 53
Charleston, North Carolina, 195
Charnock, Job, 175
chemistry, 23–24
China, 22
Ch'ing dynasty, 162–63
Christian IV of Denmark, 34
Christianity
    Japanese hatred and suspicion
        toward, 152–55
    see also Catholic Church; Protestant
        Church; religion

Cid (Corneille), 144
Clapham, J.H., 75, 77, 78–79
Clark, George, 81
Clark, G.N., 18
Clark, Kenneth, 128
Cocks, Richard, 153
Colbert, Jean Baptiste, 68, 85, 178
Commager, Henry Steele, 192
commerce. See trade
Conroy, Hilary, 164
Cook, James, 18
    claiming East Coast for England, 190
    expedition of, 186–88
    exploration and charting in Australia
        by, 188–90
    scientific mission of, 185–86
    second voyage of, 190
Copernicus, Nicolaus, 122
Corneille, Pierre, 144
Corven, Phillip, 258
Cotchett, Thomas, 98
Crete, 51
Cromwell, Oliver, 39, 40–41
Crouzet, François, 93
Crowley, Sir Ambrose, 94–95
crypto-Jews, 244–45, 246–47
Curtin, Philip, 251

Darby dynasty, 96
Day, Francis, 173, 174
Deane, Phyllis, 72
de Blij, Harm J., 262
de Champlain, Samuel, 228–29
deductive reasoning, 24, 116
    Descartes on, 119–20
    leading to superstition, 117–18
    Newton on, 124
Defenestration of Prague, 30
Defoe, Daniel, 100, 148
Delaware, 196
de' Medici, Marie, 136
democracy, 47–48
Denmark, 31–32
Descartes, René, 116
    inductive method of, 119–20
    on "I think, therefore I am," 120–21
    on logic and mathematics, 118–19
Dorgon, 161
Drowne, Samuel, 223
Duke of Bridgewater's Canal, 75, 76–77
Dunciad (Pope), 147
Dupleix, Joseph, 183
Durant, Will, 42
Dutch, the
    and American colonization, 195
    colonization by, 21
    conflicts with South Africans, 266–67
    declining power in South Africa, 267
    domination to Africa by, 264–65
    and English East India Company,
        172–73

and English East India Trading
  Company, 177–78
and English loans, 91–92
financial machinery in, 89–90
independence of, 17
settlement in South Africa under,
  263–67
see also Dutch East India Company
Dutch East India Company, 83–84, 85
  founding of, 18–19
  journey to Africa, 262–63
Dutch Northern Company, 84

East India Company. See Dutch East
  India Company
economy
  Indian, 165–66
  see also finances
Edict of Restitution (1629), 31–32
Endeavor (ship), 186–88, 189
Endicott, John, 194
England
  Australia claimed for, 190
  capture of Quebec, Canada, 235–36
  colonization by, 21, 22
  financial institutions of, 90–92
  foundation for democracy in, 47–48
  and French Canada, 241–42
  governed by Oliver Cromwell, 40–41
  hopes of restoring Catholicism in,
    42–43
  industrial development in, 22
  joint-stock companies in, 82, 83
  literature in, 144, 146–48
  migration from, 197–99
  ruled by William III, 46–47
  settlers from, in America, 192
  taxation in, 90
  and Treaty of Utrecht, 70
  William III conquering throne in, 43–46
  world trade by, 19
  see also Charles I, king of England;
    English East India Company; Great
    Fire of London (1666); Plague of
    1665
English East India Company
  European competition, 172–73, 177–78
  factory founded for, 173–74
  and Mogul empire, 174–76
  profits, 177–78
  reconstruction of, 178
Enlightenment, 23–24
Enríquez, Simón, 247
Essay on Criticism (Pope), 146–47
Essay on Man, An (Pope), 25, 147
Estrada, Escovedo, 244
Europe
  and Ottoman empire, 52–55, 268–69
  in 1648, 20
  Turkish expansion in, 50–52
  see also names of individual countries

factories
  brewing industry, 96–97
  first, 98–99
  large units of production, 94–96
  multiple tasks in, 97–98
  paper mills, 96
  small units of production, 93–94
Fagel, Kaspar, 43
Fallass, William, 226
famines, 165–66, 174
Ferdinand II (king of Bohemia), 30, 31,
  33
finances
  British taxes, 90
  Dutch superiority in, 89–90
  financing wars, 87–89
  institutions created for, 90–92
  scarcity of coined money, 88
  see also investments; joint-stock
    companies
Finn, Michael, 95
fire. See Great Fire of London
Foley family, 95
Fort Frontenac, 233
France
  acquisition of Vietnam, 183–84
  and English East India Company, 178
  expansion into Indochina, 181
  and French and Indian War, 213
  joint-stock companies in, 85–86
  literature in, 144–46
  as most powerful European nation,
    17–18
  religious influence in Southeast Asia,
    179–80
  in South Africa, 265, 266
  taxation in, 90
  and Thirty Years' War, 33–35
  trading companies of, 19
  Turkish invasion, 51–52
  see also New France
Frederick V (king of Bohemia), 30–31
Frederick William (king of Prussia), 60
Frégault, Guy, 235
French and Indian War, 213–14
French East India Company, 180–81, 183
Frontenac, Count, 232–34

Gage, Thomas, 217
Galileo, 122–23
Garden of Love, The (Rubens), 137
Gardner, Mary, 226
geometry, 118–19
George (prince of Denmark), 45
George Apaffy (prince of Transylvania),
  54
George William of Brandenburg, 33
George II Rákóczy, 51
Germany
  and King James II's overthrow, 44
  and Thirty Years' War, 29, 31, 33–35

Gioro, Aisin, 158
Glorious Revolution, 47–48
God, 126–27
government
  early American, 193
  role of, in joint-stock companies, 84–85
Grant, James, 237
grants, 197
Great Barrier Reef, 189
Great Common Brewhouse, 96
Great Fire of London (1666)
  beginning of, 110
  desertion during, 113
  effect of, 113–14
  removal of goods during, 112–13
  spread of, 110, 111, 113
  St. Paul's Cathedral after, 25
  trying to extinguish, 110–11
  witnessing, 109–10
Great Wall of China, 162
Greeks, 269–70
Green, Charles, 186
Gulliver's Travels (Swift), 147
Gustavus Adolphus (king of Sweden),
  32, 33–34

Hamlin, Talbot, 25–26
Hanbury, John, 95
Handel, George Frideric, 26, 131–33
Hapsburg Empire, 17, 44
Harvey, William, 24
Haydn, Franz Joseph, 26
Herzstein, Robert Edwin, 36
Hinduism, 168
Hobbes, Thomas, 147
Hoerder, Dirk, 218
Hohenzollern family, 17
Holland. See Dutch, the
Hooker, Thomas, 194
Hooton, Joseph, 221
Hottentots, 263, 264
House of Hohenzollern, 70
House of Savoy, 70
Hudson, Henry, 195
Hungary
  and absolutism, 17
  and Ottoman Turks, 51–52

Ieyasu (shogun), 152, 156
Iklé, Frank W., 164
Imbangala kingdom, 254–55
immigration. See migration
India, 22
  missionaries in, 179–80
  see also English East India Company;
    Mogul empire
Indian Mutiny of 1857, 170
Indochina. See Vietnam
Industrial Revolution
  and canals, 75, 76
  see also factories

Innocent X (pope), 35
Intellectual Revolution, 23
  see also philosophy
inventions, 22
investments
  in canals, 77–78, 79
  in transportation, 72–73
  see also joint-stock companies
Ireland, 41
iron industry, 94–95
The Ironworks in Partnership, 95
Islam, 168
Israel, J.I., 243

Jahan (shah of India), 165
James I (king of England), 31
James II (king of England)
  and English East India Trading
    Company, 176
  hopes of restoring Catholicism, 42–43
  overthrow of, by William III of
    Orange, 43–46
Japan. See Tokugawa family
Jesuits, 180, 181
  in French Canada, 229–30
  and global expansion, 18
Jews
  attitudes of, 247
  inquisition of, 244–45, 248
  religious life of, 247–48
  secretly practicing Judaism, 244
  urban centers of, 245
  work history of, 245–47
John III Sobieski (king of Poland), 52
joint-stock companies, 18
  and canals, 79
  formation of, 81–83
  French, 85–86
  government role in, 84–85
  see also Dutch East India Company;
    English East India Company;
    trading companies
Juarez, Melchor, 246
Judaism. See Jews
Judd, Gerrit P., 29

kangaroo, 189
Kant, Immanuel, 24
Kay, Marvin L. Michael, 217
Kennedy, Paul, 87
Kirkwood, James, 222
Kuprili, Mohammed, 50, 51

Ladies-in-Waiting, The (Velásquez),
  140–41
Laing, R.D., 123
land riots, 216–17
Landscape with the Chateau of Steen
  (Rubens), 26
Las Menianas (Velásquez), 140–41
Laud, William, 37

Laval-Montmorency, Francois Xavier, 231–32
Law, John, 85
Lenotre, André, 66
Levant Company, 86
literature
  based on reason, 25
  French drama, 144–46
  influence of classics on, 143–44
  poetic diction, 143
Li Tzu-Ch'eng, 161–62
Li Yung-fang, 160
Locke, John, 24, 147, 195
logic, 118
Lombe, John, 98
Lombe, Thomas, 98
London, 73
  see also Great Fire of London; Plague of 1665
London Company, 196–97
López de Mendizabal, Don Bernardo, 248
López Fonseca, Francisco, 246
Louis XIV (king of France)
  achievements of, 67–68
  as European role model, 67
  and New France, 230
  palace of, 25, 66–67
  passing of throne to, 65
  personal characteristics, 65–66
  and Treaty of Utrecht, 69–70
  and Turkish invasion, 52
  wars waged under, 68–69
Loyal Nine, the, 218

Machell, John, 95–96
Magdeburg, Germany, 33
Manchus
  overthrow of Ming dynasty
    Dorgon's leadership in, 161–63
    Nurhaci's leadership in, 158–60
Mango, Andrew, 268
Marathas, the, 174, 176
Márquez, Domingo, 248
Martin, Susanna, 206–12
Mary (queen of England), 43, 46
Maryland, 194, 195
Massachusetts Bay colony, 194, 197
Massachusetts Bay Company, 197
mathematics, 24, 118–19
Mather, Cotton, 206
Maximilian I of Bavaria, 30, 31
Mayflower (ship), 193
Mazarin, Cardinal, 65
medicine, 24
Mexican Inquisition, 244–45, 248
Mexico
  colonists vs. officers in, 249
  foreigners in, 243–44
  see also Jews
Middle East, 21–22

see also India; Turkey
migration
  to America, 197–99
  from France to Canada, 230–31
military
  English Parliamentary, 39
  French Canadian, 230, 236–37, 239–40
Ming dynasty
  divide-and-rule policy of, 157–58
  fall of, 162–63
  overthrowing of
    and Abahai regime, 160–61
    and Dorgon regime, 161
    Nurhaci's leadership in, 158–60
Misanthrope, The (Moliére), 146
missionaries
  and global expansion, 18
  in India, 179–80
  in Indochina, 180–82, 183
  and Japanese isolationism, 151–52, 154
  in Thailand, 180
  see also Jesuits
Mogul empire
  Aurangzeb's rule in, 167–70
  end of, 170–71
  and English East India Company, 172–73, 174
  revolts in, 168–69
  under Shah Jahan, 165–66
  succession struggle in, 166–67
Mohammed IV (sultan of Turkey), 50
Moliére, 144, 145–46
monarchy
  changing political landscape, 16–18
  global expansion under, 18–19
  king's power under, 64–65
  William III overthrowing James II of England, 43–46
  see also Charles I; Louis XIV; Peter the Great
money, 88
Monk, George, 41
Monteverdi, Claudio, 26
Moravia, 51
Mori family, 156
Morris, Jeffrey, 192
Muñoz de Sandoval, Agustin, 248
music
  and architecture, 128–29
  baroque, 26, 130–31, 132
  religion influencing, 129
Mustapha, Kara, 51–54

Nash, Gary, 214, 215
nationalism, 269
Navigation Acts, 19, 76
Netherlands. See Dutch, the
Neumann, Balthasar, 130–31
Nevins, Allan, 192
New Caledonia, 190
New East India Company, 177

New France (Canada)
and the British, 235–36, 241–42
church established in, 231–32
deterioration of public morale in,
238–39
father of, 228–29
Frontenac's protection of, 232–34
military in
deterioration of, 236–38
irresponsible and corrupt behavior
by, 239–40
sent from France, 230–31
missionaries in, 229–30
New Model Army, 39, 40
Newport, Christopher, 192
New South Wales, 190
Newton, Isaac, 24, 147
absolute clockwork universe of, 125–26
applying theory of, 127
on laws of motion, 123–24
on occult and esoteric knowledge,
124–25
on reason, 124
on role of God, 126–27
New York, 195–96
New Zealand, 190
Nguyen dynasty, 182, 183
North Carolina, 195
Northern Company, 85
Núñez Pérez, Luis, 247
Nurhaci, 158–60
Nussbaum, Frederick L., 49

Otis, James, 214, 215
Ottoman Turks
decline of empire, 268–70
defeated by European forces, 52–55
importance of, 49–50
expansion into Europe, 50–52
vs. Peter the Great, 59
Outside Lords, 150–51
Oxford Canal, 78

Packard, L.B., 67
painting, 26, 66, 135–41
paper mills, 96
Paris Seminary for Oriental Languages,
180
Parkinson, Sydney, 186, 189
Parliamentary Presbyterians, 40
Parry, J.H., 172
Pascal, Blaise, 143
Pasha, Humbaraci Ahmet, 269
Peace of Westphalia, 23, 35
Peacock Throne, 165
Peiterson, Anthony, 258
Pemberton, Samuel, 220
Penn, William, 196
Pennsylvania, 196
Pepys, Samuel, 109
Pereira Lobo, Matías, 248

Perrot, Francois, 232
Persia, 57, 58–59
Peter the Great
death of, 62
expeditions of, 56–60
final years of, 61–62
legacy of, 62–63
and Ottoman Empire, 270
and St. Petersburg, 60–61
Petition of Rights, 37
Phaedra (Racine), 145
Phaulkon, Constantine, 180
Philips, John, 97–98
Philips, Nathaniel, 97–98
philosophy, 24
on art, 142–43
deductive reasoning, 116–18, 119–20
Descartes's four rules, 119
inductive reasoning, 116–17
"I think, therefore I am," 120–21
Phips, William, 200
physics, 24
Pierpont, Robert, 222
Pilgrims, 193–94
Plague of 1665
deaths of, 100–102, 107–108
horror stories spread during, 104–105
thievery during, 104, 105–107
victims of, 102–105
Plymouth Company, 196
Podolia, 51
Poland
and absolutism, 17
and Ottoman Turks, 51, 54
and Peter the Great, 60
Pope, Alexander, 25, 146
Portuguese
crypto-Jews, 244–45, 246–47
and English East India Trading
Company, 177–78
exploration by, 18
and Mogul empire, 165
Presbyterianism, 40
Preston, Captain, 220, 225, 227
Primavera (Vermeer), 139
printing, 98
Protestant church
missionary work by, 179
see also Thirty Years' War
Providence, Rhode Island, 194
Prussia, 17
Puritanism, 36–38
Puritans, 194, 197, 198

Quakers, 96
Quebec, Canada, 235–36
see also New France

Racine, Jean, 144, 145
Rajputs, 168–69, 174
Rape of the Lock, The (Pope), 147

rationalism, 120–21
Rawlinson, William, 95–96
reason
  in literature, 25, 145–47, 148
  vs. imagination, in art, 142–43
reasoning
  deductive, 24, 119–20, 226–18
  inductive, 24, 116–17
  Newton on, 124–25
Regulator movement, 217
religion
  and American settlement, 193, 194–95
  hatred and suspicion of Christianity,
    152–55
  hopes of restoring Catholicism in
    England, 42–43
  influences on art, 129
  intolerance to
    in India, 165, 168
    in Mexico, 244–45, 248
  and opposition to King Charles I,
    38–40
  and Ottoman empire's decline, 269–70
  practiced by Jews in Mexico, 248
  toleration of, in England, 43–44
  see also Thirty Years' War
Rembrandt, 26, 137–39
Return of the Prodigal Son, The
  (Rembrandt), 138–39
Rhode Island, 194
Richardson, Samuel, 148
Richelieu, Cardinal, 18
  and Louis XIV's throne, 65
  and Thirty Years' War, 33
roads, 73
Robinson, John, 193
Rococo style, 132–33
Rodríguez de Oliveira, Mathías, 246,
  247
Rodríguez de Silva y Velásquez, Diego,
  140–41
Rolfe, John, 193
Romanov family, 17
Roundheads, 39
Royalists (English Parliament), 39
Royal Society, 185–86
Rubens, Peter Paul, 26, 136–37, 138
Russell, Edward, 44
Russia
  and absolutism, 17
  and decline of Ottoman empire, 270
  joint-stock companies in, 82–83
  at war with Turks, 51
  see also Peter the Great
Russian Company, 82

San Ignacio, Fray Joseph de, 248
Sankey Brook (canal), 76
Sansom, G.B., 150
Scarlatti, Alessandro, 128
School of Athens (Vermeer), 139

science, 23–24
  Galileo, 122–23
  see also Newton, Isaac
Scotland
  under Oliver Cromwell's government,
    41
  rebellion against King Charles I, 38
Scott, W.R., 83
sea routes, 73–75
Seven Years' War, 213–14
Shiko, Dara, 165, 166–67
Shimabara rising, 155
Shimadzu family, 156
Siberia, 57
Sidney, Henry, 44
Silesia, 51
silk, 98
Skempton, C., 75–76
slavery
  arrival of, in America, 193
  populations chosen for, 252–53
  purposes of, 251–52
  rights of slaves under, 253
  slaves petitioning for freedom, 258–61
  in South Africa, 264
  trade, 19, 246, 253–57
Smith, Adam, 74
Smith, Isaac, 188
Smith, John, 192–93
Society for Foreign Missions, 180
Solander, Daniel Carl, 186
South Africa
  decline of Dutch power in, 267
  Dutch domination in, 264–67
  Dutch settlement in, 263–64
  expansion into Europe, 265–66
  slaves imported to, 264
South Sea Company, 83, 84
Spain
  exploration by, 18
  in Indochina, 181
  and Japanese fear of invasion, 152, 155
  and Mexico, 249
  and Treaty of Utrecht, 69–70
  and Turkish invasion, 52
Spanish New Christians, 245
Spöring, Herman Dietrich, 186, 189
Stamp Act (1767), 217–19
steam engine, 22–23
Steele, Richard, 147–48
Sting Ray Harbour, 188–89
stock exchange, 21
St. Paul's Cathedral, 25–26
St. Petersburg, Russia, 60–61
Sumner, B.H., 56
Swan, Caleb, 221
Swansborough, Margaret, 221
Sweden
  and absolutism, 17
  and Peter the Great, 59–60
  and Thirty Years' War, 32–34, 35

Swift, Jonathan, 147
Syndics of the Draper's Guild
  (Rembrandt), 137–38

Tahiti, 186
Taj Mahal, 165
Talon, Jean, 230, 231
Tartuffe (Moliére), 146
Tasmania, 187, 188
taxation, 90
Taylor, Alastair M., 16, 17, 64
Taylor, John, 97
textile industry, 22, 98
Thailand, 180, 181
Thirty Years' War (1618–1648), 16–17
  end of, 34–35
  stages of, 29–34
Thurn, Count, 30
Tilly, Baron of, 30–31, 32
Tököli, Emmerich, 53, 54
Tokugawa family, 150
  fear of revolt, 151
  seclusion policy, 151–52, 155–56
  suspicion and hatred of Christianity,
    152–55
Torres Strait, 190
Tozama, 150–51
trade
  changing practice in global, 19
  colonial, 213–14
  colonies and settlements for, 21
  industrial developments for, 22–23
  institutions created from, 19, 21
  and Japanese isolationism, 155
  and scarcity of coined money, 88
  see also slavery; trading companies
trading companies, 18–19, 81–82
  financing American colonies, 196–97
  tighter controls for, 21–22
  see also Dutch East India Company;
    English East India Company; joint-
    stock companies
Transcaucasia, 57–58
transportation, 22–23
  as an investment, 72–73
  road improvements, 73
  sea routes, 73–75
  see also canals
Treaty of Barwald, 33
Treaty of Carlowitz (1699), 268
Treaty of Lübeck (1629), 31
Treaty of Prague (1635), 34
Treaty of Utrecht (1713), 69–70
Trinh dynasty, 182, 183
Turkey, 17
  and absolutism, 17
  see also Ottoman Turks

United Company of Merchants of
  England, 177
United States. *See* America
Usher, Jane, 221

Váez de Acevedo, Antonio, 246–47
Váez de Acevedo, Sebastian, 246–47
Váez de Castelobranco, Antonio, 246–47
Váez Sevilla, Simón, 245–47
van der Stel, Simon, 265
van Dykvelt, Everhard, 43
van Riebeeck, Jan, 262–65
Van Rijn, Rembrandt, 137–39
Vantrump, Peter, 258
Vermeer, 139–40
Versailles, 25, 66–67
Vietnam
  French acquisition of, 183–84
  reunited, 183
  rival dynasties in, 181–83
Villiers, George, 37
Voltaire, 146
von Stahremberg, Count Rüdiger, 53

Wailan, Nikan, 158
Wakeman, Frederic, Jr., 157
Wallbank, T. Walter, 16, 17, 64
warfare
  financing needed for, 87–89
  under Louis XIV, 68–69
  see also Seven Years' War; Thirty Years'
    War
Warnock, Robert, 17, 24, 142
War of the Spanish Succession, 68–69
Warren, Joseph, 220
Washington, John, 198
Wheeler, John, 95
Wheeler, Richard, 95
Will, Mary Ann Frese, 134
William III of Orange
  conquering English throne, 43–46
  and English East India Trading
    Company, 176
  government under, 46–48
Williams, Roger, 194
Winthrop, John, 194
witchcraft, people accused of
  attempt to stop executions for,
    204–205
  court proceedings for, 202–204
  false accusations of, 200–202, 204
  trial of, 206–12
Wren, Sir Christopher, 25–26
Wu San-kuei, 162

Yuan Ch'ung-huan, 160

Zinn, Howard, 213

ABOUT THE EDITOR

After many years of teaching British literature to high school students, Clarice Swisher now devotes her time to research and writing. She is the author of *Albert Einstein, Pablo Picasso, Genetic Engineering, Victorian England, The Glorious Revolution,* and editor of *Spread of Islam* and *Galileo.* She is currently working on a new series, *Understanding Great Literature.* She lives in St. Paul, Minnesota.